Rembrandt:
The Nightwatch

PRINCETON ESSAYS ON THE ARTS

For a complete list of titles in
the series see page 139

Rembrandt:
The Nightwatch

E. Haverkamp-Begemann

Princeton University Press • Princeton, New Jersey

Published by Princeton University Press, 41 William Street,
Princeton, New Jersey
In the United Kingdom: Princeton University Press, Guildford, Surrey

Clothbound editions of Princeton University Press books are printed on acid-free paper,
and binding materials are chosen for strength and durability

Illustrations printed by The Meriden Gravure Company, Meriden, Connecticut

Printed in the United States of America by Princeton University Press,
Princeton, New Jersey

Library of Congress Cataloging in Publication Data

Haverkamp-Begemann, Egbert.
Rembrandt, the Nightwatch.

(Princeton essays on the arts ; 12)
Bibliography: p.   Includes index.
1.   Rembrandt Harmenszoon van Rijn, 1606-1669.
Nightwatch.   I.   Title.   II.   Series.
ND653.R4A7 1982   759.9492   81-47921
ISBN 0-691-03991-7   AACR2
ISBN 0-691-00341-6 (pbk.)

To the Memory of
Jan G. van Gelder

Contents

List of Illustrations

All photographs are by the Rijksmuseum unless credited otherwise.

Preface

The *Nightwatch* first fascinated me when I was a student. Ever since, I have worked intermittently toward a monograph. In 1975, a manuscript was ready to be published as a volume of Art in Context, when this series of much needed studies on individual works of art unfortunately was discontinued. Then other duties intervened. As often, the delay became an advantage. Four friends—the late Richard S. Sylvester, Peter Gay, J. M. Montias, and J. W. Smit—were willing to read the manuscript. Their observations, suggestions, and corrections improved the text greatly. To them I am most grateful. Furthermore, restoration and cleaning necessitated by the damage inflicted on the painting in the fall of 1975 yielded new insights that I could incorporate. These events produced a new, short, and general monograph on the painting in the context of Rembrandt's work and life and the city of Amsterdam. Concurrently, Margaret D. Carroll wrote a dissertation at Harvard on the *Nightwatch* and the iconology of militia company portraiture that came to my attention in the beginning of 1978. Mrs. Carroll addresses herself to some of the same questions that are raised here, and reaches in those instances similar conclusions. Her study contains an excellent analysis of the complex history of the militia and its institutions in Amsterdam, and of their implications for the meaning of the painting. In that respect, Mrs. Carroll goes into greater detail than I can within the scope of this monograph. Some of her observations I have included, with grateful acknowledgment. Finally, in the late summer and fall of 1979, just before the manuscript was concluded for a second time, discussions with the resourceful and imaginative young archivist of Amsterdam, S.A.C. Dudok van Heel, yielded new insights, and his renewed search in the incomparably rich archives produced new data. Some of these I also have included. I should like to thank him here especially for his generosity.

The *Nightwatch* is one of those complex works of art that fascinate and puzzle, that address themselves to the viewer on many levels of feeling, thought, and association, that enrich fact with fancy, clarity with ambiguity. If this study makes the painting better understood and thereby more appreciated, its goal will be fulfilled.

Rembrandt:
The Nightwatch

Note to the Reader

Titles of books, catalogues, and articles are cited by name of author and year of publication; for full titles, see the Bibliography. In some instances of multiple authorship, publications are cited by their abbreviated titles. Unless stated otherwise, translations are the author's.

A fold-out color reproduction of *The Nightwatch* has been included as the last plate in the book.

Introduction

In 1642, at age thirty-six, Rembrandt was at the height of his career. He was one of the most sought-after painters in Amsterdam, was a successful teacher, lived in an elegant house where he had an extensive collection of art, antiquities, and other objects, and he was a wealthy man. In that year he completed the *Nightwatch*. It is no more than a group portrait of eighteen prominent citizens of Amsterdam shown as members of one of the city's militia companies in action under the command of their captain and lieutenant. Rembrandt turned this prosaic subject into one of the world's greatest and most fascinating works of art which has evoked admiration ever since he painted it.

Yet, from the beginning, this admiration was linked with censure. Rembrandt's pupil Samuel van Hoogstraeten, the first to mention the painting in print in 1678, praises it as an example of fine and lively composition, but finds it too dark and considers Rembrandt's rendering of the subject too personal.[1] Shortly after, in 1686, the Florentine abbot, academician, collector, and historian Filippo Baldinucci records what another pupil of Rembrandt's had told him about the *Nightwatch*. This pupil considered the painting the main reason for Rembrandt's fame, surpassing that of virtually all his Dutch contemporaries. This surprised him because he found the figures, with the exception of the two central ones (which in his memory had fused into one), so jumbled and confused that one could not keep them apart.[2] A similar mixture of conflicting evaluation disturbed the author

---

[1] VAN HOOGSTRAETEN 1678, p. 176; HdG 1906, no. 338; SLIVE 1953, pp. 86, 97, 98. For Van Hoogstraeten's text, see Chapter V, note 6. The *Nightwatch* is the only Dutch seventeenth-century painting mentioned by Van Hoogstraeten in his discussion of composition (pp. 174-192). Probably the most remarkable expression of disappointment, however, is frequently overlooked or misquoted, and I therefore mention it here. Sir Joshua Reynolds, upon seeing the painting in Amsterdam's town hall, noted: "If it is by Rembrandt it is the worst of him I ever saw". The statement is preserved among Sir Joshua's manuscript notes of his trip through the Netherlands (Institut Néerlandais, Coll. Frits Lugt, Paris). It was omitted from the printed *Journey to Flanders and Holland*, 1781 (JUYNBOLL 1954, p. 183; I owe the reference to J. G. van Gelder).

[2] BALDINUCCI 1686, pp. 78 f.; HdG 1906, no. 360; SLIVE 1953, pp. 104-115. Baldinucci had not seen the *Nightwatch* but obtained his information from Bernhardt

or the most memorable description of the painting made centuries later. In 1876, the painter and critic Eugène Fromentin published his brilliant evocation of the *Nightwatch* in his *Maîtres d'autrefois*. His vivid recollections of his impressions of the painting, his sensitive analysis of color, composition, and light-dark effects still impress the reader. At the same time, he unsettles us by his struggle to understand, and his final confession of being unable to accept the painting. He rejects the validity of Rembrandt's basic aim which, in his opinion, was "to illumine a true scene by a light which was not true, that is to say, to give to a fact the ideal character of a vision".[3]

Indeed, as Fromentin noted, Rembrandt merged portraiture and pageantry in this painting, juxtaposed strong light and impenetrable darkness, combined action with pose, daily costume with fantastic apparel, martial accoutrements with childlike apparitions. Fromentin found these differences irreconcilable, and thereby essentially subscribed to the verdicts of Van Hoogstraeten and Baldinucci. But for us, less hampered by rational expectations in art than Fromentin and less biased toward naturalist requirements than the seventeenth-century critics, this fusion of seemingly incompatible features, although surprising and puzzling, heightens the interest of the painting. Rather than expressing an eccentric vision, these contrasting features constitute the core of Rembrandt's thoughtful reinterpretation of a subject that had a long tradition.

The contemporary viewer was familiar with group portraits of militiamen. Knowing certain social and personal circumstances of the sitters, as well as customs, traditions, and functions of the Amsterdam militia, and being familiar with the role played by its citizen members, the contemporary viewer was able to interpret these paintings through associations that easily escape us. For him, the militia embodied the power and individuality of the city as distinct from the country and from other cities, and militiamen stood for ideas of civic virtues of the past and present. He was proud of these group portraits. We sense this from contemporary references, like the one by Joan Blaeu in his Baedeker-like description of the Dutch cities, published in 1651. Writing about the buildings of the militia companies in Amsterdam, he praises the spaciousness of their large halls and rooms and finds it a pleasure to see in them "the portraits of the distinguished commanders

---

Keil. See also the Conclusion and its note 4.

[3] FROMENTIN 1876, quoted from translation by M. C. Robbins, 1882, in reprint with introduction by M. Schapiro (New York 1963), p. 272.

and militiamen usually represented with their weapons, gathered in groups and artfully painted".[4]

Amsterdam's citizens immortalized in the *Nightwatch* were subject to similar associations, but Rembrandt endowed them with further meaning not expressed or not as clearly formulated by his colleagues. Chiefly by means of the features that upset Fromentin, Rembrandt imparted to the viewer specific images of the sitters as individuals and of the social organization to which they belonged. The contemporary viewer undoubtedly understood this interpretation as well much more easily than we do.

The main purpose of this study is to reconstruct the image that Rembrandt wished to convey to contemporary viewers and to posterity, and the associations contemporary viewers presumably experienced when seeing the *Nightwatch*.[5] To obtain clarification in these respects, we must see the painting in its relation to earlier and contemporary group portraiture.[6] Moreover, it should be studied in the

[4] BLAEU 1651, n.p. (s.v. *De Doelen*): "De huysen van de Doelen self, sijn ruym en wijt, met groote salen en kamers, in welcke men d'afbeeldingen der uytstekende Bevelhebbers en Schutters, in 't gemeen met hunne wapenen in troepen byeen kunstigh geschildert, met vermaeck kan besien".

[5] HELLINGA 1956, particularly pp. 7-9, 12, stated for the first time emphatically that efforts should be made to establish what the painting meant for Rembrandt's contemporaries rather than for the twentieth-century observer. His emphasis on symbolism in the *Nightwatch* was welcome, but his analysis too firmly based on literary parallels and emblem books, often out of context, does not convince. For criticism of Hellinga see VAN DE WAAL 1956b.; BAUCH 1957, pp. 18, 19 and 1967, pp. 140, 141; GERSON 1968, p. 76; Emmens in CHICAGO 1973, p. 79. KNUTTEL 1955, seeing no symbolism at all (like, surprisingly, also HAAK 1969, p. 179) opposed Hellinga too strongly. Of earlier writers, particularly SCHMIDT-DEGENER 1914-17 had investigated the "meaning" of the painting (which in his pre-iconological era he labeled "Ramifications of the Subject") and NEUMANN 1902 had recognized the symbolic quality of objects and motion. BAUCH 1957 and TÜMPEL 1970 correctly emphasize Rembrandt's symbolism and allusions, although the theoretical framework and the emphasis on the predominance of the visual tradition do not convince fully. The best iconological study to date of the painting, particularly of those aspects that relate to the Amsterdam militia, and of the history of the militia itself, is found in CARROLL 1976 (see also my Preface). I believe, however, that Carroll overemphasizes the degree to which the painting refers specifically and directly to triumphal entries (e.g., pp. x, 121). For the concept of associations, see below, note 7.

[6] RIEGL 1931 is still fundamental for the study of this genre as a whole, in spite of the early date of the first publication (1902) and many shortcomings, particularly the biased focus on formal characteristics and the assumption that the narrative elements depicted actual happenings. Unduly neglected is the first history of this genre written twenty years earlier (RIEGEL 1882; not to be confused with RIEGL 1902 and 1931). An excellent corrective to Riegl for the method of interpretation of these collective

context of Amsterdam society and the Dutch militia, of traditions of pageantry and rhetoricians; what is known of the individual sitters should be reviewed, and the role of costumes, weapons, architecture, movement and action analyzed. The principal method of this study, therefore, is iconological.[7]

But it is not solely an iconological study. It reviews and reinterprets traditional aspects, both factual and formal, as well. It is intended as a monograph on the painting. Many views expressed necessarily have been stated before in the voluminous literature on the subject.[8] Certain aspects, however, particularly the symbolic and associative values of the painting as a whole and of various details, especially of the startling visual center of the painting, the girl in yellow and her companion, are here interpreted in a new way.

This monograph does not aim at comprehensiveness. I do not discuss later artistic reactions and literary criticism, since both reveal less about the painting than about its critics.[9] Moreover, I discuss the technical aspects of execution and preservation only summarily because this

---

portraits was provided by VAN DE WAAL 1956a. However, these and similar "association portraits" (Riegl's *Korporationsporträts*) as a category of "role portraits" (see BAUCH 1967, pp. 145-151, with bibliography) and as distinct from "historicizing portraits" (a welcome introduction provided by WISHNEVSKY 1967) are in need of further iconological study. A step in the right direction was made by HAAK 1972 and BLANKERT 1975-79. See also Chapter VI and its note 1.

[7] The term association is used here to denote the significance imparted to objects, actions, and other phenomena in works of art by the individual and collective experience of contemporary viewers. To give an example from our own time, a Volkswagen or a painting representing one may be associated with youth, the less privileged, college faculty, or car buffs, or all four, depending on locale, time, the artist's intentions, and the viewer's experience. The study of such associations may be considered an extension of iconology as formulated by Erwin Panofsky with a shift of emphasis from the artist to the spectator in defining the meaning of a work of art.

[8] Of the monographic studies on the painting, MEIJER 1886 and DYSERINCK 1890 are still of great significance. The book by NEUMANN 1902 (and later editions) and the articles by Schmidt-Degener 1914-17 contributed much that unduly has been disregarded, partially because of a naturalistic bias of later writers, particularly MARTIN 1947. It is regrettable that Schmidt-Degener did not publish an expanded version of his articles as he intended (1916a., p. 67, note 1). WIJNBEEK 1944 and BAUCH 1957 wrote monographs, the first a lively evocation but without documentation, the latter the best single study to date. KOOT 1947 was written as a general introduction to the painting at the occasion of the recovery and cleaning of the painting after World War II and HIJMANS-KUIPER-VELS HEIJN 1976 for similar purposes after the damage and restoration of 1975-76. GERSON 1973 is likewise a general introduction.

[9] For seventeenth-century appreciation of Rembrandt, see particularly SLIVE 1953, for literary criticism BROM 1936. For a recent representative selection of early as well as later criticism of the *Nightwatch*, see GERSON 1973.

subject has been treated recently and in great detail by others.[10] To
do justice to earlier writers and to put this study in historiographic
perspective, I refer extensively to previous literature, whether I agree
with the opinions expressed or not, in the notes. In order not to
interrupt the text, discussions of tangential issues and references to
details of varied nature are also relegated to the notes.

Before I start, however, a few misconceptions should be refuted.
The first one concerns the painting's title.[11] Although keeping watch
at night, as we shall see, was the duty of some members of militia
companies at certain times, even in the 1640s, that activity is not
represented here. The title was coined only at the end of the eighteenth
century when patrolling at night was virtually the only duty left to
the city's militia. Furthermore, by that time, the painting, which from
the beginning has been darker than other group portraits of militiamen,
as Van Hoogstraeten's complaint confirms, had darkened considerably
more by the accumulation of layers of dirt and varnish. Taken literally,
the title *Nightwatch* is wrong, yet it is the best we have. Rembrandt's
unique interpretation of group portraiture in this painting has prompted
various new titles at different times, but these are also incorrect and,
worse, lack the traditional title's imaginative touch and evocative power
which do the painting justice.[12]

[10] The documentary evidence concerning the physical history of the painting and the
insights gained during the cleaning of 1945-46 are found in VAN SCHENDEL-MERTENS
1947; the restoration and cleaning of 1975-76 are discussed with candor and the results
of the investigation during that process set forth in detail and perceptively by P.J.J. van
Thiel, L. Kuiper, W. Hesterman, E. van de Wetering, and others in BULLETIN 1976.

[11] According to MARTIN 1947, p. 25, the title *De Nagtwacht* was first used in 1797
by Claessens in connection with his print after the painting, but I have not been able
to verify this. The first time the painting is called *De optocht van een burger Nachtwacht*
is in the catalogue of the collection of Cornelis Ploos van Amstel sold March 3, 1800,
where it is applied to a drawing by H. Pothoven after the painting (VAN SCHENDEL-
MERTENS 1947, p. 10; for other early references see ibidem, and SCHMIDT-DEGENER
1916a., pp. 61-63, also KOOT 1947, pp. 19, 20).

[12] The titles *Der Wachtaufzug* ("The Marching Out For a Watch") coined by RIEGEL
1882, and *De Schuttersoptocht* ("The Marching of Militiamen") emphatically defended
by Schmidt-Degener in lieu of *Nightwatch* are not in accordance with contemporary
interpretations. They overemphasize the act of marching at the expense of the element
of portraiture. KOOT 1947, p. 20, BAUCH 1957, p. 25, and others have argued on similar
grounds for acceptance of the traditional title. The correct titles of most group portraits
of militiamen are so cumbersome, that they can be managed only in abbreviated form.
This practice has been followed in this study. The correct titles of the militia pieces
decorating the same hall as the *Nightwatch* (see below, and Fig. 35) are: Jacob Adriaensz
Backer, *Officers and Men of the Company of Captain Cornelis de Graeff and Lieutenant
Hendrick Lauwrensz*; Nicolaes Eliasz, called Pickenoy, *Officers and Men of the Com-*

Secondly, the painting did not cause the public to turn its back on Rembrandt. Although the painting apparently surprised some, Rembrandt remained in demand as a portraitist, even for group portraits. The *Nightwatch* is not a pivotal work in Rembrandt's career; it marks a break neither in his own concepts nor in the appreciation he received from others.[13]

The *Nightwatch* is the subject of this book. The rest of Rembrandt's oeuvre will enter the discussion only occasionally. Commission, subject, and artistic tradition provide a more solid basis for the analysis of the *Nightwatch* than Rembrandt's other works. So much of Rembrandt's oeuvre is still obscure or subject to divergent interpretations that clarification of the *Nightwatch* with its wealth of data and the numerous parallels in contemporary and earlier paintings contributes more to a better understanding of other works by Rembrandt than *vice versa*.[14]

---

pany of Captain Jan van Vlooswijck and Lieutenant Gerrit Hudde; Govert Flinck, *Officers and Men of the Company of Captain Albert Bas and Lieutenant Lucas Conijn*; Bartholomeus van der Helst, *Officers and Men of the Company of Captain Roelof Bicker and Lieutenant Jan Michielsz Blaeuw*; Joachim von Sandrart, *Officers and Men of the Company of Captain Cornelis Bicker and Lieutenant Frederick van Banchem*. The full titles of the paintings by Cornelis Ketel and Thomas de Keyser which are mentioned frequently throughout this study, are: *Officers and Men of the Company of Captain Dirck Jacobsz Rosecrans and Lieutenant Pauw*, and *Officers and Men of the Company of Captain Allaert Cloeck and Lieutenant Lucas Jacobsz Rotgans*. These and similar titles have been abbreviated to: *The Company of Captain . . .* with the name of the captain. To be correct historically, the title of the *Nightwatch* would have to read: *Officers and Men of the Company of Captain Frans Banning Cocq and Lieutenant Wilhem van Ruytenburgh*.

[13] Both legends are nurtured particularly by NEUMANN 1902 and Schmidt-Degener in various publications. The first to deny briefly but emphatically the validity of both legends was PLIETZSCH 1939, followed by HELD 1950 and, with extensive discussion, SLIVE 1953. DVOŘÁK 1921 had given the most eloquent evocation of Rembrandt the rebel artist. I shall return to Rembrandt's reputation as a group portraitist in the Conclusion and its note 3.

[14] BAUCH 1957 and 1962 (1962, pp. 19, 24, 25) and TÜMPEL 1970, p. 164, represent the opposite point of view that the *Nightwatch* can only be understood against the background of Rembrandt's art.

I

The Painting: Commission,
Execution, Condition

What requirements was Rembrandt to fulfill, and what freedom did he have in acquitting himself of his task? Who gave him the commission? Why was it given to him and not someone else, and when? These and similar questions can be answered, at least partially.

Whatever else the *Nightwatch* represents, essentially it is a group portrait, and as such it was considered by contemporaries. Documents and literature of the time refer to militia pieces as portraits of men belonging to a certain company or, more succinctly, as companies of a named captain (without implying that entire companies were represented). The *Nightwatch* is no exception. Sixteen years after the painting had been completed, two of the sitters made a declaration about the fees they had to pay, and at that occasion, they implied that the painting, which they did not name by title, was a group portrait.[1]

---

[1] Van Hoogstraeten 1678 implies that the painting is a group portrait. Baldinucci 1686, p. 78, or rather his spokesman Bernhardt Keil, calls the subject a "formation of those companies of citizens" ("una gran tela . . . in cui [Rembrandt] aveva rappresentata un ordinanza d'una di quelle compagnie di Cittadini"). Michel 1890, p. 170, and 1893, p. 283, translated *ordinanza* with "prise d'armes", implying the action of taking up arms and forming company; Gerson 1973, p. 40, also gave the word an active meaning ("l'appel"). It appears more likely that Baldinucci used the word with its first meaning of "military formation". (Neither Hofstede de Groot, HdG 1906, nor Slive 1953 translated the word.) Statements by Jan Pietersz Bronckhorst ("dat hij . . . door Rembrandt . . . is geschildert en geconterfeyt geworden neffens andere persoonen van hunne compagnie en corporaelschaep tot sestien int getall in een schilderije, nu staende op de groote sael in de Cloveniersdoele en dat het yder van hen . . . wel heeft gekost dooreen de somme van hondert guldens, d'een wat meer en d'ander wat minder, nae de plaets die sij daer in hadden") and Claes van Cruysbergen ("dat het stuck schilderije staende op de Cleuveniersdoelen . . . daerin hy . . . mede is geconterfeyt, van schilderen wel heeft gekost de som van sestienhondert guldens") (HdG 1906, nos. 205, 206; Strauss-Van der Meulen 1980, nos. 1659/16 and 1659/19) were made in 1659 in

A second contemporary reference at first seems at variance. The caption accompanying a copy of the painting, drawn in black chalk and watercolor (Fig. 43), describes the *Nightwatch* as "the painting in the large hall of the Kloveniersdoelen, in which the Lord of Purmerland [Frans Banning Cocq], as captain, summons his lieutenant, Lord of Vlaardingen [Wilhem van Ruytenburgh], to order his company of citizens to march out".[2] In fact, however, the two statements complement each other. The copy was made for Banning Cocq himself in one of the two albums recording honors he had received, deeds he had performed, and other noteworthy facts (some of them imagined) from his life and his—and particularly his wife's—ancestry.[3] The caption, therefore, rather than accounting for the entire painting, emphasizes Banning Cocq's action. Similarly, the caption of a drawing of the Handboogsdoelen (Fig. 45) elsewhere in the same volume says about the building only that Banning Cocq was one of its governors.[4]

From the statements of the two sitters just mentioned, we can draw more conclusions. First, the sixteen men portrayed paid according to whether they were represented fully or partially, each one paying "more or less according to the place each one occupied". This was the usual procedure at the time.[5] Rembrandt had to adjust his por-

---

order to establish Rembrandt's assets at the time of Saskia's death (June 14, 1642). It is likely, therefore, that these sums were paid before that date, but this does not imply that the painting was finished by that time, because they may have paid in advance all or part of the fee (CARROLL 1976, pp. 125, 126, reaches the same conclusion on different grounds). It is even likely that they paid in advance because Jan Claesz Leijdeckers, who died in December 1640, is included in the painting (his name appears on the shield) and his widow was in strained financial circumstances (I am grateful to S.A.C. Dudok van Heel for this information, August and September of 1979; see also note 16 of this chapter).

[2] "*Schets* van de Schilderije op de groote Sael van de Cleveniers Doelen, daerinne de Jonge Heer van Purmerlandt, als Capiteijn, geeft last aen zijnen Lieutenant, de Heer van Vlaerdingen, om sijn Compaignie Burgers te doen marcheren" (HdG 1906, no. 139). For the albums, see Chapter II, note 13.

[3] SCHMIDT-DEGENER 1916a., pp. 65, 66, and 1916b., p. 31, rightly concluded that the two points of view did not necessarily contradict each other. He qualified the albums as an "egocentric production". RIEGL 1931, p. 194, considering the captain's order the main theme (and the company "reines Akzidenz, gleich einem Hinterraume oder einem landschaftlichen Hintergrunde"), misinterpreted the caption in the album as an objective description of the subject of the painting. This misinterpretation is still found in many recent descriptions of the *Nightwatch*.

[4] "St. Sebastiaens ofte handboogsdoelen binnen Amstelredam daer van de Jonghe heer van Purmerlant Overman is geworden in den Jare . . ." (Vol. I, p. 120; drawing made on separate pieces of paper and inserted; the year of appointment, 1648, was omitted).

[5] In the group portrait of members of the St. Sebastiaansdoelen in Middelburg painted

trayals to the sums paid, and the individual sitters must have known beforehand whether they could expect to be represented in full, like the man in red charging his musket, or only partially. Although they probably could not anticipate many specific features of their representation in the *Nightwatch*, there is no reason to believe that they were startled by the varying degrees of their visibility. It is not known whether the officers had more rights than the men and could make special requests, but human nature seems to allow the supposition that they did. If Banning Cocq receives more emphasis in Rembrandt's *Nightwatch* than other captains in other militia pieces, he may have asked Rembrandt to stress him. He also may have chosen a particular composition, or even asked for the representation of a company in motion.[6] Such demands cannot now be established. It is certain, however, that the central position allotted to Banning Cocq agrees with both the captain's ambitions and Rembrandt's preference for emphasizing a central figure in a crowd.[7]

From the statements, we also learn that the men who wished to be included in the *Nightwatch* had to be able to afford it.[8] This does not imply that Rembrandt charged the sitters of the *Nightwatch* more than other painters of militia pieces might have done. Rembrandt's price of 100 florins per person seems to have been in proportion with the 61 florins that one of the sitters of the much smaller *Company of Captain Allaert Cloeck* (Fig. 88) had to pay to Thomas de Keyser in 1632. In fact, the total sum of 1,600 florins must be considered low for a portrait painting of that size by Rembrandt. If the sitters had

---

by Cornelius Janssens van Ceulen in 1650 (Town Hall, Middelburg), the five seated and the fourteen standing men (all portrayed in civilian dress) are entered as two distinct categories on the painter's bill depicted on the table, implying different amounts paid, as DE STOPPELAAR 1886, pp. 209-211, supposed (with reference to a second painting with a similar differentiation in costs). The statement by Nicolaes Eliasz about his painting of the company of Captain Van Vlooswijck (adjacent to the *Nightwatch*) that it "alsoo volmaeckt was, als de geconterfeyte personen selffs begeert en geordonneert hebben" (SIX 1909, p. 147) seems to indicate that his sitters also had made their stipulations. This seems to have been their prerogative in general, in Amsterdam (see also HAAK 1972, p. 15) and elsewhere. The effect of individual payment on the presence or absence of certain officers in militia pieces by Frans Hals and others was demonstrated by VAN VALKENBURG 1958-62; see also SLIVE 1970, p. 48.

[6] GERSON 1968, pp. 72, 76, and SCHÖNE 1973, pp. 87, 88.

[7] SCHMIDT-DEGENER 1916a., pp. 66, 67, stressed this point.

[8] Group portraits of governors of the *doelens*, on the other hand, were paid from funds of the association, according to the contemporary statement by Bontemantel: "De compagniën sijn geschildert uyt de beurs van de schutters, en de overluyden apparent uyt de gemene cas" (MEIJER 1886, p. 232; BONTEMANTEL-KERNKAMP 1897, p. 188).

been portrayed by Rembrandt individually, they would have had to pay considerably more.[9] In general, group portraits must have been bargains for those who wished to perpetuate their appearance, and their proliferation may, at least partly, have been caused by the attraction of these opportunities.

Finally, the statements speak of sixteen men portrayed in the painting, whereas a framed shield in the painting, about which more is said below, contains a reliable list of eighteen names. How can this discrepancy be explained? Probably, in speaking about the company, the two witnesses were referring to its men, not to its chief officers. Banning Cocq and Van Ruytenburgh may have made their own arrangements with the artist.[10] In that case, Rembrandt would have received considerably more than 1,600 florins.

According to these sources, and there is no reason to doubt them, the painting is a group portrait of men represented as members of a militia company in the process of starting to march under the command of their captain and lieutenant. Not long after Rembrandt had completed the *Nightwatch*, the names of eighteen men portrayed were inscribed on the framed shield that was added to the archway as if it were hanging from its cornice (Fig. 28). The names have been verified, and are correct; furthermore, the men are listed in order of seniority, and the shield therefore has authority.[11] Only eighteen of the twenty-

[9] Jan Vogelesangh, one of the six most prominent sitters out of the sixteen in De Keyser's painting, had to pay 61 florins. De Keyser's painting is less than two-fifths the size of the *Nightwatch*. For Vogelesangh's payment, and a comparison with the *Nightwatch*, see VAN EEGHEN 1965. About 1642 Rembrandt charged 500 florins for one double portrait (or perhaps two companion pieces, now lost) with an additional 60 florins for canvas and frame (HDG 1906, no. 209); for one single portrait, that of Andries de Graeff, as much as 500 florins in or shortly before 1642 (probably the large *Standing Man* in Kassel; see HDG 1906, no. 208, and DUDOK VAN HEEL 1969). NEUMANN 1902, p. 220, and HAAK 1969, pp. 179, 180, considered 1,600 florins a low price, and so does TÜMPEL 1977, p. 85 (*contra*: SLIVE 1953, p. 6, "Rembrandt was well paid").

[10] Were their fees also paid from the budget of the *doelen* as were those of the governors (see note 8)? That the captain or both he and the lieutenant might not have been included in the count of sixteen was supposed by respectively SCHMIDT-DEGENER 1916a., p. 67, and VAN SCHENDEL-MERTENS 1947, p. 38 (also HAAK 1969, p. 179a; HIJMANS-KUIPER-VELS HEIJN 1976, p. 55).

[11] MEIJER 1886, p. 209, already concluded that the shield was later; DYSERINCK 1890, p. 249, and others agreed. VAN SCHENDEL-MERTENS 1947, pp. 36-39, established it beyond doubt (unconvincingly suggesting Gerbrand van den Eeckhout as its painter). The shield originally seems to have been included in the copy by Lundens and subsequently to have been overpainted (MACLAREN 1960, p. 346). In that case, it dates from before 1655, probably even from before 1649, rather than "from the third quarter of

nine figures in the painting are portraits; the others are included for other reasons. Although only six or seven names can be assigned to specific figures, there can be little doubt as to which of the eighteen men are portraits (see diagram with key, Fig. 2). Difficulties are provided only by the man (no. 27) whose face is partly hidden behind an arm (Fig. 25), since it could be mistaken for a portrait, and by the absence of two portraits that were lost at the very left when the canvas was cut down (Fig. 26).[12] The extra figures were crucial for Rembrandt in conveying the image of the sitters in their various roles as citizens and militiamen.

Why Rembrandt? For some he may have been the most eminent, for many certainly one of the two or three best known portrait painters in Amsterdam. He already had a very successful group portrait to his name, *The Anatomical Demonstration of Dr. Tulp*, had contact with the militia, one of whose members he had portrayed individually, and, to judge by the armor he donned in some of his self-portraits, he

---

the century" (MARTIN 1947, p. 19) or from about 1690 (SCHMIDT-DEGENER, *in litteris*, *ibidem*). VAN DIJK 1758 was the first to print a list of sitters, undoubtedly transcribed from the shield, with numerous inaccuracies and omissions; Van Dijk's list in its turn was copied on the reverse of Lundens' painting (MEIJER 1886, p. 209; MACLAREN 1960, pp. 343, 347; transcription corrected by DYSERINCK 1890, pp. 249-251 and VAN SCHENDEL-MERTENS 1947, pp. 36-38). The list now reads: "Frans Banning Cocq / heer van Purmerlant en Ilpendam / Capiteijn / Willem van Ruijtenburch van Vlaerding / heer van Vlaerdingen' leutenant / Jan Visscher Cornelisen' vaendrich. / Rombout Kemp' Sergeant / Reijnier Engelen' Sergeant / Barent Harmansen / Jan Adriaensen Keyser / Elbert Willemsen / Jan Clasen Leijdeckers / Ian Ockersen / Jan Pietersen bronchorst / Harman Iacobsen wormskerck / Jacob Dircksen de Roy / Jan vander heede / walich Schellingwou / Jan Brugman / Claes van Cruysbergen / Paulus Schoonhoven". That the men are listed in order of seniority of membership in the militia was concluded by S.A.C. Dudok van Heel, chiefly on the basis of the time of their taking up residence in the second precinct (letter, November 26, 1979; I again express my gratefulness). For a slightly different reading, see STRAUSS-VAN DER MEULEN 1980, no. 1642/11.

[12] That the man at the very left (no. 32) was portrayed is most likely because of his musket and musket rest, and because of the care with which his features and costume are rendered. His bareheadedness does not exclude him as a portrayed member of the company since many militiamen in other militia pieces are without headgear. Some writers on the *Nightwatch* considered him to be an addition and instead interpreted no. 27 as a portrait, thus reaching the total of eighteen portraits. In no other militia piece, however, is a portrait face partly obscured by an arm or other part of the body. The rejection of no. 32 as a portrait probably was due to the reluctance to accept the fact that the painting was cut. MEIJER 1886, p. 209, DYSERINCK 1890, p. 252, and SCHMIDT-DEGENER 1916b, p. 40, correctly interpreted no. 32 as a portrait (but the latter considered no. 27 also a portrait, and no. 24 as only a "supernumerary"). There is no reason to entertain the thought that no. 27 might be a self-portrait of Rembrandt as HIJMANS-KUIPER-VELS HEIJN 1976, p. 52, do.

apparently had a personal interest in the militia.[13] Yet, fame and vague
affiliations do not explain why Rembrandt and not Thomas de Keyser
or one of the other successful portraitists was chosen. The captain and
lieutenant may have had a stronger voice than the members of the
company, also in matters of portraiture. Banning Cocq's ambition
matched Rembrandt's stature, but we do not know how the two found
each other. The members of the company, who all paid individually,
must have had considerable influence on the choice. Possibly some
tentative suppositions about the reasons for the choice may be drawn
after we have reviewed the sitters and some of their activities.[14]

We know that Rembrandt completed the painting before the end
of 1642, because he placed that year after his signature (Fig. 27). He
presumably was paid before June 14 of that same year, as we may
conclude from the declarations of some of the sitters, mentioned above,
which were made to establish the extent of Rembrandt's possessions
at the time of Saskia's death, which occurred that day. It has not been
established, however, when he received the commission. It can have
been given only after Frans Banning Cocq's appointment as captain
of the militia, but that year is not available either.[15] A recent find by
the Amsterdam archivist Dudok van Heel allows us now to conclude
that the commission was given to Rembrandt before December 1640.[16]
One of the men portrayed in the painting, Jan Claesz Leijdeckers, was
buried December 27 of that year. His appearance among Banning
Cocq's men—although we do not know which of the portrayed men
he was—does not imply that he was already painted before he died,
but it does indicate that Rembrandt had received the commission by

[13] Both *The Anatomical Demonstration of Dr. Tulp* (BREDIUS 1935, no. 403, Mauritshuis, The Hague) and the *Portrait of Joris de Caullery* in San Francisco (BREDIUS
1935, no. 170) date from 1632. De Caullery wears a metal collar and carries a musket;
a sword is attached to his side. The sitter lived in The Hague where he was lieutenant
of one of the six militia companies in 1635. My doubts about the identity of the sitter
and the nature of his weapon (HAVERKAMP-BEGEMANN 1980, p. 205) were superfluous
(letter of J. Bruyn with opinions of B. Kist and R. Scheller, August 14, 1980). Rembrandt
represented himself and other sitters at various times with a gorget (BREDIUS 1935,
nos. 6, 20, 24, 25, 132).

[14] See Chapter II and its notes 29 through 34.

[15] Banning Cocq was appointed captain after August 1638 (Maria de' Medici's entry;
KOK 1967, p. 118).

[16] S.A.C. Dudok van Heel established, in discussion August 27-28, 1979, that Jan
Claesz Leijdeckers, who lived *op het Water* ("on the Damrak") in the fifth house north
of the Zoutsteeg, made his will December 20, 1640, and that he was buried one week
later, December 27 (also letter February 5, 1980, and ms. 1981). One may conclude
that Banning Cocq was apointed captain before December 1640.

that date. He therefore probably started considering the artistic problems posed by the commission already before December 1640, and may then have begun the painting. We assume that he worked at it during the year 1641 and part of the first half of 1642.[17]

How did Rembrandt accomplish this demanding task? We know little about preparatory work for group portraits of militiamen, and virtually nothing about that for the *Nightwatch*. Rembrandt's pupil Govert Flinck sketched, in 1648, some figures in black chalk, either from nature or from memory, in the attitudes they would occupy in the painting, *The Company of Jan Huydecoper* (Amsterdam, Rijksmuseum), introducing the likenesses of the sitters only in the painting itself. He apparently also painted an oil sketch for the entire painting.[18] Jan van Ravesteyn made earlier, in 1618, a large and detailed drawing for his painting *The Magistrates of The Hague Receiving the Officers of the Militia* that may have served the purpose of a modello or a *vidimus*. Thomas de Keyser's drawings for his group portrait of 1632, to be discussed later, may also have been submitted to the patrons.[19] Whether Rembrandt submitted a detailed drawing for approval, we do not know. Neither is it clear whether he made studies of individual figures the way he would do later for the *Syndics*. He must have made quick, rough, preliminary lay-out scribbles for the *Nightwatch* that were soon discarded.[20] The only drawings that are related to the *Nightwatch* and that preceded it are two studies of individual militiamen, one in the Louvre and one in the Museum in Budapest (Figs. 4 and

[17] It took Thomas de Keyser also more than a year (from November 1630 to sometime in 1632) to complete his *Company of Captain Allaert Cloeck* (see Chapter V and its note 11).

[18] For Flinck's drawings for *The Company of Jan Huydecoper*, see MOLTKE 1965, nos. D.39 and D.40, ill.; for Flinck's oil sketch and his procedure, BLANKERT 1975-79, p. 124.

[19] J. A. van Ravesteyn's painting of 1618 is in the Gemeentemuseum, The Hague, his drawing for it in the Institut Néerlandais (Coll. Frits Lugt), Paris. Painting and drawing are reproduced side by side in LA VIE EN HOLLANDE 1967, plates 86-88; for De Keyser's drawings, like van Ravesteyn's more advanced in movement and composition than the corresponding painting, see Chapter V and its note 11.

[20] For such drawings, see J. Rosenberg in CHICAGO 1973, p. 140, who characterizes them as "fugitive drawings". One by Rembrandt for *The Conspiracy of the Batavians* is preserved in the National Gallery of Scotland, Edinburgh (HAVERKAMP-BEGEMANN 1970, pp. 31-43). Rembrandt's extremely summary compositional outline sketch in red chalk for his etching *Joseph Telling His Dreams* of 1638 (BARTSCH 1791, no. 37) was recently found on a corner of the reverse of another drawing by GILTAY 1977. It certainly was not intended to be preserved.

5). These are related to the *Nightwatch* in a general sense rather than as studies for specific individual figures, yet Rembrandt may very well have drawn them with the *Nightwatch* in mind.[21]

One painting for the same hall as Rembrandt's *Nightwatch* is known to have been executed elsewhere in Amsterdam rather than in the hall itself. Nicolaes Eliasz' portrait of the company of Captain Jan van Vlooswijck was brought to the Kloveniersdoelen shortly before July 29, 1642, and placed in the hall.[22] It is likely that Rembrandt also painted the *Nightwatch* elsewhere. The hall had been in use since 1631, and the artists therefore probably all had to do their work outside the building.

Rembrandt used three horizontal strips of canvas, of a width of 141.5 centimeters, sewn together, allowing for a maximum height of about 420 centimeters.[23] After having covered the sized canvas with a brownish ground, he sketched the subject roughly with black and brownish strokes, thus making the lay-out of the painting. He subsequently sketched, rapidly although with greater definition, the light areas with whitish paint, applied rather thickly, and then painted the entire painting from that basic design.[24] Photographs using X-rays made in 1945-46 and 1975-76 indicate a number of changes, but they are all comparatively small.[25] Frequently he changed the contour or

---

[21] The officer in the drawing in the Louvre (Walter Gay Bequest, Inv. no. 29031; LUGT 1933, under no. 1317; BENESCH 1954-57, IV, no. 661) and probably also the one in Budapest (Inv. no. 1586; ALTENA 1955, p. 418, fig. 12 [as by Rembrandt]; VAN GELDER 1961, p. 151, note 17; not in Benesch) may be captains, since they seem to hold a baton. A third drawing sometimes connected with the *Nightwatch*, perhaps representing a standing officer, in black chalk, also in the Louvre (LUGT 1933, no. 1161; BENESCH 1954-57, IV, no. 663; WIJNBEEK 1944, ill. p. 66), may postdate the *Nightwatch* (see also LUGT 1933, no. 1317).

[22] The circumstances of the painting of Eliasz' group portrait (DE GELDER 1921, pp. 51, 140) are now described in great detail, with use of new documents, by BLANKERT 1975-79, no. 140.

[23] According to COPPIER 1922; in his opinion 141.5 cm. (five Amsterdam feet of 28.3 cm. each) was the maximum width of canvas available in 1642. The width of the canvas of *Jacob Blessing* of 1656 in Kassel, which has preserved its original woven edges, measures approximately 175.5 cm. (SONNENBURG 1978, pp. 221, 230).

[24] This summary of Rembrandt's working method is based on the detailed analysis by E. van de Wetering and his co-authors C. M. Groen and J. A. Mosk (BULLETIN 1976, pp. 68-79). Their reconstruction partly confirms, partly invalidates the earlier ones of Doerner and Laurie. I do not believe, however, that Van de Wetering's supposition that Rembrandt worked from background to foreground can be substantiated (the same doubt is expressed by SONNENBURG 1978, with further valuable observations on Rembrandt's technique).

[25] VAN SCHENDEL-MERTENS 1947 published conclusions drawn from X-rays made in 1945-46, E. van de Wetering *et al.* and G. van de Voorde did the same from the

placement of a helmet (particularly the one of the shooting figure in the center was originally much larger), or the border of a hat (that of Van Ruytenburgh, for instance). The changes in Rombout Kemp (no. 5) seem to indicate that he originally was wearing a helmet,[26] and that he first held his halberd in a vertical position, to the left of his head. By making him carry it over his shoulder and letting it stick forward, Rembrandt emphasized the three-dimensionality of space.[27] Similarly, Rembrandt enlarged the silhouette of the musket on the dress of the girl in gold (no. 13) and adjusted the foreshortening of Van Ruytenburgh's partisan by lengthening its blade twice (Figs. 13 and 14). These changes, however significant their visual effect, do not concern basic features of the composition. The figures seem to have been painted in place from the beginning. Apparently, Rembrandt had established the painting with its essential details in the preliminary compositional brush drawing on the canvas itself.

Of course, Rembrandt could draw from his store of previous experiences in representing crowds in complicated spatial arrangements as well as defining individual figures and architectural settings. He had used the central arch as an accentuating and unifying element[28] and walls to close off space before, but never had he emphasized these elements as strongly as in the *Nightwatch*.[29] The movement of figures in front of static groups was another device which he had developed earlier.[30] And the historical, social, and political background of the Amsterdam militia was familiar to him. Simultaneously with the

---

1975-76 radiographs (BULLETIN 1976). The following remarks, which by and large agree with theirs, are based on my own reading of the x-ray photographs of 1945-46 (I am grateful to P.J.J. van Thiel for giving me access to them), and, for Van Ruytenburgh's partisan and the shooting militiaman's helmet, on the 1975-76 radiograph, BULLETIN 1976, p. 53, and Van de Wetering's article.

[26] If that is the case, then the "lost" feathers behind his hat could be explained as a remnant of the painted-out helmet. Apparently, Rembrandt frequently introduced changes in helmets and other head-coverings in the *Nightwatch*, some of which can be seen with the naked eye: the top hat of the man in the center above Banning Cocq originally was lower in front; the point of the helmet of the man blowing the pan has been changed more than once; the collar of the ensign was first higher.

[27] The fingertips of Banning Cocq's outstretched hand were first a little higher; his hand was therefore slightly more curved.

[28] For instance, in the etchings of *The Great Jewish Bride* of 1635 (BARTSCH 1791, no. 340), *The Beheading of St. John the Baptist* of 1640 (BARTSCH 1791, no. 92), and *The Angel Departing from the Family of Tobias* of 1641 (BARTSCH 1791, no. 43). For these and other antecedents see NEUMANN 1902, pp. 268, 269 (1924, pp. 292, 293) and WEISBACH 1926, pp. 342, 343.

[29] As stated by GERSON 1968, pp. 75, 76.

[30] This concept was analyzed by H. van de Waal in 1967 (according to BREDIUS-GERSON 1969, p. 584).

Nightwatch or shortly afterwards, he painted the oil sketch of *The Concord of the State* for a project, probably an etching or else a painting, that was never executed.[31] This complicated allegory, whatever its exact meaning, could only be represented with a thorough knowledge of the struggle between Spain and the Netherlands and of the role of Amsterdam, its political power and armed might within the Northern Netherlands. He had also fused portraiture and action in a group portrait, *The Anatomical Demonstration of Dr. Tulp*, and used the action to define the nature of the sitters.[32] Yet, even if Rembrandt had already come to terms with some of the problems of form and subject posed by the commission for the *Nightwatch*, it is surprising that no preparatory studies for the painting have been preserved.

The *Nightwatch* has not come down to us unscathed. The painting unfortunately is smaller than it originally was.[33] It was cut down at the left and, less seriously, at the other three sides.[34] This was done

[31] The last digit of the year 1641 on the sketch has been disputed, most recently by J. G. van Gelder, who reads it as five (CHICAGO 1973, p. 9) and the Amsterdam group of Rembrandt researchers who by September 1975 had reached the preliminary conclusion that six is more likely than any other digit (letter of J. Bruyn, September 24, 1975). For the subject matter, see the bibliography listed by BREDIUS-GERSON 1969, p. 593, no. 476, and J. G. van Gelder, CHICAGO 1973, pp. 6-10. Although the date 1641 seems preferable to 1645, the suggestion of SCHMIDT-DEGENER 1912 and 1914a., pp. 3-17, to consider the painting a study for the *Nightwatch* cannot be accepted; his later supposition (1917a., pp. 28, 29) that it might have been projected as a chimney piece for the assembly hall of the Kloveniersdoelen is not supported by any other instance of a political allegory at such a location. The wall space over the fireplaces in assembly halls of *doelens* was reserved for the portraits of the governors. I do not accept Van de Wetering's supposition that *The Concord of The State* is an unfinished painting rather than a sketch (BULLETIN 1976, p. 80).

[32] TÜMPEL 1977, p. 81.

[33] The curtailment was already mentioned as a regrettable fact by VAN DIJCK 1758 (p. 61 of 1760 ed.); yet Jan Veth and others (most recently MOES-VETH 1960), unable to accept the shattering of an idol, have tried to deny it. (According to MEIJER 1906, p. 446, Jan Veth "felt upset by the statements of some foreign writers that *The Nightwatch* had lost a great deal of its artistic value by this curtailment"). For further literature concerning this question, see VAN SCHENDEL-MERTENS 1947, p. 12, and KUIPER-HESTERMAN 1976, p. 48.

[34] The *Nightwatch*, now 363 × 437 cm. large (ALL THE PAINTINGS 1976, p. 469; VAN SCHENDEL-MERTENS 1947, p. 27, give 363 × 438 cm.), measured originally ca. 402 × 510 cm. according to DE HAAS 1927 (on the assumption of a present width of 435 cm.). NEUMANN 1902, p. 275, came to an original size of 387 × 502 cm.; COPPIER 1922 to one of ca. 412-414 × 523 cm.; J. Six to one of 358.7 × 497 cm. (according to MARTIN 1933, p. 224) and KOOT 1947, p. 22, to one of at least 388 × 479 cm.

in or shortly after 1715 in order to fit the painting between two doors in the Small War Council Room in the Town Hall when it was moved there from its original location in the Kloveniersdoelen. Fortunately, soon after the painting was finished, Frans Banning Cocq had a reduced copy made by Gerrit Lundens (1622-ca. 1683).[35] Lundens painted this copy (Fig. 3) probably in or before 1649, because his *Country Wedding* of that year is, in composition, a paraphrase of the *Nightwatch* (Fig. 90).[36] From Lundens' copy, we learn that two men and a child were cut off at the left (Fig. 26), a narrow strip of the drummer at the right, the crown of the archway at the top, and some space in front of the figures at the bottom. However regrettable, the effect of the cutting

---

The discrepancies probably result from the rough and partly oblique edges of the canvas caused by the cutting of 1715 (KUIPER-HESTERMAN 1976, p. 48). Because of these oblique edges, the painting was slightly tilted (first noted by COPPIER 1922) until it was straightened in 1975-76.

[35] The traditional attribution of this copy on panel, 66.8/67 × 85.4/85.8 cm., now on loan from the National Gallery, London, to the Rijksmuseum, was questioned unnecessarily by MACLAREN 1960, p. 345. It is confirmed by three minature portraits, all signed and dated 1650 (*Portrait of a Young Man* and *Portrait of a Woman*, Rijksmuseum, nos. A4337 and A4338, and *Portrait of a Man* in the collection of H. M. the Queen of the Netherlands). Furthermore, Lundens' relationship with the Amsterdam militia is confirmed by his portrait of Reier Pietersz Elias with musket and slowmatch, unfortunately destroyed by fire in 1864 (64 × 47 cm., signed but not dated, described in BESCHRIJVING BOYMANS 1862, no. 192). That Banning Cocq commissioned the copy (as MARTIN 1951, p. 5, stated without substantiating his assumption) may be concluded from its provenance; from the circumstance that a drawing of the *Nightwatch* in Banning Cocq's albums was made from this copy rather than directly from the large painting; and from the fact that Banning Cocq also owned a copy of a second group portrait that included him (*Governors of the Handboogsdoelen*, now in the Louvre, also by Lundens; see Chapter II, notes 12 and 13). Banning Cocq may have chosen Lundens for his talents as a miniature portraitist since those were probably already developed by 1649. Lundens' ability to provide an accurate record is also apparent from his painting *The Fire of the Old Town Hall* (Amsterdams Historisch Museum). The fire occurred July 6-7, 1652. For provenance and literature on Lundens' copy of the *Nightwatch*, see MACLAREN 1960, pp. 343-349, and ALL THE PAINTINGS 1976, p. 473, no. C1453. The date before 1655 is derived from the fact that the drawing in Banning Cocq's albums was executed before that year (DYSERINCK 1890, p. 240); for the probable date of 1649, see next note.

[36] GLÜCK 1907, pp. 18, 45, pl. after p. 16, pointed out the relationship and concluded that Lundens' copy of the *Nightwatch* preceded this *Country Wedding* (panel, 84 × 112 cm., signed with monogram and dated 1649; later sold in Vienna with the collection of VON AMERLING, December 1-4, 1920, no. 39; present location unknown). It is indeed difficult to find another explanation of this unusual borrowing, in spite of the skepticism of VAN SCHENDEL-MERTENS 1947, p. 12, and MACLAREN 1960, p. 345 (WEISBACH 1926, p. 614, accepted the hypothesis; others passed it over). A variation of this *Country Wedding*, also signed by Lundens although not dated and somewhat further removed from the *Nightwatch*, was in 1973-74 with the David M. Koetser Gallery in Zürich.

could have been worse, since the greatest loss occurred in the least significant areas of the painting. Yet, for questions concerning composition and space, the Lundens copy should be consulted.[37]

Equally important for the study of the *Nightwatch* is the excellent preservation of the colors of Lundens' copy. Since it is painted on panel, the thinly applied brown and other dark areas have darkened less in time than the corresponding passages in the *Nightwatch* itself, and the color balance of Lundens' copy reflects the original state of the large painting in many respects better than the painting itself in its present state.

This is particularly true since the most recent cleaning and restoration of the *Nightwatch* after its damage by an unbalanced person. The man cut through the paint and even the canvas in various places, particularly in the lower part of the costume of Captain Banning Cocq.[38] The expert restoration carried out by L. Kuiper and W. Hesterman and their staff at the Rijksmuseum has completely obliterated the damage. The cleaning carried out concurrently has left virtually no traces of any of the previous varnishes or retouchings.[39] Since their own retouching has been kept to a minimum, the present balance of tones is that of the original paint and of discolorations caused by time, and, particularly in the thinly painted areas, by the many wax relinings of the past. Those areas that presumably have changed very little, like the many heavily painted light-colored costumes, are virtually the same in the Lundens copy. These areas lead to the conclusion that originally the *Nightwatch* looked very much as the copy does now; that is, there was less contrast, with lighter shadows and a lighter background. In spite of being only one thirty-sixth the size of the original, Lundens' copy is a remarkably trustworthy document.

[37] I suggested once it would do justice to the painting to add around it a reconstruction of the missing parts matching it in colors yet recognizable as an addition (HAVERKAMP-BEGEMANN 1947). This was impractical as A. van Schendel, then curator of paintings at the Rijksmuseum, pointed out in a postscript to my note. Our imagination must make up for the loss.

[38] The damage was caused on September 14, 1975, the restoration completed during the summer of the following year. The restoration has been described with admirable candor by the restorers, and concurrent analyses have been reported by E. van de Wetering and others in BULLETIN 1976.

[39] I do not think this is the place to discuss the merits or demerits of the restoration. Let it suffice to state that the original, or what time has left of it in some areas, has been admirably respected, but that in some thin areas, the painting, and therefore Rembrandt, could have been assisted if a few more damaged passages (thin shadows, a few faces) had been retouched further. I fully realize that borderlines are difficult to draw. I am also of the opinion that the painting is now closer to its original state than after the cleaning of 1945-46.

II

The Men Portrayed:
Regents and Merchants

The contemporary viewer knew many of the citizens portrayed in the *Nightwatch* by name, particularly the most prominent ones, and if he did not recognize them, he associated them with their level of society, the type of activities they performed, their role in the life of the city. For a reconstruction of the meaning of the painting, these associations need to be traced.

The list of names in the shield added to the painting starts with captain and lieutenant, adding the lofty-sounding title of "Lord of Purmerland and Ilpendam" to the name of Captain Frans Banning Cocq, and that of "Lord of Vlaardingen" to the name of Lieutenant Wilhem van Ruytenburgh.[1] Captain Banning Cocq and his lieutenant clearly stand out in the painting (Fig. 6). The former, dressed in black, holds the captain's baton in his right hand, and wears a red sash and, barely visible under his white collar, a gorget made of steel. Van Ruytenburgh, holding a partisan in his left hand as attribute of his rank, is dressed in yellow and wears a white sash and a polished, finely decorated gorget.

Frans Banning Cocq was born in 1605, and was therefore about thirty-seven years old when Rembrandt finished his portrait in the *Nightwatch*.[2] His father, Jan Cock, had come to Amsterdam from

---

[1] For the shield and the names see the preceding chapter and its note 11. After this chapter was written, new investigations by S.A.C. Dudok van Heel in the Amsterdam archives provided additional data concerning the sitters. He completed the record of their birth and death dates, of their residences (except for two), of their professions, and found other additional data concerning their lives and relatives. I am very grateful to Mr. Dudok van Heel, who will publish a compilation of all known and new data in the near future, for having made these *curricula vitae* available to me (verbal communications, letters November 26, 1979, February 5 and May 9, 1980, and part of his ms. DUDOK VAN HEEL 1981).

[2] For Frans Banning Cocq, see ELIAS 1903-05, I, p. 406 and index; BONTEMANTEL-KERNKAMP 1897, index and p. 193; WIJNBEEK 1944, pp. 83-101; MEIJER 1968; and

Bremen at the age of fifteen.[3] Jan Cock did well; he soon owned his own apothecary shop, and in 1631 was estimated for tax purposes to be worth 60,000 florins. He married Lijsbeth, the daughter of Frans Benningh, a wealthy merchant. In accordance with an old custom, Frans Banning Cocq was named after his maternal grandfather, with both given name and family name. This naming may be an expression of his parents' ambitions concerning his future career. The Benninghs had been members of the city council (Vroedschap), and the visibility of Frans' parentage later would support his claims to a seat in this self-perpetuating body of the city government. Another relationship that helped his career was his multiple ties with the distinguished family of burgomaster Cornelis Pietersz Hooft (1547-1628). He followed in his father's footsteps by marrying, in 1630, the wealthy Maria Overlander, daughter of the merchant and shipowner Volckert Overlander, who was burgomaster in 1628 and at one time governor of the Kloveniersdoelen.[4]

As a wealthy father-in-law, Overlander came to mean much to Banning Cocq. In 1609, Overlander bought one of the most distinguished houses built in Amsterdam in the first quarter of the seventeenth century, the sumptuous double house "The Dolphin", built by Hendrick de Keyser for the poet-merchant Hendrick Laurensz Spieghel between 1595 and 1606 (Fig. 46; presently at Singel 140-142); in 1612 he acquired the manor of Purmerland and Ilpendam north of

---

now with full detail DUDOK VAN HEEL 1981. According to JOCHEMS 1888, p. 29, Cocq became lieutenant in Precinct I in 1635 and still occupied that rank there in 1638. The customary spelling of the name is maintained here although he himself seems to have preferred "Banninck-Cocq" toward the end of his life (signature under letter of August 28, 1654, Gem. Archiefsdienst, Amsterdam, and under the ordinance of the same year [see below]). In 1628, on his doctor-of-law diploma, he is called "Franciscus Bannink".

[3] Like other immigrants from Germany, Jan Cock (1575-1633) and/or his parents may have come originally from Flanders (FREDERIKS 1892, p. 28). Pieter de Graeff's statement that Jan Cock, after coming from Bremen, "is said to have gone begging from door to door" ("ostiatim mendicasse dicitur"), sometimes repeated, has to be taken *cum grano salis* (MEIJER 1906, p. 427; ELIAS 1903-05, I, p. 406; and others). DUDOK VAN HEEL 1981 points out that when Jan Cock arrived in Amsterdam he took advantage of his relationship with the Hooft family. Frans Banning Cocq, therefore, cannot be called an upstart.

[4] For Volckert Overlander (1571-1630), see BONTEMANTEL-KERNKAMP 1897, p. 175, ELIAS 1903-05, I, p. 274, MEIJER 1906, and DUDOK VAN HEEL 1981. He is portrayed as lieutenant in the militia piece *The Company of Captain Jonas Cornelisz Witsen* painted by Cornelis van der Voort for the Kloveniersdoelen (Rijksmuseum no. C748; BLANKERT 1975-79, no. 484) and copied for Banning Cocq's album (see below note 13). The estate of Volcker Overlander's widow was evaluated in 1631 at 150,000 guilders. His daughter Maria was born in 1603 and died in 1678.

Amsterdam, with the title Heer, and ten years later he built there an elegant old-fashioned country house, Ilpenstein, resembling a medieval castle (Fig. 47), which his son Frans enlarged.[5] Overlander must also have had an interest in art, even if his involvement may have been primarily financial: the publisher of Karel van Mander's *Schilderboek* dedicated the second edition to him in 1618.[6]

When Overlander died in 1630, Maria Overlander inherited both houses and a considerable fortune, and Frans Banning Cocq himself was invested with the title of lord of Purmerland and Ilpendam. Another honor befell him in 1648 when he received the order of St. Michael from the king of France. He was also a man of great achievement. He studied law and received a doctor's degree in the subject in Poitiers in France in 1626. In 1632, he started his ascent of the administrative ladder by becoming administrator of marriage contracts for the city of Amsterdam ("commissaris van het college van huwelijkse zaken"); two years later, at the age of twenty-nine, he was elected a life member of the Vroedschap, the city's oligarchic, self-perpetuating advisory council of thirty-six men. In 1637 he became alderman, a position he also held in 1640, 1642, 1645, 1646, 1648, and 1649. Then, in 1650, he was elected burgomaster for the usual term of one

[5] A pen and watercolor drawing of De Dolphijn is found on page 38 of volume one of Banning Cocq's albums (reproduced by KERNKAMP 1897, I, pt. 1, opp. p. 129, and by MEIJER 1906, p. 428). A print of the facade was included in the book of De Keyser's designs ARCHITECTURA MODERNA 1631, pl. 33, its merits qualified in an introduction by Taverne (ibidem, ed. 1971, p. 7). The house was restored in 1966-67 (VAN EEGHEN 1967). As Miss Van Eeghen points out, the house was named by Spieghel, since Arion riding the dolphin was his emblem. On October 24, 1975, a plaque honoring Banning Cocq was affixed to the facade.

Ilpenstein, razed in 1877, is known from drawings by A. Schouman and C. Pronk, from a lithograph by J. C. Backer after F. H. Sypkens (MEIJER 1906, ill. p. 444), and from two watercolor drawings and a ground plan in Banning Cocq's albums (here reproduced is the one on page 136 of volume two); it is represented in its rural setting in Joris van der Hagen's beautiful *View of Ilpendam* in the Louvre (no. 2382, canvas, 37 × 42 cm.; according to STECHOW 1966, p. 49, fig. 83, from the later 1650s). The most comprehensive history of the country house was written by OSINGA 1961; further observations in VAN AGT 1953, p. 63, and MEISCHKE 1978, pp. 88, 89 (VAN ENST KONING 1836 is rather chatty). DUDOK VAN HEEL 1981 points to the need for Amsterdamers who had no land to acquire properties and titles, and the availability of both when during the Twelve Years Truce (1609-21) many South Netherlanders sold their properties in the north. The preference for medieval styles manifest in Cocq's country house and others, and its meaning for the owner's interpretation of the Dutch past, needs to be investigated further.

[6] The publisher Jacob Wachter dedicated this edition to Overlander and Jean ten Grootenhuys (pointed out by MEIJER 1906, p. 444).

year, and thus joined the body of four that made the ultimate decisions
in Amsterdam. What is more, the next year he was allowed to stay
on as presiding burgomaster—normally, burgomasters had to skip a
year before being eligible. In 1653 he was again elected burgomaster,
and once more he became presiding burgomaster the next year.

He moved up quickly in Amsterdam's militia. He was appointed
lieutenant of Amsterdam's first precinct in 1635, captain of the second
precinct before December 1640; in 1646 he became one of the two
colonels in charge of all twenty militia companies in the city (and by
law had to resign as captain); in 1648 he was appointed governor
(*doelheer* or *overman*) of the old and distinguished Handboogsdoelen.
As colonel, he initiated, with Andries Bicker, in 1647 a description of
the twenty precincts of Amsterdam, and he issued in 1650 over his
signature a new ordinance for the Amsterdam militia (Fig. 50).[7] This
effort to revitalize the militia undoubtedly was not a mere gesture.
Andries Bicker, one of the strongest opponents of the power of the
Prince of Orange, and Banning Cocq, himself a protagonist of the
freedom and independence of Amsterdam, the republic city, knew that
a well-organized militia could only help their cause and the cause of
Amsterdam.

His interest in the militia was indeed intense. The four governors
of the Handboogsdoelen requested a certain "Colin" (probably Jacob
Colijns) to make drawings after all the paintings in their building and
to record the names of the sitters, "so that people forever would know
who they were". We may suppose that Banning Cocq was the one to
initiate this project.[8] These drawings indeed fulfilled their purpose:

[7] The appointment as lieutenant according to JOCHEMS 1888, p. 29, and KOK 1967,
p. 118. The date *post quem* of the appointment as captain is based on the absence of
his name on the list of captains as of August 1638 (KOK, ibidem), the date *ante quem*
from the hypothetical date of the commission of the painting (Chapter I and its note
16). The appointment to colonel occurred in January 1646 (BONTEMANTEL-KERNKAMP
1897, p. 193; therefore not in 1647, as JOCHEMS 1888, pp. 5, 11, stated; ELIAS 1903-
05, I, p. 406, "1647 or earlier" was closer to the truth). This appointment implied that
he had to step down as captain. The year 1648 for the appointment as governor of the
Handboogsdoelen appears in ms. Egerton 983, f°2 (see following note). For the description of the precincts, see below, note 27. A copy of the ordinance of 1650 is
preserved in the "Historische Verzameling der Schutterij te Amsterdam", presently in
custody of the K.O.G., Amsterdam (JOCHEMS, CATALOGUS 1888, no. 25[bis]). JOCHEMS
1888, p. vii, gave a (not fully accurate) transcription of the ordinance.

[8] SCHAEP 1630-50s, see SCHELTEMA 1885, p. 131 ("ad perpetuam memoriam quoad
in posterum reperiri poterit"), without reference to Banning Cocq. For the album of
drawings (British Museum, London, ms. Egerton 983), see DEL COURT-SIX 1903. That
it probably was Banning Cocq who proposed the project is suggested by the following:

thanks to them, we are very well informed about the sitters of the paintings in the Handboogsdoelen. We know for certain that it was Banning Cocq who proposed to shorten the tenure of governors of the Kloveniersdoelen, presumably to make the governorship more active.[9] He did so in 1654, but nothing came of it, perhaps because of his death on the first day of January 1655. He died without issue.[10]

Banning Cocq's share in the *Nightwatch* was not his only commission to artists, though it was by far the most important one. In the same year that the *Nightwatch* was finished, he had stained-glass windows installed in the churches of Purmerland and Ilpendam.[11] The Purmerland window presented the coats of arms of Frans Banning Cocq in the center suspended in an aedicula with a *memento mori* under it and a personification of Fame in the canopy above (Fig. 48). The date was inscribed on a cartouche formed partly by two dolphins. The other window, presented to the church at Ilpendam, showed coats of arms only. He gave commissions to other artists also *ad majorem suam gloriam*. For that reason, he asked Gerrit Lundens to make a copy of the *Nightwatch*, and a second one of the group portrait that Bartholomeus van der Helst painted in 1653 of the four governors of the Handboogsdoelen, including, of course, himself (Fig. 44).[12] He

---

(1) he had an interest in having militia pieces copied; (2) the album contains a duplicate of the drawing after Van der Helst's painting of Banning Cocq and the other governors of the Sebastiaans-doelen; (3) the drawings are probably by the same hand as the copy of the *Nightwatch* in Banning Cocq's personal album (see below and note 13). I suppose that the lost detailed list of the paintings in the Doelens mentioned by MEIJER 1906, p. 444, without source (repeated by SCHMIDT-DEGENER 1916a., p. 66) refers to this volume. "Colin" mentioned as author of the volume by COMMELIN 1693, p. 664 (also by SCHELTEMA 1885, p. 131) probably was Jacob Colijns (1614-1686) because he specialized in genealogical subjects, and ms. Egerton 983 is full of coats of arms (on the artist see OLDEWELT 1942, pp. 101-106); the authors of BLANKERT 1975-79, p. 448 came to the same conclusion.

[9] BONTEMANTEL-KERNKAMP 1897, p. 176.

[10] Banning Cocq's widow was taxed in 1674 for property to the amount of 200,000 guilders (ELIAS 1903-05, I, p. 406); her wealth may have stemmed partly from the inheritance of her father.

[11] The windows have not been preserved, but they are known from watercolor drawings made for Banning Cocq's albums (see note 13). The watercolor depicting the window in Ilpendam is pasted in on pp. 81, 82, the one after the window in Purmerland, dated 1642, on pages 55, 56 of volume one. The captions to both state specifically that they were "given by the Lord of Purmerland". VAN AGT 1953, while describing the churches, does not mention the windows.

[12] See Chapter I and its note 35 for Lundens' copy of the *Nightwatch*. For *The Governors of the Handboogsdoelen* by Van der Helst in the Rijksmuseum (Cat. no. C3) see DYSERINCK 1893 and DE GELDER 1921, pp. 235, 236, no. 838; for the identity

also had two volumes made of drawings recording the works of art he commissioned, the paintings in which his father-in-law and he himself were represented, the houses he owned, and various achievements of his wife's ancestors and himself.[13] The *Nightwatch*, of course, appears in these albums, copied after Lundens' version (Fig. 43), and so does Van der Helst's *Governors of the Handboogsdoelen*, also after Lundens' copy. One sumptuous work of art, a sculptural decoration planned for the new town hall, was never executed. Only a terracotta sketch was completed. Designed by Artus Quellien or his studio, it represents the coats of arms of Banning Cocq and his ancestors, and includes the chain and medal of the order of St. Michael. Contrary to the truth, it pretends in the coats of arms of Banning Cocq's ancestors

---

of the sitters, DEL COURT-SIX 1903; for the likeness of Banning Cocq, DYSERINCK 1893 and MEIJER 1886, pp. 232-234; for the effect of the painting's location on the representation of figures and space, VAN DE WAAL 1956a., pp. 67, 68. The painting is partly overpainted and is trimmed at the bottom. The attribution of the copy in the Louvre (Fig. 44; canvas laid down on panel, 50 × 67 cm., Cat. 1922, no. 2394, and 1979, p. 69, as by Van der Helst) to Lundens rests on its similarity with the copy of the *Nightwatch* and on the likelihood that both were in the possession of Frans Banning Cocq (**Bredius** 1912; for its later history see BILLE 1961, I, p. 74, II, pp. 15, 96, no. 61). MEIJER 1886, p. 234, accepted the traditional attribution to Van der Helst himself (Cat. Louvre 1855, no. 197); DE GELDER 1921, under p. 235, stated "copy probably by Lundens"; **Martin** 1947, p. 23, referred to it as a work by Lundens. Van der Helst's authorship is still defended in LA VIE EN HOLLANDE 1967, no. 301, on the basis of Van der Helst's "signature" which, in fact, is copied from the original with the inscription of which it is part, and accepted in ALL THE PAINTINGS 1976, p. 268, under no. C3.

[13] The two albums belonging to the De Graeff family and on loan to the Rijksmuseum are entitled: *Geslacht / Register der Heeren en Vrouwen / van / Purmerlandt en Ilpendam. / Zoo in consanguiniteijt, als affiniteijt.* The pages of the albums apparently were filled consecutively with notes and drawings but without specific order. Some drawings were made on the pages of the albums, others were pasted in. The volumes are not dated, but were begun before December 1649 (Volume one contains a copy of the decree of the King of France of November 26, 1648, bestowing the order of St. Michael on Banning Cocq; this copy was authenticated in December 1649), terminated after 1653 (because volume two contains a drawing after Van der Helst's *Governors of the Handboogsdoelen* of that year), and before 1655 (because ms. notes in both volumes have been attributed by N. de Roever to Gerard Schaep who died in the summer of that year and by W. R. Veder to Banning Cocq himself who died January 1, 1655; these attributions of two successive archivists are found in volume one). The copy of the *Nightwatch* was drawn onto p. 142 of volume one after the copy of the decree had been pasted in, therefore shortly after December 1649, and well before 1655; "about 1650" seems a justifiable guess. The three drawings after paintings seem to be by the same hand as those in ms. Egerton 983 in London (see above note 8), therefore by Jacob Colijns. VEDER 1914 was not available to me.

displayed on the wooden frame that his father had been Lord of Purmerland, rather than his father-in-law (Fig. 49).[14]

In commissioning these works of art and ordering these albums, Banning Cocq must have been motivated by pride, vanity, and political ambition. To be successful in government in Amsterdam, the first prerequisite was to have the right family ties. In the stained-glass windows, in the selection of facts and portraits for his two volumes of records, he emphasized these ties, and drew attention to honors received and worldly possessions owned by him. Among the works of art in his life, the *Nightwatch* was by far the most significant in spite of being only a joint commission. He must have felt that his presence in the painting, while enhanced by the past glory of the militia, expressed his concerns for its strength and for the power of Amsterdam that it served; he undoubtedly also was gratified not only by the way it supported his personal ambitions, but also by the manner in which it paid tribute to his own achievements.

Wilhem van Ruytenburgh (1600-1652) had a similar, although somewhat less successful career.[15] His father, Pieter Gerritsz van Ruytenburgh (1562-1627), was a wholesale merchant in products of the Indies (*kruidenier*) and founded a trading company dealing with Rio de la Plata; he apparently managed it with great success. In 1611 he bought the manor of Vlaardingen from Karel, Prince of Ligne, Count of Aremberg, and in 1615 bought a second manor, that of Ter Horst near Voorschoten, from Lamoral, Prince of Ligne, and thus acquired land and titles, as Volckert Overlander did. On his property in Vlaardingen he built, in 1619, the country house, Het Hof te Vlaardingen. Like Banning Cocq, Van Ruytenburgh inherited these from his father, and he also enlarged the building. He likewise became a member of the Vroedschap, although not until 1639, and an alderman in 1641. He was appointed lieutenant in the second precinct in 1639 to succeed Gerbrand Claesz Pancras who in that year was elected burgomaster. He married Alida Jonckheyn who provided him with influential in-laws, but they were not so powerful as those of his captain; he lived

[14] His father's coat of arms was equally unjustly embellished in Banning Cocq's hatchment (Rijksmuseum, no. N.G. 87); the liberty taken was pointed out by VAN LUTTERVELT 1951. The terracotta sketch (Rijksmuseum; LEEUWENBERG 1973, p. 232, no. 306) was executed as a design for one of the coats of arms of burgomasters and exburgomasters in the Vierschaar of the Town Hall (1658; FREMANTLE 1977, pp. 30, 81). For further interpretation, see DUDOK VAN HEEL 1981.

[15] For Wilhem van Ruytenburgh, see ELIAS 1903-05, I, pp. 425, 534, Index, and DUDOK VAN HEEL 1981.

in 1642 in an elegant house on the Herengracht, the so-called Blue
House, but it was owned by his mother-in-law; he was never appointed
colonel, never elected burgomaster; and he was not a lifelong Amsterdamer.[16] In 1647, he moved to The Hague and Vlaardingen for
good. Although very successful, he did not fully measure up to Banning
Cocq.

Both were members of the small group of administrators and their
relatives who wielded the power in Amsterdam and who constituted
a caste rather than a class at the upper level of the social structure, a
true patriciate in the Roman sense. Banning Cocq and Ruytenburgh
belonged to this patriciate, called *regenten* ("regents"). The other
members of this militia company, however powerful many of them
were by means of their wealth and influence, did not. The others may
have aspired to the position of regents, but they had not reached it.

The third most significant person of any militia company had always
been the ensign. Traditionally, ensigns had to be bachelors, undoubtedly because preceding soldiers in battle, they were exposed to great
danger and should not risk leaving widow and children behind. In
spite of changed circumstances, few exceptions were made to this rule
in the seventeenth century. The honor to be chosen usually befell only
members of well-to-do families high on the social ladder.[17] Jan Cornelisz Visscher (1610-1650), the ensign of the *Nightwatch* (no. 3; Fig.
15), was thirty-one when portrayed in the *Nightwatch*. He lost his
father at an early age, and as an only child he grew up, with his
mother, in the house of his grandmother, who also was widowed at
an early age. His relatives had been merchants, and he was destined
for the trade, but there is no evidence that he followed their example.
He lived surrounded by art—more than fifty paintings decorated the
home where he lived; he enlarged a substantial library he had inherited
from an uncle, and, to judge by his estate, he was interested in music

[16] At the time of his marriage (1626) Van Ruytenburgh lived in the house "in ruytenburgh" on the Oude Zijds Achterburgwal (ELIAS 1903-05, I, p. 425; acc. to KOOT
1969, p. 48, the number is 45); his residence on the Herengracht in 1642 in " 't blaeuwe
Huys" (nos. 196-198) I owe to S.A.C. Dudok van Heel (from a discussion in August,
and a letter, November 26, 1979). In 1631, his mother-in-law was taxed on property
of 210,000 florins, his wife of 34,000, and he himself of 60,000. In 1632, Van Ruytenburgh seems to have tried to pass himself off as a descendant of a noble family of
this name in Brabant (ELIAS 1903-05, I, p. 435).

[17] The awe experienced by a young man just before assuming the responsibilities of
ensign is clearly expressed by G. A. Brederode in his poem "Een zekere hartstocht oft
ontroeringe, waargenomen uit mijn woelende gedachten, rechts voor mijn optrekken,
met het vaandel" (*Aendachtigh Liedt-boeck*, 1622). I owe this reference to J. W. Smit.

and drawings. He probably became an ensign in 1637. He died a bachelor in 1650 a few days before William II planned his attack on Amsterdam which was never carried out. His mother survived him and became his sole inheritor.[18]

Fourth and fifth in line were the two sergeants, both recognizable by the halberd, the weapon of their rank.[19] Rombout Kemp (1597-1654), then forty-five years old, stands at the right, one arm stretched out as if giving an order, resting his halberd on his shoulder (no. 5; Fig. 17). Of the Reformed Church, and its deacon in 1625 and 1631, Kemp was from 1635 to 1653 one of the six *regenten* of the Nieuwe Zijds Huiszittenhuis, one of the two charitable organizations that took care of those poor who were not in residence in various other institutions in Amsterdam. In that role he was portrayed by Jacob Backer about 1650 (Fig. 18). He obviously was a devout man, and also must have had a penchant for reading; his mother bequeathed him, in 1641, all the family's Latin books. He and his wife, married in 1623, had

[18] I am grateful to I. H. van Eeghen (letter June 25, 1975) for pointing out that Jan Visscher Cornelisz probably was the same as the person of that name baptized on June 22, 1610, in the Nieuwe Kerk and also the same as Jan Visscher, *Jongman* ("bachelor") buried in the same church on July 29, 1650. MEIJER 1886, p. 209, correctly applied the following poem by Jan Vos to the ensign of the *Nightwatch*:

"Dus ziet men VISSCHER, die het vaandel heeft gezweit:
Maar toen het woeste heir de Stadt aan 't Y deed vreezen,
  Heeft hy van spyt zyn vaan en leeven afgeleit.
Zoo toont de jongling zich van BIKKERS bloedt te weezen:
  Dien BIKKER, die zijn Staat, tot heil van 't volk, verleit.
Een Vrye ziel gedoogt niet dan een vry gebiedt".

Vos refers to a portrait of Visscher, therefore probably to his likeness in the *Nightwatch* since no other portraits are mentioned in his or his relatives' estates (Dudok van Heel, letter, May 9, 1980). Data about his mother I owe to S.A.C. Dudok van Heel (during a discussion, August, 1979); she was buried in the Oude Kerk October 15, 1654. The other facts are found in DUDOK VAN HEEL 1981. Jan Visscher lived on the east side of the Nieuwe Zijds Achterburgwal, the northern corner of the Molsteeg.

[19] After unsuccessful efforts by Schmidt-Degener and Sterck, VAN DILLEN 1934 incontrovertibly identified the two sergeants in the *Nightwatch* as Rombout Kemp and Reijer Engelen and established their professions. The exact dates of baptism (January 19, 1588 in the Nieuwe Kerk for Reyier, son of Jan Enghels and Al Reyiers, and January 4, 1597, in the Oude Kerk, for Rombout Kemp), which were not known to Van Dillen and Van Schendel, were kindly provided by I. H. van Eeghen (letter, June 25, 1975). Miss Van Eeghen informs me also that Reijer Engelen, when posting the bans on April 5, 1625, for his marriage with a woman who was fifteen years younger (Willemken Wynes), gave his age as thirty-two rather than thirty-seven. Numerous data, particularly concerning Kemp, are found in DUDOK VAN HEEL 1981, who also refers to Engelen's brush with the law.

no less than twelve children, of whom seven reached maturity. He was a successful and distinguished cloth merchant, as we shall see, and also a successful member of his company and respected citizen of his precinct: having become a sergeant by 1640, he succeeded Wilhem van Ruytenburgh as lieutenant, perhaps in 1646. His family had a certain wealth, his mother being taxed on 60,000 florins in 1631. But he never reached the top administration of the city, because he did not belong to the patriciate, and the influence of his relatives was not sufficiently powerful.

Reijer Engelen (1588-1651), seated at the very left on a parapet and seen in profile (no. 4), was also a cloth merchant, then aged fifty-four (Fig. 16), but he apparently was not as successful as the others. Neither was he as stalwart as Kemp. In 1624 he was fined because he sold unleaded cloth, and at another time, when marrying a much younger woman, he misrepresented his age by subtracting five years.

Of the remaining thirteen persons, one more can be identified with confidence. The man holding a shield (no. 8, Fig. 19) to the left of the banner above the musketeer in red was portrayed again eleven years later by Bartholomeus van der Helst (Fig. 20).[20] In this portrait of 1653, the head was copied from the *Nightwatch*, and a new body was added, undoubtedly because the sitter had died. Herman Jacobsz Wormskerck, born in Deventer in 1590 and therefore fifty-two years old at the time the *Nightwatch* was painted, died in the very year 1653, in the month of January.[21] We may conclude that he is the man to the left of the banner.

Like Engelen and Kemp, Herman Wormskerck was also a cloth merchant. A wealthy man, and a conscientious member of the Reformed Church, he lived in the house Het Groninger Wapen, later

[20] Museo de Arte, Ponce, Puerto Rico (no. 60.0158); DE GELDER 1921, no. 402; HELD 1965, pp. 82, 83, fig. 72, with reference to the figure in the *Nightwatch* and to a forthcoming study by him on the subject. The identification of (no. 8) in the *Nightwatch* with Wormskerck has not been proposed previously.

[21] About Wormskerck, see ELIAS 1937, pp. 86-91; ELIAS 1944, ALINGS 1962 and DUDOK VAN HEEL 1981. I am grateful to I. H. van Eeghen for having referred me to the articles by Elias and Alings (letter, June 25, 1975). The other militiaman who is a candidate for the portrait of which Van der Helst made a new version is Jan Ockers. As S.A.C. Dudok van Heel informed me (letter, November 29, 1979), Ockers, who was baptized in the Oude Kerk January 22, 1599, was buried there on March 19, 1652. He was therefore also eligible for a posthumous portrait in 1653. He was forty-three at the time of the *Nightwatch*, Wormskerck was fifty-two. The latter seems more likely, since the man with the shield appears a little older than Kemp, who was forty-five, rather than of the same age or younger.

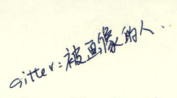

sitter: 被画像的人

called Den Oyevaer on the Nieuwendijk and owned a second house in the same street, a shop elsewhere in Amsterdam, and drying grounds for his textile business outside the city. In 1642, the same year he was portrayed by Rembrandt in the *Nightwatch*, Wormskerck bought the new, extremely elegant house, Soli Deo Gloria, for 36,000 florins; and moved there that same year (the address is Herengracht 166; Fig. 51). At that time, he retired and set a son of a sister-in-law up in business in his house Het Groninger Wapen on the Nieuwendijk, providing him with 60,000 florins in capital for his trade in wool and linen. This nephew associated himself with none other than Rombout Kemp, who was his neighbor. At the time of the death of Wormskerck's wife, their estate was valued at 370,150 florins. By his last will and testament, he established a fund to support students wishing to become ministers in the Dutch Reformed Church. This fund still provides fellowships today.

Other identifications are more tenuous.[22] The names of the sitters, however, have made it possible to gather information about the occupations and the circumstances of the lives of most of them.[23] Besides

[22] Jacob Dircksz (or Dercksen) de Roy is known from a portrait (with wife and two children) by Gerrit Bleeker, presumably dated 1641, in Museum Amstelkring, Amsterdam (GERSON 1950, p. 80, fig. 3). On the basis of similarity with that portrait, Sterck proposed to identify the man between Banning Cocq and Van Ruytenburgh (no. 22), others (SCHMIDT-DEGENER 1916b., p. 50; MARTIN 1947, p. 37; KOOT 1969, pp. 45, 46, 56, 57; and HIJMANS-KUIPER-VELS HEIJN 1976, p. 63) the pikeman (no. 25) as Jacob de Roy. Neither identification seems justified. The date on the painting, if read as 1641, does not accord with the ages of the children, according to Otto van der Aa (letter J. Leeuwenberg, December 31, 1974; S.A.C. Dudok van Heel, on the same grounds, supposed in a discussion, August 1979, that ca. 1631 may be closer to the truth). In need of further support is also the suggestion of VAN SCHENDEL-MERTENS 1947, p. 38, that no. 20 would be Walich Schellingwou, based mainly on his age of twenty-eight or twenty-nine. Equally unsubstantiated is the supposition of MEIJER 1886, p. 209, and of DYSERINCK 1890, p. 252, that the man without a hat at the very left (no. 32) and of SCHMIDT-DEGENER 1916b., p. 40, that the second one from the left (no. 33) was Claes van Cruysbergen.

[23] Some of the occupations of the men listed on the shield and their residences were established by N. de Roever (in DYSERINCK 1890, p. 251), most of the others by VAN DILLEN 1934, whereas further data about the sitters were provided by VAN DILLEN 1934 himself, by ELIAS 1937 and 1944 (about Wormskerck), VAN SCHENDEL-MERTENS 1947, pp. 37, 38 (about Schoonhoven and Schellingwou, provided by Aldewelt and I. H. van Eeghen), by I. H. van Eeghen in correspondence (June 25, 1975), and especially by DUDOK VAN HEEL 1981. To sum up (and to provide birthyears): Rombout Kemp (1597), Reijer Jansz Engelen (1588), Jan Ockers (1599), Jan Pietersz Bronckhorst (1587), Herman Jacobsz Wormskerck (1590), Jacob Dircksz de Roy (1601), Jan Brughman (1614) were cloth merchants; Paulus Harmensz Schoonhoven (1595) was a broker in hemp and other goods; Jan Adriaensz Keijser (1595) was a broker in wine (and for the

the two sergeants and Wormskerck, four other men were cloth merchants; an eighth was a broker in hemp, rope, and similar goods. Three others were *kruideniers* (merchants in spices and other products from the East Indies, for many a lucrative business at the time); two were wine merchants, one of them being a descendant of cloth merchants; two were dealers in unspecified goods, one of them being an owner of bleaching grounds. Apparently only the ensign had no specific profession.

Not only Sergeant Kemp fulfilled social obligations toward the lower classes; Jacob Dircksz de Roy, a Catholic, was also *regent* of an institution taking care of the poor. He also served in the City Theater in a similar capacity.[24] The profession of the man in the right bottom corner is obvious; he was a drummer, but not a member of the company, and therefore not one of the men who payed to be portrayed. Drummers were hired. His name was probably Jacob Jorisz, his age fifty-two.[25]

---

last ten years of his life from 1654 to 1664, *kastelein* ("steward") of the Handboogs-doelen, which then was named after him Keizers Doelen, see DAPPER 1663, p. 448; he probably owed his appointment to Banning Cocq); Walich Schellingwou (1613), descendant of generations of cloth merchants, was himself also a wine merchant, and a very successful one; Claes van Cruysbergen (1613), the grandson of a cloth merchant, became himself a merchant and *kruidenier*, but apparently gave up business in 1651 when he became *provoost* of the Amsterdam militia (with responsibility for keeping order); Barent Hermansz Bolhamer (1589) and Jan Aertsz van der Heede (1610) were also *kruideniers*; Elbert Willemsen (*alias* Elbert Willem Louwerisz, Elbert Willemsz Swedenrijck; 1589) and Jan Claesz Leijdeckers (1597) dealt in unspecified goods, the former owning bleaching grounds, the latter having a brother Willem Claesz Leydeckers who was a cloth merchant. Only the profession of the ensign Jan Cornelisz Visscher (1610) is not stated anywhere.

[24] De Roy was regent of the Catholic Oude-Armenkantoor (as pointed out by STERCK 1927, p. 54, ill. p. 51), from 1628 to 1654 (acc. to DUDOK VAN HEEL 1981). TÓTH-UBBENS 1975, pp. 388, 406, pointed out that De Roy in 1641-42 and 1651-52 was one of the *regenten* of the City Theater (Stadsschouwburg).

[25] The drummer, therefore, was not included in the shield. VAN DIJK 1758 called him, for no good reason, Jan van Kampoort. He seems to have misread the extremely poorly legible last two lines, and interpreted "Claes van Cruysbergen / . . . Sch . . ." as "Jan van Kampoort / Tamboer" (SCHMIDT-DEGENER 1916a., p. 66, could only decipher "Sch" on the last line). On July 30, 1646, a drummer by the name of Jacob Jorisz stated that he had worked for Banning Cocq when the latter was still captain (therefore before January 1646; see note 7 of this chapter). Jacob Jorisz was then fifty-five years old, and may well be the same as the one represented in the *Nightwatch* ([DE ROEVER] 1887, p. 38, referring to the statement, pointed out that Jorisz was a drummer of Banning Cocq; the exact wording of the relevant passage of the document, not given by De Roever, was provided by S.A.C. Dudok van Heel, letter, November 29, 1979). MEIJER 1886, p. 210, who seems to have known of Jacob Jorisz, points out that Van Kampoort lived on as a drunkard in the work of Maxime Du Camp.

These merchants had more in common than their occupation. All of them—except for the captain and the lieutenant—lived in the same precinct, most of them in close proximity to each other in the same streets, some of them being neighbors. Seven of them lived on the Nieuwendijk, and three *op 't Water* (presently Damrak).[26] The precinct in which they all lived was the second one of the twenty into which, from 1620 to 1650, the city was divided for the sake of the organization of the militia. This precinct was a small area north of the Dam and the Nieuwe Kerk, bordered by the Singel and the present Damrak (Fig. 52).[27] The most important houses in this precinct were located on the Nieuwendijk, *op 't Water*, and on the east side of the Singel.

Not all of these merchants were as wealthy as Herman Wormskerck, but wealthy they were. The cloth merchants bought cloth in large quantities from abroad, mainly from England, in order to have it dyed and manufactured, and then resold it in the Netherlands and abroad. By the time they were portrayed in the *Nightwatch*, three (Kemp, Ockers, and De Roy) had been members of the distinguished and powerful committee of overseers of trade and manufacture of cloth, and they would be re-elected to that post various times afterwards.[28] As *waardijnen van de lakenen*, or "wardens of the linen industry", they were predecessors of the men immortalized in Rembrandt's so-

[26] It was known that the men portrayed in the *Nightwatch*, except for captain and lieutenant, lived in one precinct, but recently S.A.C. Dudok van Heel was able to establish the exact residences of all of them except for two (Jan Adriaensz Keijser and Claes van Cruysbergen, letters, November 26 and 29, 1979). For the residences, see Fig. 52.

[27] The area, according to the description of the twenty precincts printed by Jacob Colom in 1647 upon the request of the colonels Andries Bicker and Frans Banning Cocq (only copy in Archief, Amsterdam, SCHAEP 1630-50s, f°.16vo, 17ro and ^{vo}, almost completely reprinted, precinct by precinct, by JOCHEMS 1888, pp. 29-40), was bordered on the south side by the Zoutsteeg, Gravenstraat, Molsteeg, and Torensteeg, to the west by the Singel, to the north by the Nieuwstraat, Lijnbaansteeg, and O. L. Vrouwssteeg, and to the east by the Amstel River (*'t Water*). The map of which a detail is reproduced (Fig. 52) is the second updated edition of 1647 of *Amstelredamum emporium hollandiae primaria totius europae celeberrium* made by Balthasar Florisz (first edition was of 1625; D'AILLY 1934, no. 134, 2nd ed. of no. 117).

[28] I owe this information to S.A.C. Dudok van Heel (letter, November 26, 1979; and DUDOK VAN HEEL 1981); Kemp was "waardijn van de lakenen" in 1631, '33, '34, '36, '37, '40, and '41; Ockers in 1638, '39, '44, '45, '46, '48 and '51; De Roy in 1630, '43, '46, '47 and '49; Jan Theunisz Schellingwou (1579-1657), father of the wine merchant Willem Schellingwou, had been cloth merchant and "waardijn van de lakenen" in 1609, '10, '13, '14, '18, '19, '21, '23, '24, '26 and '27. Reijer Engelen never became warden, although his father had held the position (DUDOK VAN HEEL 1981).

called *Syndics*. These were truly successful merchants and distinguished citizens.

  Did any particular relationship exist between Rembrandt and these cloth merchants, and why did they select him? The nature and history of such relationships tend to be evasive, yet links between cloth merchants and Rembrandt, which preceded the commission of the *Nightwatch*, may have been part of the delicate fabric of rapport between the painter and his patrons. Between 1631 and 1640, Rembrandt painted a double portrait of the cloth merchant Jan Pietersz Bruyningh and his wife, and between 1631 and 1635 a portrait of her father, Jan Pietersz Moutmaker. Jan Bruyningh, who was a Mennonite, lived until the summer of 1639 on the Nieuwendijk, therefore in the same street where the cloth merchants of the *Nightwatch* lived.[29] Furthermore, in 1641, Rembrandt finished the etched portrait of Cornelis Claesz Anslo and the painted portrait of him and his wife (now in Berlin); in the painting he is shown addressing himself to an imaginary listener, and she sitting next to him (Fig. 80). Rembrandt dated his drawings preparatory to the painting and the etching both 1640, and therefore knew Anslo about the time he received the commission for the *Nightwatch*. In these works, Anslo is represented as a minister, but besides a prominent Mennonite preacher, he was also a successful cloth merchant. Until shortly after 1636, he owned and operated a store and home on the same Nieuwendijk.[30] In spite of the Mennonites' opposition to arms and warfare—none of the sitters of the *Nightwatch* was a Mennonite—these men may have spoken in favor of Rembrandt when the moment came for their neighbors to select an artist.[31] Com-

[29] The documents concerning the Bruynigh and Moutmaker portraits were published by VAN EEGHEN 1977b. However attractive the idea, both Van Eeghen (pp. 68, 69) and DUDOK VAN HEEL 1980, p. 112, are reluctant to identify the double portrait of 1633 in the Isabella Stewart Gardner Museum with the "conterfeitsel van Jan Pietersz Bruyningh ende sijn huysvrouwe zal: van Rembrant" because of the difficulty in reconciling the costume of the woman with Mennonite preference for simplicity.

[30] For Anslo and Rembrandt's portraits of him, see VAN EEGHEN 1969. According to Miss van Eeghen, Anslo lived in the house De Kalkoense Haan ("The Turkey Rooster") on the Nieuwendijk until shortly after 1636 when he left the management of the store to his son Gerbrant and moved to the Rokin; in 1641, he moved to the O. Z. Achterburgwal. For the drawings, see BENESCH 1954-57, IV, nos. 758 (London, British Museum; for the etching) and 759 (Paris, Louvre; for the painting). For the painting (BREDIUS 1935, no. 409), see BERLIN 1978, pp. 356-57, and the bibliography listed there. The speaking gesture of Anslo's left hand in the second drawing and the painting is virtually identical to the gesture of Banning Cocq in the *Nightwatch*. Rembrandt worked simultaneously on the Berlin double portrait and the *Nightwatch*.

[31] The role of Bruyningh and Anslo was first suggested (with more emphasis than I give) by DUDOK VAN HEEL 1980, pp. 113, 114.

cloth merchent.
(old customer.

bining ministry with commerce, and portrayed with his wife by Rembrandt in an action portrait, Anslo seems to be an appropriate link between the history and portrait painter and the cloth merchants who were portrayed in the painting which was as much a history piece as a group portrait. Some cloth merchants portrayed in the *Nightwatch* may have supported the selection of Rembrandt partially because they knew the artist personally. Paulus van Schoonhoven was a neighbor of the painter Claes Moyaert, and Jan Claesz Leijdeckers was an uncle of Gerbrand van den Eeckhout. He and his brother (who was also a cloth merchant) witnessed, in 1621, the baptism of Rembrandt's later pupil.[32]

Whatever the reasons for Banning Cocq's and the merchants' selection of Rembrandt as their artist, contemporary viewers, looking at the painting, must have noticed the marked distinction between the two central figures and the members of the company, and undoubtedly were reminded of corresponding social differences. Banning Cocq and Van Ruytenburgh belonged to the group of regents, the patriciate, the others to the wealthy, powerful upper middle class. Knowing who the sitters were, contemporary viewers associated them with their achievements and place in Amsterdam. To the extent that they read the painting as a group portrait, they saw the captain and lieutenant as regents and the men as successful, well-to-do merchants, some of them trustees of civic institutions, all living in a small precinct not larger than a few city blocks. They knew that they all belonged to the Reformed Church (except for two who were Catholic and one who was Arminian) and that all of them were ambitious citizens striving for power while carrying out their civic duties.[33]

Furthermore, those contemporaries who were at all aware of the recent history of the Dutch Republic and the particular role of Amsterdam in it and in the world—and who was not aware, yes, proud of those circumstances—realized that those who were portrayed in this painting and in other similar group portraits of militiamen of those years were the very representatives of those who a generation earlier had overthrown the old, Catholic powers and had instituted a completely new regime. These men now carried out what their predecessors had initiated. Their effective mercantile and financial policies,

---

[32] These data I also owe to Dudok van Heel (letter, November 26, 1979, and DUDOK VAN HEEL 1981).

[33] Barent Hermansz Bolhamer and Jacob de Roy were Catholic, Jan van der Heede, Arminian (*Remonstrant*; DUDOK VAN HEEL 1981).

combined with smart politics, endowed the city with unprecedented growth and power, and made it virtually independent of other powers within the Netherlands, particularly the Prince of Orange. They turned Amsterdam into a city-republic holding a veritable world empire of trade in her own right.[34]

[34] This last paragraph is written with grateful acknowledgements to BARBOUR 1950, p. 13, RENIER 1944, VAN HAMEL 1946, and particularly to J. W. Smit.

pride of Amsterdam.
Honor independence.

III

The Role Enacted:
Historic Honor and
Active Service

Since the citizens portrayed in the *Nightwatch* are represented as members of the militia, their image is strongly affected by the views contemporaries had of this institution. If we want to read this aspect of the painting, it is necessary to discuss the nature of Amsterdam's seventeenth-century militia. Because of the decisive impact of traditions going back to the Middle Ages, these traditions must be taken into consideration wherever relevant.[1]

In the Middle Ages, and particularly in the German-speaking countries, as soon as serfs became free men and cities emerged, all free citizens had the duty to protect themselves. For that purpose they formed an armed citizens' militia that should act whenever necessary. In addition, certain groups of citizens associated themselves voluntarily in permanent groups that received privileges and the status of guild from local or regional rulers.[2] The former citizens were far more numerous than the members of these militia guilds, and often less well trained. The membership of these militia guilds became an honor and

[1] REINTGES 1963 provides a good survey, with ample bibliography, of the history of militia guilds in Europe. Very useful for the Northern Netherlands is still SICKESZ 1864 (whereas HOFDIJK 1874-75 and TE LINTUM 1910 must be approached with caution for clarification of group portraits of militiamen because both use the paintings as sources for their study). CARROLL 1976, pp. 1-12 ("From Shooting Guilds to Militia Companies") gives a fine survey. Fundamental for Haarlem is TE LINTUM 1896, for Middelburg DE STOPPELAAR 1886, and for the various regional guilds of Gelderland, Zeeland, and Brabant a series of books by [J.] A. Jolles of the 1930s. Numerous data for France and Belgium are provided by DELAUNAY 1879, for Germany by EDELMANN 1890.

[2] For the distinction between armed citizens' militia and militia guilds, see especially NOORDKERK 1744 and WAGENAAR 1767, III, pp. 169-174, also SICKESZ 1864, pp. 4, 8, 11, 23.

a distinction, and those enjoying these prerogatives constituted an armed elite. The militia guilds (*schutterijen*) built shooting ranges and buildings (together called *doelens*) for practice and meetings of their members (*schutters*).[3] Each guild had its proper weapon, originally either the longbow (*handboog*) or crossbow (*voetboog*), later one or another type of firearm. The guilds were named after their weapons, and they kept these names after they all had adopted firearms.

Amsterdam, by 1384, had one militia guild that stood under the patronage of St. George and which had the crossbow as its weapon.[4] The city grew, membership increased, and probably by 1436 it had three: the first had been split into an "old" and a "new" guild (the *oude schutterije* and the *jonge schutterije van de voetboge*), and one more had been added whose members handled the longbow under the patronage of St. Sebastian. To keep up with the times, the original *oude schutterije* was replaced in 1522 by a militia guild using firearms.[5] This was the guild of the Kloveniers.[6] All the belongings of the superseded guild, including its shooting range, its treasury and its altar in the

[3] Whatever the origin of the words *schutter* and *schutterij* (which have been debated), in the seventeenth century they were felt to convey the meanings of "to shoot" (*schieten*) as well as of "to guard" (*schutten, beschutten*); *doelen* for buildings as shooting ranges stems from the Dutch *doel* ("target"). I prefer the term "militia guild" to "shooting guild", although both terms can be defended.

[4] Most useful for the history of the militia guilds and their successors in Amsterdam is the coherent survey written by NOORDKERK 1744 and published by SCHELTEMA 1844 (erroneously as by J. Wagenaar rather than H. Noordkerk). Additional data are found in WAGENAAR 1765-67, III, pp. 164-194, TER GOUW 1880, etc., KERNKAMP 1897, and later multivolumed books on Amsterdam. The "History of the Amsterdam Schutters-doelens and their Activities" in CARROLL 1976, pp. 199-254 ("Appendix") is a good analysis. Important sources are the notes by SCHAEP 1630-50s, never fully published, and by Bontemantel (1613-1688), published by KERNKAMP in 1897. Invaluable for the seventeenth century are also the publications by JOCHEMS, particularly his book of 1888. Outstanding are the collections of contemporary pamphlets of the "Historische Verzameling der Schutterije te Amsterdam" (K.O.G., Amsterdam) and of the New York Public Library. The recent catalogue BLANKERT 1975-79 brings new data on the Amsterdam militia in some entries on individual paintings.

[5] The ordinance of 1522 establishing the Kloveniers was published by SCHELTEMA 1844, pp. 115-118.

[6] Literally the word means "someone who shoots with a 'klover' ", a *klover* or *kolover* being a simple kind of firearm (French: *couleuvrine* and *coulevrine* according to the etymological dictionaries; see also VAN HOBOKEN 1971). BLAEU 1651, n.p., s.v. Amsterdam, *in margine* Doelen, observes that the Kloveniers should be called *coleuvriers*, "nae het Fransche woordt *Coleuvre*, 't welck by onse Voor-ouders een busse oft roer betekende". Because the *kloveniers* carried a claw as emblem (see next note), already in the seventeenth century some derived the word *klovenier* wrongly from *klauw* ("claw"). Although DAPPER 1663, p. 444, already noted this erroneous derivation, it is continuously repeated (e.g., TÜMPEL 1977, p. 84).

Oude Kerk, were transferred to the Kloveniers in the same year. The emblem, which the old guild had carried since at least 1412, a claw, was also transferred to the Kloveniers.[7] Although in fact, this guild was the youngest one, it was seen as the successor and heir of Amsterdam's oldest militia guild and was often referred to as the *oude schutterije*.

In 1522 the Kloveniers were given the tower Svych Wtrecht and some adjacent buildings on either side of the Nieuwe Doelenstraat with a shooting range for the purpose of practice and meeting, and for storage of arms. Shortly before, the other two guilds had built ample meeting places on the Singel (on the site of the present University Library) with shooting ranges behind them stretching as far as the Kalverstraat. The premises of the first were known as the Kloveniersdoelen, those of the crossbow militia guild as the Voetboogsdoelen or St. Joris-doelen, those of the longbow militia guild as the Handboogsdoelen or St. Sebastiaansdoelen.

The three militia guilds and their *doelens* functioned without major interruptions until 1567, when the fierce political and religious struggles with Spain and the Catholic church led to their temporary dissolution. Because the guilds were suspected of siding with the Protestants, their belongings were confiscated, their members disarmed.

About ten years later, however, once the Protestant and anti-Spanish powers had established themselves, the militia was fundamentally reshaped. Amsterdam's entire male citizenry, not its elite, was now organized according to the structure of the old guilds. The centuries-old distinction between the general armed citizens' militia and the distinguished militia guilds was eliminated, and every new militiaman could feel himself successor to his privileged ancestor.[8] It was a meaningful change: it paralleled the dismissal of the old families from the gov-

[7] This appears from the context of the ordinance of 1522 (see note 5), the "claw" being mentioned in the middle of the paragraph listing the transfer of objects and rights from "den ouwe Schutters" to the "Cloveniers" ("Item, dat de voirsz[egde] twee hondert Cloveniers sullen hebben d'altaer van de ouwe Schutters in Sint Niclaes-kercke en[de] voeren de claeuwe en[de] voirt bruijcken en[de] besijghen ornamenten, kelck, juweelen en[de] anders, die ouwe Schutters pleghen to ghebruijcken"); and from the presence of a claw alongside the coat of arms and a crossbow painted with the date 1412 onto a beam of the chapel of the crossbow militia guild (the St. Joriskapel) of the Oude Kerk in Amsterdam (BIJTELAAR 1959, p. 19; illustrated in JANSE 1969 and WEGENER SLEESWIJCK 1970, fig. 17; see also JANSE 1970).

[8] The fusion of militia guilds and citizens' militia has been outlined clearly by NOORDKERK 1744, pp. 74-81, SICKESZ 1864, pp. 70-76, and SCHMIDT-DEGENER 1916a., pp. 68-71. In the Southern Netherlands militia guilds (*schutten gilden*) continued to exist side by side with citizens' militia (SICKESZ 1864, p. 75). Now also clearly summarized by CARROLL 1976.

ernment of the city and expressed the power of the new citizenry taken
over from the old.

The take-over of the old militia guilds by the new citizens' militia
was complete, and their fusion was total. Although the old guilds lost
most of their privileges, their properties, among them the *doelens* and
the treasury, were restored to the new organizations and even the
words *schutterij* and *schutter*, originally used exclusively for the militia
guild and its members, gradually came to be used officially for the
citizens' militia and the citizens serving in it. Let us look at the organization and customs of the re-established militia against the background of the past by which it was strongly influenced.

In 1579, in accordance with the new egalitarian principles, the city
was divided into precincts and the militia organized by precinct. The
number of eleven precincts of that year had increased to twenty by
the time the *Nightwatch* was painted, each with its own militia company (*burger-compagnie* or simply *compagnie* or *vendel*). Each of these
companies was under the command of a captain and a lieutenant, and
usually two or three sergeants; and each company had an ensign, one
or two drummers and perhaps a piper. Each was usually subdivided
into four smaller units (*corporaalschappen*).[9]

In the beginning of the sixteenth century, each guild had about
seventy-five members. This number increased to about two hundred
in the 1560s, or six hundred for the entire city. After 1579, the total
number of militiamen increased. In the first half of the seventeenth
century at times there may have been about two hundred per company,
which added up to a city-wide total of about four thousand.[10] According to law, a still much larger part of the male population should
be members, but many may have served in case of emergency only.

[9] In October 1579, Amsterdam was divided into eleven precincts; in 1620 the number
was changed to twenty, in 1650 to fifty-four (JOCHEMS 1888, suppl. II, pp. III-IX; pp.
1, 2). The wrong term *korporaalschap* for a militia piece (*schuttersstuk* is correct) is
based on the phenomenon that the number of men in a *korporaalschap* is about the
same as that of men portrayed, whereas the paintings actually represent rather a selection
of men from the entire company (MEIJER 1886, who also pointed out that the error is
already found in the inventory made in 1670 of paintings of the Crossbow Militia Guild
where the writer substituted *compagnien* for the crossed-out *corporaalschappen*).

[10] The strength of companies is difficult to establish. According to BARLAEUS 1639,
p. 13, the Amsterdam militia had more than four thousand members in 1638. SCHMIDT-
DEGENER 1916b. concluded that a *corporaalschap* consisted of about thirty men, which
would bring a company to about one hundred twenty. In 1672, the average number
of men in the sixty companies then in existence was 166 (BONTEMANTEL-KERNKAMP
1897, p. 201).

Undoubtedly not all members participated in the activities of the companies on the same level, and those who had the means to participate in expensive social events—and enjoy the distinction of being portrayed—belonged to the higher level of society in the same precinct as the materially less well-endowed members.

The chain of command around 1640 was clear. The captains were responsible to two colonels who were in command of all the twenty companies and who in their turn were responsible to the burgomasters. New was the institution of the Krijgsraad (the "War Council") composed of the four burgomasters, the two colonels, and all the captains (substituted by their lieutenants if they could not be present). The Krijgsraad had to decide on matters of policy and to appoint captains, lieutenants, ensigns (and perhaps also sergeants). This greater share in decision making for the captains may have seemed larger than it was because the Krijgsraad met less than once a year.[11] As in so many realms of life, the burgomasters had the true power.

Captains and lieutenants invariably were chosen from the ruling patriciate, the regents. The position of captain was most prestigious *rank.* and was often a step toward the position of burgomaster: seven of the twenty captains of 1642 and ten of the twenty of 1649 were elected burgomaster in later years.[12] Also in keeping with tradition, the ensign had to be a bachelor, and had to resign if and when he married.

Virtually all activities of the seventeenth-century militia were strongly affected by traditions. Before 1567, the militia guilds defended the cities against enemies (together with the armed citizens' militia). They practiced regularly at the *doelens*, staged yearly, usually around Pentecost, the "Shooting the Parrot", added liveliness and color to kermisses, lent festive decorum to triumphal entries or solemn dignity to funerals of royalty and rulers, and competed with other guilds in other towns at so-called *landjuwelen.* At all these occasions, the men generally wore prescribed costumes. And they loved to dine with ceremonial pomp. All these activities were continued after the reorganization. Certain administrative structures even remained when they made no real sense anymore. Before 1567, the guilds had been presided

costume

---

[11] Chain of command and appointment procedures are based on BONTEMANTEL-KERNKAMP 1897, pp. 191-199, 203, 209 (here, however, he states that sergeants were chosen by colonels, captains, and lieutenants). Bontemantel also points out that practically everyone belonging to the magistrature in Amsterdam at one time or another had been a member of the Krijgsraad. JOCHEMS 1888, p. 185, lists the years the Krijgsraad met (eighteen times from 1630 to 1655).

[12] BONTEMANTEL-KERNKAMP 1897, pp. 197, 198.

over by governors (*overlieden*) responsible to the burgomasters and the city council. After the reorganization, the institution of four governors for each *doelen* was continued even when there was no longer a guild to be governed, but only a building and its activities.[13] The governors were proud of the honor and fared well by their appointment (which by 1650 had tended to become for life), partly because the stewards of the *doelens* had to pay a franchise fee to them. They did not fail to have themselves portrayed in their role as governors, in the case of the Kloveniersdoelen by Govert Flinck (Fig. 36).

High points for the militia companies and for the city as a whole in the sixteenth century, as before, were the annual competitions of Shooting the Parrot. In origin, this *papegaai-schieten* may have been a spring rite, but the target usually was a brightly colored wooden bird. Elaborately wrought chains and scepters of precious metals were awarded to the winner, the "king", and additional objects were made for other prizes. These and ceremonial drinking horns and goblets, which symbolized and emphasized the sense of fraternity of the members, as well as other precious objects, came to constitute veritable "treasures".[14] In Amsterdam new chains, drinking horns, and similar objects were made in the beginning of the sixteenth century and added to the treasury. Some of these are preserved in the Rijksmuseum, for example, a scepter and chain of the "king" of the Handboogschutters and Voetboogschutters, and the drinking horns of all three guilds; all except one date from the first half of the sixteenth century (Figs. 58, 59).[15] These ceremonies were so costly that the guilds at one point decided to take turns staging them every year.

In the seventeenth century, "Shooting the Parrot" continued to be a popular spring festival around Pentecost, and new "kings" were proclaimed victor, the last one perhaps as late as 1663.[16] The objects

[13] For the governors and their tenure, see Kernkamp's notes in BONTEMANTEL-KERNKAMP 1897, pp. 170-175.

[14] A wealth of information about such objects, not only in Germany but also in the Netherlands, is found in JACOBS 1887 and in its continuation by HOBUSCH 1927; useful in this respect is also DELAUNAY 1879 and SCHATTEN 1966-67 with numerous illustrations of such objects in private collections and museums. Probably one of the largest treasuries of a militia guild, that of the Zwinger-und-Werderschützen in Breslau (Wrocław), is known from the more than thirty-two prints made from an inventory painted by Georgius Hauer in 1613 (JACOBS 1887, p. 113; HOBUSCH 1927, pp. 204-213). For such objects belonging to the Kloveniers in Amsterdam in 1569, see STERCK 1900.

[15] AMSTERDAM 1952, nos. 20, 24, 25, 26, 35, 39, 40. The only later object is the drinking horn of the Voetboogschutters (no. 39).

[16] AMSTERDAM 1952, p. 10, no. 25.

from the treasury were reused each year, and the chains were provided with name plates of the new winners. The events were spectacles full of traditional lore.

Ever since the Middle Ages, the militia had the decorative and honorific task of lending luster to triumphal entries of national and foreign royalty. This duty and privilege also was taken over from the earlier militia guilds. The Count Palatine was welcomed in 1613, Prince Maurice in 1618, Prince Henry in 1628; in 1638 Maria de'Medici, in 1642 Henrietta Maria, Queen of England, with the Prince of Orange and their children. The city magistrates considered the performance of the *schutters* of great importance, and imposed stiff fines for those who did not appear.[17] About the participation and appearance of the Amsterdam militia at Maria de'Medici's entry in 1638 we are particularly well informed, thanks to the lively descriptions of Caspar Barlaeus and the illustrations of his book commemorating the event.[18] The companies of the twenty districts marched out for the occasion, and lined the streets through which the queen and her retinue passed. Triumphal arches were erected in various places, dumb shows and pantomimes were enacted on stages above them. The triumphal procession and the festivities related to the queen's entry served to honor the distinguished guest, to commemorate and confirm old privileges the city had received from the Emperor Maximilian, and to propagate the power and greatness of Amsterdam. The festivities expressed pride in Amsterdam's achievements of past and present.[19]

Many a kermis in the sixteenth century and before was made more colorful, and perhaps safer, by the presence of militiamen in uniform. The practice was continued in the seventeenth century. At a certain

[17] Already Schaep 1630-50s, f°. 41ro, and Coster 1642 listed triumphal entries into Amsterdam; for an exhaustive discussion, see Snoep 1975. Additional illustrations and data are found in Bokhoven 1976 and Adèr 1976-77.

[18] Barlaeus 1638, 1639. The prints were mainly made by S. Savry and P. Nolpe after drawings by S. de Vlieger, C. Moyaert, J. Martsen de Jonge and others. For a detailed analysis of the events commemorated, the decision making behind the production of the book, and the trustworthiness of the prints, see Snoep 1975, pp. 39-64. See also Carroll 1976, pp. 88-96, with a good analysis of the political background and impact of traditional triumphal entries.

[19] Snoep 1975, pp. 63, 64, and Carroll 1976, pp. 91-94, give good analyses of the often exaggerated significance attached to Amsterdam and its institutions by these performances and Van Baerle's description of them, but Snoep's characterization of this pride as chauvinism introduces an anachronistic derogatory element. Parallels between the *Nightwatch* and the joyous entry of Maria de'Medici are discussed below in Chapter VI, under "Portraits of Officers and Men", "Arms and Costumes . . .", "The Archway", and "Action", and its notes 34, 63, 103.

moment another performance was added to the repertory. Every Sunday during the summer and on the days of the kermis in September, the members of two companies had to march in proper costume to a central point in the city, usually the Dam Square, where they charged and shot firearms. Since there were twenty companies and approximately ten Sundays, we may assume that each company had a turn at performing this duty, undoubtedly for the sake of the spectacle rather than for practice. When this custom originated is not known, but it did exist before 1650, and most likely already by the time Rembrandt painted the *Nightwatch*.[20] It is probably this ceremony that is represented in the painting of ca. 1620-30 in the Graf von Schönborn'sche Gemäldegalerie at Castle Weissenstein in Pommersfelden (Fig. 67).[21]

In the fifteenth and sixteenth centuries the militia guilds were closely associated with the guilds of the rhetoricians. This association should not surprise us, given the similarity between many of the activities of both organizations. Both were engaged in public competitions and both participated simultaneously in public performances. Moreover, many members of the militia guilds and later the militia companies were also rhetoricians, certain militia guilds had rhetoricians perform on their premises, and others had departments within their own organizations that devoted themselves to acting. Like the rhetoricians, the militia guilds went by invitation to other cities and towns for competitions, and the procedures of invitation, performance, and awarding of prizes were the same. The name *landjuweel* was used for such festive competitions of both groups, and some believe that they were first developed by the militia guilds, then taken over by the rhetoricians.

[20] BONTEMANTEL-KERNKAMP 1897, p. 212; NOORDKERK 1744, p. 91. Although the custom is mentioned first in the resolutions of the Krijgsraad of 1650 (according to Noordkerk), Bontemantel states specifically that it existed before that year. That the men were costumed can be concluded from Bontemantel ("De schutters . . . pleegen . . . cierelijk in de waepenen to comen en op te trecken"), that they charged and fired muskets on the Dam (and elsewhere), from NOORDKERK 1744, p. 91.

[21] Panel, 80 × 122 cm., by an unidentified artist, according to the costumes ca. 1620-30 (Collection of Count Schönborn-Wiesentheid, FRIMMEL 1894, no. 380). The subject depicted agrees with the periodic Sunday march as described by Bontemantel and Noordkerk. The procession in the painting terminates on the Dam Square, and, at the very right, one militiaman who has reached the end of the course fires his musket. The woman in the left bottom corner wears a hat often seen on women in churches; she probably wears a Sunday costume. The exhibition catalogue DUTCH CITYSCAPE 1977, no. 10, supposes that the picture was made about 1620 to commemorate "the civic guard procession" (without reference to the specific custom of *uittrecken* on Sundays).

At the time of the *Nightwatch*, the militia companies from various towns and cities did not come together any more for *landjuwelen*. Yet, the connections between them and the rhetoricians were not severed. For example, both the companies and the rhetoricians simultaneously, although separately, performed in Amsterdam at the occasion of the triumphal entries of Maria de'Medici and Henrietta Maria, the former by standing guard and marching, the latter by enacting scenes from history or the Bible and allegories on triumphal arches and stages. In both associations citizens acted out specific roles in honor of the same occasion.[22]

The strong link between the new militia companies and the centuries-old militia guilds was sustained by the *doelens*. Each six or seven of the twenty companies were affiliated with one of the three *doelens*, and the members of these companies gathered for their social occasions in the *doelens*.[23] The companies felt themselves successors and were considered heirs to the old squads (*rotten*) that, also six or seven, occupied those same buildings before the reorganization of the militia.[24] The age and style of the buildings, the two on the Singel ample Gothic structures built expressly for the purpose early in the sixteenth century, the one of the Kloveniers, a tower of the former ramparts of the city dating from the late fifteenth century, must have reinforced the awareness of tradition in the members of the militia and the other citizens as well.

Each *doelen* had received its coat of arms and its colors centuries ago. We know them from a sketch after one of the pillows on which they were all embroidered (Fig. 55). The Voetboogsdoelen had a red

[22] For the relationship of militia guilds and rhetoricians, see SCHOTEL 1871, I, pp. 166-168; DE STOPPELAAR 1886, pp. 180-184 (on *landjuwelen* of the militia guilds); MAK 1944, pp. 11, 92; VAN AUTENBOER 1962, pp. 79-86 ("schutterij en toneel"). Among art historians, SCHMIDT-DEGENER 1916a., pp. 71, 72, 78, 80-84 and GUDLAUGSSON 1938, pp. 44, 45, referred to these relationships and their significance for subject matter in Dutch art. For the *landjuwelen* of the rhetoricians and the similar, although less elaborate, *haagspele*, see SCHOTEL 1871, I, pp. 193-308; WORP 1904, 1908, I, pp. 165-171. The book by G. J. Steenbergen, *Het landjuweel van de rederijkers* (Louvain, 1950), was not available to me. For the rhetoricians' parts in the triumphal entries, see SNOEP 1975, p. 38.

[23] SCHAEP 1630-50s gives on f°. 54 a "Lijste vande 20 Compagnien Burger Vaendelen onder wat Doelen ijder is sorterende" in the years 1630-36, and lists the company of Precinct II, then under Captain Pieter Reael, as the first of the six that were affiliated with the Kloveniersdoelen. The remaining fourteen companies were equally distributed over the Voetboogsdoelen and the Handboogsdoelen.

[24] In 1569 the Kloveniers comprised twelve *rotten*, lettered A through M (STERCK 1900); in 1578 these were reduced to six (NOORDKERK 1744, p. 63).

cross on a white field, the Handboogsdoelen, a gold cross and four smaller crosses on a red field, and the Kloveniers, a golden claw on a blue field. The coat of arms of their superior administrative body, the War Council (Krijgsraad) showed the words *Regno pro Patria* in gold on a blue field.[25] Kloveniers and Krijgsraad thus shared the colors gold and blue, possibly because the Kloveniers were the oldest militia organization in the city. As we have seen, as early as the beginning of the fifteenth century, the claw had been the emblem of the crossbow guild that was the immediate predecessor of the Kloveniers. Apparently at the time of the foundation of the latter in 1522, the musket was added to the claw, since an embroidered claw holding a musket is found on costumes in three militia pieces of the Kloveniers, of the years 1529 (Fig. 82), 1532, and 1557.[26] Both claw and muskets, although not attached to each other, are also shown on the name stone of the tower of the Kloveniers (Fig. 53). The claw was included in the decoration of the drinking horn and the chain (Figs. 58, 59) and was still held in high esteem in Rembrandt's time. It appears as a large, framed and gilded emblem hanging on the wall in Govert Flinck's *Governors of the Kloveniersdoelen* (Fig. 54) and it was represented in stained glass windows of the *doelen*, probably in the very assembly hall where the *Nightwatch* and the other militia pieces were hanging, and elsewhere.[27] In clear and detailed renderings, the claw is that of

[25] The coats of arms and colors of the three *doelens* are known from a description and pencil sketch with indication of colors made by Schaep 1630-50s, f°. 18ro, of the pillows in the Krijgsraad in Amsterdam. The pillows made ca. 1600 were decorated with crossbow, longbow, and musket in the center, the coats of arms of the three *doelens* and those of the Krijgsraad in the corners (clockwise beginning left top: Voetboogsdoelen, Kloveniersdoelen, Handboogsdoelen, and Krijgsraad). None of the pillows seems to have been preserved. The coat of arms of the Kloveniers and its colors, to my knowledge, have been referred to only by Ter Gouw 1880, p. 378, and D'Ailly 1947, p. 48; both repeated Schaep's description.

[26] In the oldest preserved militia piece of 1529 by Dirck Jacobsz (in gold; Rijksmuseum, no. C402); in one of 1532 also by Dirck Jacobsz (Hermitage, Leningrad; acc. to Schmidt-Degener 1916b., p. 46, in silver), and in *The Company of Squad F* of 1557 (Historisch Museum, Amsterdam; Cat. Rijksmuseum no. C424; acc. to R. Ruurs in Blankert 1975-79, no. 112, painted by Cornelis Jacobsz van Delft). Details of the embroidered emblems of the first two paintings ill. by Tümpel 1970, p. 171, figs. 128-131 (claw and musket, however, were not combined for etymological reasons). Beudeker, II, f°. 141vo, related that the newly established Kloveniers received the right to carry as "blasoen of wapen . . . een klauw houdende een vuurroer". Bontemantel-Kernkamp 1897, pp. 186, 187, already mentioned the embroidered emblems.

[27] Dapper 1663, p. 444, wrote that in his day, one could see a claw "depicted" in the windows. It is likely, although not certain, that he was referring to the windows of the new structure. Dapper stated here that pewter and silverware of the Kloveniers were

a bird of prey, probably of an eagle if one can judge by its size.[28] An eagle's claw seems an appropriate heraldic sign for a crossbow guild, where marksmanship was at a premium.

Group portraits of militiamen were not merely incidental decorations of the *doelens*. On the contrary, since the beginning of the sixteenth century, they had been an essential part of their image. Whenever contemporaries described the *doelens*, they referred to the militia pieces as one of their main points of interest. Blaeu did so in 1651, Dapper and Commelin followed him, and Bontemantel noted that they were "worthy . . . to be observed closely and attentively by residents of Amsterdam and any other city".[29] This long tradition of group portraiture of militiamen culminated in the large assembly hall of the Kloveniersdoelen with its seven large paintings of slightly over-lifesize figures, among them Banning Cocq, Van Ruytenburgh, and the members of the company of the *Nightwatch*.[30]

The militia and the *doelens* gradually came to an end in the course of the second half of the seventeenth century. The shooting ranges of the Voetboogsdoelen and the Handboogsdoelen were sold in 1650 and built up with houses and the one of the Kloveniers was used less and less.[31] After 1650, serving meals to outsiders became the main source of income for the *doelens*, along with lodging guests. As hostels, the *doelens* soon suffered from competition with newly established inns.[32] The lack of interest in traditional activities like practice shooting and Shooting the Parrot and the inability of the *doelens* to make ends meet, aggravated by the curb on spending by the city government around 1672 caused by the war with France, meant the complete

---

also decorated with a claw. Furthermore, the entrance gate to the shooting range on the other side of the Nieuwe Doelenstraat was decorated with a claw (acc. to WAGENAAR 1765, II, p. 75; destroyed).

[28] TER GOUW 1880, p. 378, and later others (e.g. BIJTELAAR 1959), assumed, probably correctly, that the claw in the coat of arms is that of an eagle.

[29] BONTEMANTEL-KERNKAMP 1897, p. 188 ("waerdich . . . bij de inwoonders en vreemdelingen met opmerckinge bespeculeert te werden"). For Dapper's laudatory description of the Kloveniersdoelen and its paintings, see the next chapter and its note 33.

[30] For this tradition and the place of the *Nightwatch* in it, see Chapter V.

[31] BLAEU 1651, n.p., s.v. Amsterdam, *in margine* Doelen ("dwars door de hoven van de twee eerste [doelen] sijn onlangs twee nieuwe straten gemaeckt, die met fraye huysen alree bynae gantsch betimmert sijn"); DAPPER 1663, p. 447.

[32] BALDINUCCI 1686, p. 78, thought that the Kloveniersdoelen was an inn for foreign gentlemen ("Allogio de'Cavalieri forestieri"); this may already have been the opinion of Bernhardt Keil, his spokesman, who was in Amsterdam only until about 1656.

demise of the *doelens* and the end of traditions.[33] The *doelens* were
gradually taken over for other purposes, and were partly used as
warehouses. Already Bontemantel, writing about this decline in the
third quarter of the seventeenth century, was worried about the fate
of the paintings.[34] Some of them were transferred to the Town Hall
as early as 1683.

It would be incorrect to think that the company of Banning Cocq
and the other nineteen in Amsterdam were purely social organizations
without any military or paramilitary responsibilities. Officially, their
duties were even quite heavy. According to law, the companies had
to guard the city at various points, including the gates, day and night
and had to assist in the extinction of fires and in keeping order. These
duties were defined in the original ordinance establishing the citizens'
militia in 1580 and were repeated later. Reality, however, was not
always that grim. The day-to-day routine work was taken care of by
hired soldiers and by other bodies of citizens (particularly the *ruiter-
wacht* and the *ratelwacht*).[35] Members of the militia companies that
did not fulfill their duties had to pay fines, and we must assume that
many for whom the fine was not a hardship preferred to pay. In times
of political unrest, however, the companies had to participate together
with mercenaries in truly military actions to defend the Dutch Republic
against attacks from abroad (1622 expedition to Zwolle; 1632 to
Nijmegen).[36] These events caused casualties and deeply disturbed contemporaries. In 1650, when the animosities between Amsterdam and
the Prince of Orange came to a head, William II marched up to Amsterdam to attack it. The city prepared itself for a siege and closed
and manned the gates. It was necessary to avoid slackness in the
application of the rules for the militia, and these were reprinted in
that year over the signature of Banning Cocq (Fig. 50).[37] A fight was

[33] BONTEMANTEL-KERNKAMP 1897, pp. 181-182; the shooting ranges of the two
doelens having been built up with houses in 1650, only the Kloveniersdoelen had one
left. According to BEUDEKER II, f°. 145ro, some Kloveniers still used their range at the
time of his writing (ca. 1730).

[34] BONTEMANTEL-KERNKAMP 1897, p. 188.

[35] SCHELTEMA 1853, p. 101 (with the names of the captains of the two bodies,
respectively Simon Gerritsen and Willem Last).

[36] Others were planned in 1625 and 1629, but it is not certain whether these *uittochten*
took place (NOORDKERK 1744, p. 92).

[37] The ordinance of 1580 was published in NOORDKERK 1748, pp. 142-146, and
separately by Isaak Tirion in Amsterdam in 1747. The ordinance remained valid in
principle, although it was changed in details incorporated in new versions issued in
1590, 1618, 1650, and later years. Concise information is provided in JOCHEMS 1888.
For Banning Cocq's ordinance, see also Chapter II and its note 7.

avoided, and a compromise reached, not without sacrifices on the part of Amsterdam where some of the staunchest anti-Orangist Republicans, among them Andries Bicker, had to leave public office (Banning Cocq, somewhat more moderate, stayed on). An event like this one of July 1650 must have been constantly envisaged as a possibility in the 1640s. Even if the militia rarely fought, it embodied Amsterdam's aspirations to be a city-republic, independent of the Prince of Orange, a world power in its own right—and with its own mercantile and military might. *Its own power symbol from Orange.*

The citizens' militia embodied, traditionally and undoubtedly in the minds of Rembrandt's and Banning Cocq's contempories, the power of their city as distinct from other cities and the Dutch Republic in general. From their origins in the Middle Ages, the militia had defended the rights of the citizens in the original, narrow sense of the word, that is, the free inhabitants of a city, and in the seventeenth century they still symbolized the individual rights, character and achievements of the cities. In 1638, Van Baerle calls Amsterdam's companies "twenty standards of select citizens, the old garrison of the city, the nerves and strength of the Commonwealth", adding that "strong cities always see to it that they can rely on native soldiers rather than on foreign ones".[38] The militia of the various cities in Holland, of Alkmaar, Hoorn, The Hague, Haarlem, Amsterdam, and so many others, symbolized the individual cities.

To sum up, Banning Cocq, Van Ruytenburgh, and their men were proud to be associated with the past and with the present of the Amsterdam militia and its institutions.[39] The viewers of the painting shared these feelings, and understood the image these citizens wished to project. The militia had helped to free the Netherlands from Spanish domination, had traditionally protected the city against invaders, kept order within its walls, lent luster to triumphal entries, and had otherwise contributed to the city's political and cultural life. Their pride was primarily local, only secondarily national; the militia and the *doelens* reinforced the feeling of identity of the city and its inhabitants. The militia embodied not only a proud past, but also an even more glorious present. Amsterdam had adopted the role of Venice, and felt

[38] BARLAEUS 1639 (Dutch edition), p. 13. For Amsterdam's efforts to become independent see VAN HAMEL 1946.

[39] This retrospective attitude was recognized by SCHMIDT-DEGENER 1914-17 and emphasized by TÜMPEL 1970, but neither associated this interest in the past with a pride in the city of Amsterdam and its achievements. HELLINGA 1956 was aware of this pride, but did not define it.

supreme in its mercantile independence. The militia was its potential
army, which only occasionally had to act but continually symbolized
the will to defend itself against those who threatened it. Banning Cocq's
company, strong and ready to act, was a visual metaphor for the might
of Amsterdam and its willingness to protect its rights.

IV

The Setting: Constraint
and Enhancement

The *Nightwatch* was painted for the assembly hall of the newly constructed wing of the Kloveniersdoelen where members of Banning Cocq's company and of five other companies gathered for festive events and for occasional target practice on the adjacent shooting range. The painting shared the walls of the assembly hall with five other group portraits of militiamen of other precincts of Amsterdam, and a group portrait of the governors of this doelen.

This hall was not decorated according to a definitive program, yet the paintings were to some extent coordinated. Some of their features were preconditioned by their placement. The artists had to adjust to these requirements.[1] Even more important is the meaning the paintings derived from their setting. They were made to decorate a building that had a specific image; while contributing to that image they were also affected by it.

The original section of the Kloveniersdoelen consisted mainly of the tower Svych Wtrecht ("Utrecht, Be Silent") which had been built in 1480-90 as part of the city ramparts along the river Amstel, and some smaller structures on the other side of a street running parallel to the city wall (the Nieuwe Doelenstraat); the shooting range was also across the street, and stretched toward the Gasthuis.[2] These premises had

---

[1] MARTIN 1923-24b., pp. 193-198, and 1935, pp. 160-165, discusses in general some of the requirements painters of militia pieces had to fulfill. HAAK 1972 pointed out that group portraits of regents and regentesses were bound by similar requirements of size and location as militia pieces. See further below, and note 27 of this chapter.

[2] GIMPEL 1918 and RAM 1964 together provide a brief and incomplete summary of the history of the Kloveniersdoelen. The painting is first mentioned in this location in 1653 (after February) by SCHAEP 1630-50s, f⁰. 22ᵛᵒ (see also SCHELTEMA 1885, pp. 135, 136; HdG 1906, no. 144; VAN SCHENDEL-MERTENS 1947, pp. 11, 12).

served Banning Cocq's predecessors and their men, members of the
militia guild of the Kloveniers, ever since that guild had been established in 1522.[3] The tower had few windows and looked sturdy and
forbidding, as we know it from various drawings, among them one
by Rembrandt (Fig. 33).

The street between the tower and the shooting range, although
within the medieval confines of the city, looked like a rural road until
1631 when the first houses went up on either side of it. Because of
the elegance of these houses, the neighborhood soon became known
as the Rijkebuurt.[4] Rembrandt lived briefly in one of the brand new
houses, in or about 1636, one house removed from the Kloveniersdoelen.[5]

The stylish new wing of the *doelen* was the main building in the
street and must have contributed greatly to the status of the neighborhood. The new wing adjoined the tower and was bordered by the
river on one side and the street on the other. It was separated from
the street by a courtyard that gave entrance to the building. Virtually
the entire second floor was taken up by the large assembly hall with
six large windows overlooking the Amstel River (Fig. 31). Construction started in 1631 or shortly thereafter and was completed by 1636;
in that year, the city government held its annual banquet for the first
time in the Kloveniersdoelen, undoubtedly in the assembly hall on the
second floor.[6] Although the *Nightwatch* and the other group portraits

---

[3] See Chapter III. The tower was also called the Kloveniers Tower (D'AILLY 1947,
p. 47, drawing by Claes Jansz Visscher of ca. 1630 inscribed *Cleveniers Toore*).

[4] BEUDEKER II, f°s. 142vo, 145ro, states that both sides of the street were built up with
elegant houses in 1631, and that these gave the neighborhood its name. For Christoffel
Beudeker (ca. 1675-1756) and his undated informative manuscript description of Amsterdam (Gemeentelijke Archiefdienst), see OLDEWELT 1942, pp. 106-110.

[5] Rembrandt signed his undated letter to Constantijn Huygens, written probably in
February 1636, "naest den pensijonaeris boreel nieuwe doelstraet"; the property of
Willem Boreel adjoined the Kloveniersdoelen. See GERSON 1961, pp. 18-24, and H. F.
Wijnman in WHITE 1964, p. 146, note 30.

[6] BEUDEKER II, f°s. 142vo, 143ro, provides the date of the beginning of the construction
without being explicit ("Toen . . . in . . . 1631 deze straat aan bijde zijden met deftige
huisen wierd bebouwt, waardoor zij de naam van Rijkebuurt verkreeg, heeft de Magistraat aan dezen tooren / mede een aanzienlijk Gebouw doen timmeren"). The Heerenmael ("Gentlemen's Dinner") of 1636 is mentioned by Gerrit Schaep (see BONTE-
MANTEL-KERNKAMP 1897, p. 184). Beudeker's passage was probably the source for the
statement of JOCHEMS 1892, p. 90, that the wing was added in 1631; MEIJER 1900,
p. 92, gave ca. 1633 as date of construction (mentioning neither source nor reason);
BARLAEUS 1639, p. 32, wrote with more enthusiasm than precision that it was "zeer
cierlijk van nieuws gebouwt" (see also KOK 1967, p. 119). After this had been written,
DUDOK VAN HEEL 1981 moved the construction date convincingly back further to
before December 19, 1630 (his ca. 1627-28 seems less certain).

later lining the walls of the hall were not yet there, some of the paintings that the *doelen* already owned may have been placed there temporarily. It was the first time that the city fathers gathered for the Heerenmael outside their town hall, which had grown too small for the occasion.

In fact, the new wing was built mainly for social purposes, both for the meetings of militiamen and for the entertainment of other people, including members and guests of the city government. This was not a new development. When by the end of the sixteenth century the income of the *doelens* had diminished, the city allowed the building to be rented for banquets, keeping the right of first refusal for its own burgomasters and judges (1594). Providing meals and staging banquets had always been important and profitable for the *doelens*, but these activities had now increased to the point that a new building was needed. Various factors contributed: the phenomenal growth of population and wealth in Amsterdam, the talents of good stewards, and particularly the city government's need for more space to fulfill its social responsibilities. It is therefore not surprising that the new wing was added at the expense of the city.[7] That the Kloveniersdoelen was chosen for expansion rather than the two other *doelens* in Amsterdam may partly be due to the talents of the steward, as one contemporary observer states, but certainly also must have been prompted by the availability of space along the river where city walls had become obsolete.[8]

The new building contrasted sharply with the two other *doelens* in Amsterdam, which dated as far back as the beginning of the sixteenth century and which were built in a late Gothic style. On the river side the building was decorated with sophisticated classicizing double brick pilasters between windows, and the blind wall on the second floor at the side of the courtyard was enlivened by simulated windows separated by similar pilasters.[9] From across the river, the well-proportioned, elegant building with a double row of six windows adjoining the solid, medieval tower provided an attractive motif for artists through

[7] The reasons for building the wing are deduced from Bontemantel's statements and Kernkamp's annotations (BONTEMANTEL-KERNKAMP 1897, pp. 182-184). Bontemantel (p. 182) states specifically, and Beudeker (see previous note) implies that the city paid for the building.

[8] Bontemantel states flatly that "Steward Bartel [of the Kloveniersdoelen] got so many customers that the 'groote sael' was added" (BONTEMANTEL-KERNKAMP 1897, p. 182).

[9] In 1977-78 one of these windows with its pilasters, now on the second floor within the Doelen Hotel, was uncovered. For views of the street side of the building, see the drawing by Jan de Beijer in the Gemeentelijke Archiefdienst, Amsterdam (Atlas Splitgerber 564), and a similar view by R. Vinkeles, reproduced in KOOT 1969, p. 31, and elsewhere.

the centuries (Figs. 31, 32). Rembrandt himself, however, was not sufficiently interested in the new building to sketch it. The historical attracted him more than the contemporary. Thus, in the 1650s, he made a drawing of the original elevated section of the tower Svych Wtrecht, omitting its new roof and barely suggesting the adjacent building where his painting was hanging, only summarily indicating the edge of its facade by means of a few penlines (Fig. 33).[10]

The large assembly hall, or *groote sael*, on the second floor was the core of the new wing, and thereby of the entire complex. With its generous size of approximately nine by eighteen meters, and the unusually high ceiling (about five meters), the hall was one of the largest interior spaces in Amsterdam before the, for Amsterdam, enormous new town hall was opened in 1655.[11] The hall of the Kloveniers was excellently suited for meetings of large groups. The militiamen themselves gathered in it, and here the government of the city held its annual banquet, the so-called Heerenmael, as already mentioned above.[12] The new wing attracted many other activities, like the meetings of a supervisory body of the Amsterdam militia companies, the so-called *schietcollege*, and of the members of the Order of St. Michael, which apparently had its seat in the Kloveniersdoelen.[13] The city used the doelen to entertain distinguished guests.[14] Not only the size of the

[10] The river side is particularly carefully rendered in the etching by Moucheron (see below) and the watercolor *The 's-Gravelandse Veer with the Kloveniersdoelen in the Distance* of 1779 by H. P. Schouten (Splitgerber 716). The print (perhaps by Jacob van Meurs) in DAPPER 1663, after p. 444, and taken over by COMMELIN 1693, p. 95 (reproduced by KOK 1967, fig. 2, and elsewhere) is not accurate. Rembrandt's drawing is now in the Rijksprentenkabinet, Amsterdam (BENESCH 1954-57, p. 134; see BOON 1969).

[11] In the opinion of BEUDEKER II, f°. 145ro, the hall was unparalleled in size. MEIJER 1886, p. 204, supposed that the measurements had been: ca. 19 × 11 m., probably without checking *in situ*; J. J. de Gelder (acc. to MARTIN 1947, p. 14): 18 × 9 m.; KOOT 1947, p. 30, correctly estimated the length at about 18 meters.

[12] See above in this chapter, and note 6.

[13] Little is known of the *schietcollege*, mentioned in the poem of TENGNAGEL. Banning Cocq was a member of the order of St. Michael since 1648. The order was eulogized in a poem printed in 1659 as a broadsheet, entitled "Aan de edele Gebroederschap der schuttersorde van Sint-Michiel, in de Kloveniers doelen"; it appears among Vondel's works in the standard editions of the poet, and was already mentioned as a work of his by WAGENAAR 1767, III, p. 169, but one copy (Fig. 56; also reproduced in HIJMANS-KUIPER-VELS HEIJN 1976, p. 41) is signed S. D.

[14] The guests were usually housed in the Prinsenhof. Particularly in 1638, the Kloveniersdoelen was enlisted for entertaining distinguished guests of the city (CARROLL 1976, p. 250; TÜMPEL 1977, p. 81 states that Maria de'Medici was entertained here; I assume this is an assumption, probably a correct one).

groote sael, but also the sweeping view over the wide stretch of the Amstel River and its activities was an attraction for those gathered in the hall. An etching by Isaac de Moucheron gives us an impression of this view at a special occasion (Fig. 31). With precise attention to detail, he recorded the spectacular fireworks performed in 1697 in honor of Czar Peter the Great on a temporary artificial island. He represented the spectacle as seen by the public against the backdrop of the Kloveniersdoelen where the czar and his company were banqueting at the time.

As a spacious hall built and used for official and public meetings and banquets, situated on a second floor and decorated with some of the best paintings of the period, the *groote sael* in the Amsterdam of the 1640s must have made an impression similar to London's Banqueting House in the 1620s. Although the hall for which Rembrandt painted his *Nightwatch* cannot be considered as grand and monumental as the British one for which Rubens created one of his most ambitious and most successful ensembles, it was its Dutch parallel. And as the seat of a paramilitary establishment fostering the best art of the day, the building had another distinguished parallel. While the Amsterdam Kloveniers were building their new wing, their Antwerp colleagues who in 1611 commissioned Rubens to paint the triptych of the *Descent from the Cross* for the cathedral, were constructing a new meeting place in elegant classical style adjacent to Rubens' house and garden.[15]

The tower and the new wing remained virtually intact until about 1870, when two stories were added on top of the assembly hall. Previously, the courtyard on the street side had been built up, and some low structures on the water side had been added, but these additions had not seriously affected the main features. Before the stories were added, an anonymous photographer recorded the building (Fig. 32). In 1882, the complex was further and now completely transformed in order to better serve its function as a hotel, as it is still used today. The tower was largely demolished to make room for an ample stairwell, which incorporated part of its walls and preserved the original round exterior, and the seventeenth-century building containing

---

[15] Construction of the ambitious Kloveniershof in Antwerp started in the second half of 1631; its roof was placed late in 1632; its interiors were finished at a slow pace by 1637 (BAUDOUIN 1973-75). One wonders, I should add, through what twist of fate Rembrandt also was a neighbor of his Kloveniersdoelen, albeit for a much shorter time than Rubens (see above); also, both artists bought real estate from the same family, and shared other circumstances (VAN EEGHEN 1977).

the assembly hall was remodelled in the same style as the stairwell
and buildings adjoining the tower on the other side. In the interior,
the *groote sael* still exists, although defaced to such an extent that its
preservation has been overlooked by students of Rembrandt and of
Amsterdam. It is now subdivided into three large rooms and a corridor,
and the ceiling has been lowered, but the walls still stand, and the six
windows, although somewhat enlarged and changed, still open onto
the Amstel River. Walking through the hotel rooms where formerly
the *Nightwatch* and the other paintings hung, one can imagine the
ensemble of Amsterdam's best group portraits as it presented itself to
the viewer in the seventeenth century.[16]

Although we have no view of the interior of the assembly hall at
the time it housed the *Nightwatch* (1642-1715), we gain some idea
from the view made by an unidentified printmaker in or shortly before
1748, after the paintings were removed (Fig. 34). Furthermore, the
location of the paintings, which have all been preserved, was precisely
described in 1653. This description and what remains of the hall itself
make it possible to reconstruct the original situation (see plan with
key, Fig. 35).[17] The only entrance to the hall was from the old tower
through a door in the short wall built against the tower. The door
was at the side, the rest of the wall between door and windows being
taken up by an immense fireplace. A second, smaller fireplace occupied
the center of the opposite short wall. All the wall space, also above
the fireplaces, was covered by seven large paintings. Three of approximately the same size (including the *Nightwatch*) were placed opposite
the windows, three on the short wall (above and to either side of the

[16] The Rembrandt literature speaks of the Kloveniersdoelen as having stood on the
site of the present Doelen Hotel in the Nieuwe Doelenstraat, creating the impression
or implying that it was razed or totally transformed. In fact, the structural walls are
still in place, and the interior spaces, particularly the *groote sael*, have been preserved.
It should be comparatively easy to bring back this hall to its original state—and make
it again a landmark in Amsterdam. Since the interior decoration of the hall is of great
significance for a reconstruction of the original appearance of the *Nightwatch* and the
other paintings, an effort should be made to find out what is preserved behind the
lowered ceilings and the new facings of the walls. The original beams and corbels of
the ceilings and vertical dividers of the walls may still be there, at least in part.

[17] SCHAEP 1630-50s; Schaep and BEUDEKER II also described the lay-out of the rooms
in the new wing. The print in FOKKE 1748 representing the interior after the removal
of the *Nightwatch* seems to render the architecture inaccurately, yet gives an impression
of the general aspect of the hall, as pointed out by DE BRUYN KOPS 1976, pp. 101-
104, fig. 2; it is also reproduced in MARTIN 1947, fig. 3. The reconstructed ground plan
was taken over from KOOT 1969, p. 63, with kind permission of the author and the
publisher.

central fireplace), and the last one, the very long and narrow *Company of Roelof Bicker* by van der Helst (Fig. 42), over the wide fireplace on the western wall next to the entrance to the hall. Except for the two paintings over the fireplaces, they were placed with their lower edges approximately 75 centimeters to one meter above the floor. They all reached to the ceiling. The three paintings largely covering the long wall probably were not framed separately but encased, above a wainscot, in woodwork that separated them from each other, the ceiling and the side walls.[18]

Apparently, the seven paintings including the *Nightwatch* were loosely coordinated.[19] One, by Govert Flinck, representing the governors of the Kloveniersdoelen (Fig. 36), was appropriately made to be hung over the central fireplace opposite the entrance. The remaining six were group portraits of members of the six companies that were affiliated with this *doelen* and that enjoyed the privileges of using the hall for meetings.[20] They were painted in a comparatively short period of time, five of them between the years 1639 and 1642, the last one, the *Company of Captain Albert Bas*, also painted by Flinck, in 1645 (Fig. 38). Since, in spite of earlier suppositions, the commission was not given in connection with a special occasion, like a triumphal entry into the city of Amsterdam,[21] we may assume that the availability of the new hall and the wish to decorate it were the reasons for having the group portraits made.[22] It was an old tradition to decorate meeting

[18] The distance between painting and floor was, according to SCHMIDT-DEGENER 1917a., p. 6, at least 75 cm.; according to MARTIN 1947, p. 16, one meter. The convincing hypothesis that the paintings were encased rather than framed is due to DE BRUYN KOPS 1976, p. 103. Investigation of the actual walls of the hall, not carried out by any of the writers, should clarify these questions.

[19] MARTIN 1935-36, I, p. 164, seems to have been the first to speak in this connection of a certain "program".

[20] We know from SCHAEP 1639-50s, f°. 54vo ("Lijste van de 20 Compagnien Burger Vaendelen onder wat Doelen ijder is sorterende") that in the years 1630 and 1636 six companies (of districts II, III, IV, V, XIV, and XX, using JOCHEMS 1888 as a key) were affiliated with the Kloveniersdoelen. Although only three of the six companies portrayed in the hall between 1639 and 1645 (of districts II, IV, V, VIII, XVIII, XIX) agree with those listed by Schaep (II, IV, V) for 1630-36, the number of companies notably did not change between 1636 and 1639-45. An error may have crept into the accounting, or the affiliation with individual *doelens* changed. The twenty companies were evenly distributed over the three *doelens*, with six in one and seven in the others.

[21] For these hypotheses, see Chapter VI, under "Action".

[22] This supposition was already made by MEIJER 1886, pp. 203, 204, and is now generally accepted (e.g. VAN GELDER 1946, pp. 259-261; KOOT 1969, pp. 63, 64; particularly KOK 1967; also TÜMPEL 1970, p. 173, but there is no evidence that the appointment of three new captains provided an additional reason).

halls with militia pieces in Amsterdam, where the two other *doelens* had them, as well as elsewhere in the Netherlands, and the Kloveniersdoelen could not lag behind. However, commissioning a series of militia pieces for one hall in a comparatively short time was an exception, not only in Amsterdam. There was one precedent: in 1626, Joris van Schooten painted seven militia pieces for two different rooms of the St. Jorisdoelen in Leiden.[23] But that was a true program rather than an informal coordination. As for the *groote sael*, we may imagine that the six companies and the governors of the *doelen* agreed to have the assembly hall decorated with militia pieces, that they established which company would be portrayed where, and that companies and their captains arranged further matters with the artists of their choice, who had to see to it that their works satisfied the company as well as fit into the ensemble of the hall.

The artists apparently knew the size and placement of their paintings and the light conditions before they started their work. They did pay attention to the condition of the hall and the particular requirements of the location of each group portrait. Collocation was as serious a concern of Dutch theorists and painters as it was of Italian writers and artists at the time, as appears, for instance, from a set of rules written by Pieter de Grebber for young artists and printed in 1642.[24]

The unusual height of the ceiling of the assembly hall, probably about sixteen feet, introduced totally new opportunities for the artists and had a profound effect on these militia pieces.[25] Life-size figures

[23] Six measure approximately 174 × 192 cm., a seventh one (lost; perhaps dated 1628) measured 158 × 271 cm.; each sitter had to pay twelve florins (PELINCK 1949, pp. 246-256). BAUCH 1960, p. 40, noted the parallel between Van Schooten's series and the paintings in the *groote sael*. In Haarlem, militiamen (i.e., only officers) had themselves portrayed in group portraits at the time their tenure ended (VAN VALKENBURG 1958-62, p. 64).

[24] VAN THIEL 1965, pp. 126, 131. If the sheet with eleven rules was printed as proof of mastery of the printer Pieter Casteleyn rather than to publish a deliberately chosen set of rules, as Van Thiel considers possible, it nevertheless proves the existence of this concern for collocation at that time: "For various reasons it is necessary to know the place where will be hung what will be made: because of the light; because of the height of the place; in order to take distance and establish the horizon; for which purpose it is also necessary that all composers are thoroughly acquainted with the rules of perspective". VAN HOOGSTRAETEN 1678, pp. 235, 236, also has some good advice along the same lines for young artists. For other seventeenth-century discussions of the concept, see the treatises by Lomazzo, Baldinucci (*Vocabulario*), and Du Fresnoy (verses 398-405 of the Latin text).

[25] As first observed by SIX 1893, pp. 98, 99, and repeated by NEUMANN 1902, p. 275 (also in later editions).

had been customary for such paintings since Cornelis Ketel had represented a company in this manner in 1588 (Fig. 83), with little space to spare above or under them. The same was still true for Thomas de Keyser in 1632 (Fig. 88). Now the artists could rearrange the figures, using the extra space above them. Some used this opportunity, including Rembrandt; others strung the figures along horizontally as they and their predecessors had been doing before, now trying to fill the space above them with accessories.

The width of the individual paintings was based upon the total length of wall space and the number of companies sharing it. In this case, the space over the smaller of two fireplaces was reserved for the group portrait of the governors (Fig. 36), but the other walls were available for the six companies. Certain wall sections asked for specific compositional solutions. Joachim von Sandrart arranged his sitters in a triangle with its top to the left (Fig. 37) and Govert Flinck in one with its top to the right (Fig. 38) to fit on either side of the small fireplace and to balance each other. They both let the light fall from the left, as it did in the assembly hall. Bartholomeus van der Helst, for the *Company of Captain Roelof Bicker* (Fig. 42), had only the narrow space above the large fireplace on the entrance wall at his disposal, and could not do much else but align the members of the company. His light is coming from the right, again in accordance with the natural light in the hall.

Rembrandt, Backer, and Eliasz shared the wall, about eighteen meters along, opposite the windows. Eliasz painted his *Company of Captain van Vlooswijck* (Fig. 40) for the center of the wall, and arranged his men predominantly in horizontal isocephalic fashion. Backer had the right third of the wall, took advantage of the height of the canvas, and arranged his sitters partly in a semicircle, partly on a flight of steps towards the right (Fig. 41). The *Nightwatch* was to be placed on the left third of this wall, therefore in the corner of the hall, for what reason is uncertain. The center may have been reserved for the company of the senior captain, Jan van Vlooswijck.[26]

[26] MEIJER 1896, p. 242, seems to have been the only one to suggest that seniority might have been a factor in the placement of the three paintings. Given the sense of hierarchy among civic guard companies and their officers at the time, his suggestion is attractive. Accordingly, the company of Jan van Vlooswijck, captain by 1628 (JOCHEMS 1888, pp. 10, 31) or perhaps 1617 (BONTEMANTEL-KERNKAMP 1897, p. 196), belonged in the center, those of Cornelis de Graef, captain since 1638 (JOCHEMS 1888, p. 10, 32) and of Banning Cocq, appointed captain after August 1638 and before 1642, at the sides. In that case, there would be no grounds to fear that Rembrandt was slighted by not being assigned the center of the wall. The supposition by HIJMANS-KUIPER-VELS

Like the other painters decorating the assembly hall, Rembrandt took the location into consideration.[27] But in contrast to them, he was the only one to take full advantage of the height of the canvas.[28] Since the far left side of the *Nightwatch* would be least visible, he placed there only two portraits and closed the composition at this side with the seated figure of Sergeant Engelen two feet inside the border of the canvas. Whoever in 1715 made the decision to curtail the painting at the left more severely than at the right recognized the lesser significance of the left side. The ensign with his banner, counterbalancing that of the ensign in the painting by Backer on the other side of the wall, may owe his place to the location of the painting. Partly because the *Nightwatch* would be seen from an angle, but also because Rembrandt generally wished to avoid the central placement of main figures for the sake of a livelier effect, he placed the chief officers off center. The movement of the men from the arch towards the viewer and then to the left, as if going to bypass him, becomes even more pronounced if the painting is seen from an angle. Rembrandt must have had this effect in mind (Fig. 39). In at least two other paintings he took the location into consideration, in *The Syndics* and *The Conspiracy of the Batavians*.[29] That the light in the *Nightwatch* falls from the left as it

---

HEIJN 1976, p. 48, that the placement of the paintings was established by drawing lots is speculative. The selection of companies, as DUDOK VAN HEEL 1981 convincingly proposes, was based on their having joined the Kloveniersdoelen recently; they therefore were not yet represented among the paintings.

[27] DE GELDER 1921 (in first thesis to the dissertation edition of his book) stressed the effect of location on the composition of Amsterdam militia pieces. MEIJER 1896 had already supposed that Rembrandt took the location of the *Nightwatch* into consideration; MARTIN 1935-36, I, pp. 162-165 (also 1947, pp. 14, 15) and MOES-VETH 1960 stressed the point further. See also KOOT 1947, p. 131, and 1969, pp. 63, 64. DYSERINCK 1890, pp. 264, 265, pointed out that the effect of movement of the central group was reduced by the curtailment of the painting; SCHÖNE 1972, p. 86, made a similar point. DE GELDER 1921, p. 52, demonstrated the effect of placement on Van der Helst's painting for the assembly hall. HIJMANS-KUIPER-VELS HEIJN 1976, p. 59, indicate briefly various adjustments Rembrandt made to the location of the painting.

[28] Judging from those early works in which he reformulated Lastman's horizontal compositions into vertical ones, Rembrandt already developed in Leyden a special feeling for the opportunities offered by high formats.

[29] The adjustment of the composition of these two paintings (Rijksmuseum, Amsterdam, and Nationalmuseum, Stockholm) to their location is a fact. Rembrandt may also have proceeded in the same way with *The Anatomical Demonstration of Dr. Tulp* (Mauritshuis, The Hague), therefore as early as 1632. According to Zacharias von Uffenbach, the latter painting hung in 1711 "rechter Hand des Kamins" ("at the right-hand side of the fireplace") in the anatomical theater in Amsterdam (HDG 1906, no. 389). If this location in 1711 (which may not have been the original one) indicates that

does in the two adjoining paintings by Eliasz and Backer, on the other hand, may reflect a general practice.[30]

The relationships between the individual paintings of the hall imply a certain coordination with room for individual differences.[31] These differences between the paintings were largely due to the concepts of the artists, as we shall see in the next chapter, but they resulted also from the prevailing custom in Amsterdam, Haarlem, and elsewhere at the time that militia pieces were paid for by the sitters. Rembrandt had to accommodate their wishes and particularly the requests from the captain and the lieutenant. Although the specific demands of the patrons cannot be established, they did have an effect on the paintings, including the *Nightwatch*, as we discussed in an earlier chapter.[32] Yet, the painting was also influenced by its location.

Not only the formal appearance of the painting was affected by its setting, but also its image. Since the painting was one of seven decorating the same hall, it participated in the overall impression a visitor received. The eighteen men portrayed in the *Nightwatch* shared the walls with more than one hundred other influential and successful Amsterdamers. They were all approximately life-size, represented in martial roles, dressed in elegant, often colorful costumes on canvases that virtually covered the walls all around like murals, from a little above the floor to the ceiling. The impression must have been staggering. We sense this from the brief description made twenty years later by Olfert Dapper. In these "large, artfully painted pieces" in the *groote sael* of the Kloveniersdoelen, he wrote, "virtually entire companies of militiamen with their captains, lieutenants . . . are shown larger than life-size, as if they were standing and living, fully armed and appareled (however not in the old-fashioned way, but as the militiamen were dressed and as they marched a few years ago)".[33] He

---

Rembrandt had painted it to hang on the left of the fireplace (heraldically on its right), the lack of balance of the composition may partly have been an answer to the requirements of the placement (compare the paintings by Sandrart and Flinck in the Kloveniersdoelen).

[30] As DE GELDER 1921, pp. 51, 52, pointed out, seventeenth-century Dutch painters preferred to represent the light as coming from the left unless the future location of the painting demanded otherwise.

[31] The coordination does not imply that the paintings were executed in the hall itself (see Chapter I and its note 22).

[32] See Chapter I and its notes 5, 6 and 7.

[33] "Op de groote zael van deze Doelen, die, behalve d'oude tooren, een nieuw en treffelijk gebouw is, staen ook aen de muuren, en voor de schoorstenen ongemene groote, en kunstigh geschilderde stukken. By na hele troepen schutteren, met hun Hop-

noted the unusual size of the paintings and the modernity of arms and costumes, all features distinguishing these paintings from their predecessors. The exaggerations that Dapper allowed himself in his enthusiasm tell us much about his interpretation and presumably that of his contemporaries. By enlarging the size of the companies—they were far from "virtually entire"—he stressed the point that not only officers were represented, as in Haarlem, but officers and men; by calling the figures "over life-size", he conveyed their impressiveness compared to the much smaller figures in average Dutch painting including portraiture; by exaggerating the degree to which the men were armed, he stressed the cardinal point of their being portrayed as militiamen.

The interpretation of the painting was also partly dependent on the purpose, use, style, and even location of the building where it hung. Built in a new style as an extension to a fortified tower of the medieval city walls, the building symbolized the rejuvenation and continuation of traditional values: the defense of Amsterdam's citizens and the protection of their privileges. The social distinction and civic success of the sitters were supported and intensified by the elegance of the building and the level of social entertainment fostered within its walls. The building placed Amsterdam's painted elite in a tradition-oriented framework of civic virtue, acquired affluence, and collective pride.

Finally, contemporary viewers could not but see the painting as partaking in the traditon of a specific well-defined category of portraiture. In 1642 it was one of more than eighty group portraits of militiamen in the three *doelens* in Amsterdam, the earliest one dating from 1529. These group portraits were the Dutch equivalent of paintings of *uomini illustri* developed particularly in Italy in the fifteenth and sixteenth centuries.[34] Although not including philosophers, doctors or poets *per se*, they shared the patriotic and civic virtues and pride conveyed by series painted by Uccello, Castagno, Justus van Ghent, and others. The Amsterdam citizens, whatever their function in civil life, were the Dutch *capitani*, *condottieri*, and other heroes.

---

mannen, Lieutenants, Vendrigs, Korporalen, en Serjanten, worden in de zelve meer als levens groote, en, als ofze daer stonden en leefden, in volle geweer en rustingh (niet evenwel na d'oude tijdt, maer zoo als de Schutteren voor eenige weinigh jaren gekleet gingen en optrokken) vertoont. Hier heeftmen ook het beeltenis hangen van Maria de Medicis, die in den jare zestien hondert acht-en-dertigh, deze Stadt quam bezichtigen" (DAPPER 1663, p. 444). COMMELIN 1693, pp. 664, 665, adopted this description.

[34] Fine introductions to the subject of *uomini illustri*, with bibliographies, are found in RAVE 1959, and PRINZ 1971, pp. 17-22.

The paintings embodied and elicited patriotic feelings toward the city. They were worth a visit for these reasons, but also for artistic enjoyment. When Dutchmen or foreigners visited Amsterdam, they went to see the militia pieces, as Buchelius did in 1592, when he went to the Sagittariarum hortus (the Voetboogsdoelen) particularly to see "the lifelike paintings artfully made by Dirck Barendsz".[35]

[35] "picturas ad vivam similitudinem artificiose factas per Theodorum Bernardum". Buchelius mentioned his visit to the Voetboogsdoelen in his diary (BUCHELIUS 1928, p. 8).

V

The Form: Tradition
and Innovation

In the *Nightwatch*, Rembrandt both adopted and radically transformed fundamental aspects of traditional group portraiture and created a painting that, much as it resembles older and contemporary militia pieces, differs substantially from them.

In contrast to other traditions affecting the militia guilds and companies, the custom of painting collective portraits of members of militia guilds and companies (militia pieces, *schuttersstukken*) was exclusive to the Northern Netherlands. The first of the numerous preserved militia pieces dates from 1529 (Fig. 82) and was painted for the Kloveniersdoelen; the tradition survived the reformation of the militia guilds and ended ca. 1650 with the last such group portrait by Johann Spilberg (Fig. 89). The custom was of great significance, not only for those who were portrayed, but for the cities and their cultural life. Apart from townhall decorations, these militia pieces, together with group portraits of governors of other civic organizations, were the only official institutional commissions in Holland in the seventeenth century.[1] Conservative partly because they were meant to preserve the appearance of distinguished citizens for future generations, partly because they projected the image of defense of freedom and preservation of peace and order, these paintings adhered to compositional and representational themes that changed only moderately and slowly.

Various well-defined types developed to which artists rigidly adhered: men at ceremonial meals, men standing in a row or seated around a table, men gathered behind their captain in preparation for

---

[1] The few other occasions were provided by town halls and temporary decorations for festive entries and the like. BAUCH 1957, p. 21, went further by stating that these large "Gruppenbildnisse sind ja die eigentliche Monumentalkunst der holländischen Malerei".

a march, etc.[2] There were local characteristics: for instance, in Haarlem the habit of representing only officers and in Amsterdam officers and men in each individual painting. The origin for the different types must be sought in differences in circumstances, among them artistic preferences. The frequently chosen ceremonial meal may well have answered the need of the artists for unified action in representing a group of men, rather than properly reflecting the significance of those gatherings.[3] In general, one has to beware of interpreting the paintings in a naturalistic vein. Many of the objects symbolize the role of the sitters as militiamen, their duties, activities, privileges, and pride of belonging. Properties like fish and wine on tables in Amsterdam's militia pieces of the sixteenth century refer to fishing rights and income from selling wine rather than gustatory preferences.[4]

Shortly before coming to an end ca. 1650, this tradition experienced a last, short-lived flowering in the commission for no less than seven paintings for the new hall of the Kloveniersdoelen. One of these was the *Nightwatch*. The other six groups of militiamen painted for the same hall as part of the same program represent similar merchants and regents in similar roles, and yet are totally different.

A comparison of the *Nightwatch* with the six other paintings was first made by Samuel van Hoogstraeten.[5] He had been a pupil of Rembrandt, probably at the time when the latter was painting the *Nightwatch*, and he obviously knew both the Kloveniersdoelen and the painting well. Writing about composition in his theoretical and educational treatise published in 1678, Van Hoogstraeten warned students that they should not align figures next to one another, "as one finds them too often in Holland in the 'doelen' ". Elsewhere he wrote that they should avoid a situation in which "you can behead them all at once". Instead, real masters should unify their work: "Rembrandt has observed this requirement very well in his piece in the 'Doele' in Amsterdam, but in the opinion of many he went too far, making more

---

[2] The types are described by SCHMIDT-DEGENER 1916b., pp. 30, 31, and MARTIN 1935-36, I, pp. 158 ff.

[3] WAETZOLDT 1908, p. 294.

[4] The fish (perch) and wine in the so-called *Pos-eters* (*Militiamen of Squad L*) of 1566 by Dirck Barendsz (Rijksmuseum, no. C365) and the fish in *The Company of Captain Hasselaar* by Pieter Pietersz (ibidem, no. C404) should be interpreted in this sense; for these privileges, see BONTEMANTEL-KERNKAMP 1897, pp. 177-179; also CARROLL 1976, pp. 230-233.

[5] The seventh painting, *The Governors of the Kloveniersdoelen* by Govert Flinck (Fig. 36), is of a different type, that of the Regents and Syndics.

work of the overall subject he preferred to depict than of the individual portraits he was commissioned to do. However, this painting, no matter how much we may criticize it, will survive all its competitors because it is so painter-like in thought, so ingenious in the varied placement of the figures, and so powerful that in comparison, according to some, all the other pieces there [in the Kloveniersdoelen] look like decks of playing cards".[6]

Van Hoogstraeten's scorn of motionless standing figures in a horizontal isocephalic arrangement would be justly applied to the militia piece hanging next to the *Nightwatch*, painted by Eliasz in the same year, 1642 (Fig. 40).[7] Officers and members of the company of Jan van Vlooswijck are neatly standing next to each other in a row on either side of the captain and the lieutenant, both of whom are seated, with the ensign standing almost in the center of the painting. In this respect, Van Hoogstraeten might have been more approving of *The Company of Cornelis de Graeff* on the other end of the same wall,

---

[6] "Ten is niet genoeg, dat een Schilder zijn beelden op ryen nevens malkander stelt, gelijk men hier in Hollant op de Schuttersdoelen al te veel zien kan. De rechte meesters brengen te weeg, dat haer geheele werk eenwezich is . . . *Rembrandt* heeft dit in zijn stuk op den Doele tot Amsterdam zeer wel, maer na veeler gevoelen al te veel, waergenomen, maekende meer werks van het groote beelt zijner verkiezing, als van de byzondere afbeeltsels, die hem waren aenbesteet. Echter zal dat zelve werk, hoe berispelijk, na mijn gevoelen al zijn meedestrevers verdueren, zijnde zoo schilderachtich van gedachten, zoo zwierich van sprong, en zoo krachtich, dat, nae zommiger gevoelen, al d'andere stukken daer als kaerteblaren nevens staen. Schoon ik wel gewilt hadde, dat hy'er meer lichts in ontsteeken had" (VAN HOOGSTRAETEN 1678, p. 176). The expression "zwierich van sprong" is generally given the meaning of "[oeuvre] élégante d'agencement" (VOSMAER 1877, p. 220) or "dashing in movement" (SLIVE 1953, p. 98). I have used (as BAUCH 1957, p. 17, did) the clarification Van Hoogstraeten himself gave of *sprong* on p. 190: "Neem een aerdige sprong waer, dat is een welkunstige, maer in schijn ongemaekte plaetsing uwer beelden: op dat menze niet, bij wijze van spreeken, al te gelijk (als in sommige Doelstukken) de hoofden kan afslaen" ("Observe a pleasant *sprong*, *i.e.*, an artful yet seemingly effortless placement of your figures: in order that one could not, so to speak, behead them all at once—as in some militia pieces"). Van Hoogstraeten used the word *sprong* in the same sense also on pp. 173, 175, 191. Van Hoogstraeten meant neither "daring forward motion" (SCHMIDT-DEGENER 1942, p. 11) nor "complicated composition" (TÜMPEL 1977, p. 87). The supposition that "het groote beelt zijner verkiezing" would refer to Banning Cocq (DYSERINCK 1890, p. 273) is unfounded; the efforts of SCHMIDT-DEGENER 1917a., p. 4, and MARTIN 1947, p. 19, to vindicate the *Nightwatch*, the former supposing that Van Hoogstraeten used "light" in the figurative sense of the word, the latter suggesting that the painting was already dirty when Van Hoogstraeten criticized its darkness, were well intended but do not convince.

[7] For this and the following militia pieces and their placement in the assembly hall in the Kloveniersdoelen, see Chapter IV.

painted by Jacob Backer, who in his youth had been influenced by Rembrandt (Fig. 41). Here about half of the men portrayed are arranged in an arch starting at the left with the seated captain and standing lieutenant holding his partisan next to him. The other men are placed above the arch at both sides, some of them descending steps at the right, undoubtedly in order to avoid the horizontality Van Hoogstraeten did not like. Van der Helst, still a young artist at the time, had the most difficult task of all the painters working for this hall. Since he was allotted the space above the wide mantelpiece on the entrance wall, the height of his painting was severely limited, while his number of sitters was larger than of the other militia pieces. He tried to place some figures behind others without sacrificing visibility, but he could scarcely avoid giving the impression of an alignment of figures.

Indeed, by organizing the scene through one basic idea, Rembrandt unified his group portrait in the sense Van Hoogstraeten wanted his readers to appreciate. As a principal motif he emphasized the movement of the central group coming forward toward the viewer, and subordinated the lateral groups to the men placed in the center. He apparently tried to avoid mere juxtaposition at all cost, made people stand and move in different attitudes and on various levels, and made those placed next to each other look in different directions. In contrast to the additive alignment that characterized the group portraits by his contemporaries in the assembly hall, Rembrandt preferred a scene with action, and with differentiation between individual figures and their portraits.

Van Hoogstraeten's complaint that he "should have wished that Rembrandt had used more light in his painting" is fully understandable if the *Nightwatch* is compared with the other paintings. Instead of distributing light evenly so that it would illuminate every figure equally, he introduced an entire scale of light values, from bright to dark. The nature of the light, often described and commented upon, was clearly understood by an artist who wrote about it in the beginning of the nineteenth century. Quirinus van Amelsfoort noted that the light in the *Nightwatch* was not sunlight, but rather a mysterious light that was appropriate for religious scenes (and, he added, not for militiamen, who were no saints).[8] Rembrandt's distribution of light and dark, his

---

[8] The artist (1760-1820) worked in Den Bosch. The passage about the *Nightwatch* reads partly (translated from VERREYT 1897, p. 543): "that is not sunlight, but a mysterious light. If you imagine those finely dressed and armed men removed, and if you substitute a *Transfiguration of Christ*, a *Nativity* or another religious subject for

emphasis on some figures and areas by means of light as applied in the *Nightwatch* is indeed found in paintings and etchings of religious subjects that he made about that time. Similar in this respect are, for instance, the paintings *The Visitation* of 1640 (Detroit) and *Christ and the Woman Taken in Adultery* of 1644 (London), and the etchings *The Triumph of Mordecai* of ca. 1642 (Fig. 76), and *The Presentation in the Temple* of ca. 1639.

The wall with archway and window as background serves as another powerful unifying instrument. The arch accentuates the center and creates a source of forward movement, the walls help to link the figures in front of them, strengthen their presence by bringing them closer to the viewer and eliminate the distraction of space and scenery beyond them. In the other paintings in the hall, the presence of air and space above and behind the figures is felt even when a building is represented, since the building is placed to one side of the composition only.

It is not only the integration of all the figures in a carefully orchestrated ensemble, achieved by means of composition, movement, light, and background, that distinguishes the *Nightwatch* from the other paintings in the assembly hall. In contrast to his colleagues, Rembrandt sacrificed colors and details of costumes and apparel of many of the sitters and of the background to that integration by submerging them in deep shadows and dark tones. Rembrandt's execution of the painting is also totally different from that of any other one in the hall, and for that matter, of any other group portrait painted in the Netherlands. Rather than carefully delineating and smoothly polishing the subject, Rembrandt defined the figures and objects with broad and suggestive brushstrokes, and applied the paint thickly, particularly in light areas. Details like the embroidered border of Van Ruytenburgh's yellow jerkin stand out, literally and figuratively. It is this *impasto* that, not surprisingly given the utter difference from the smooth, enamel-like surface of the paintings by Van der Helst, Eliasz, and others, gave rise to astonishment, then criticism, and, ultimately, to legendary interpretation.[9]

However different the *Nightwatch* may be from these other paintings, its composition and main theme owe much to tradition. Rembrandt adopted and changed a composition that had been used for

---

them, then that light could be called magnificent, but applied to the Amsterdam festive militiamen it is misplaced. These men were not perfect, and there is no reason for them to be painted in a light as if they were saints". This verdict precedes Fromentin's almost identical criticism (see the Introduction) by more than fifty years.

[9] See SLIVE 1953.

the last time only a decade before, in 1632, by Thomas de Keyser for
a painting that was hanging in the same Kloveniersdoelen, over the
stairway leading to the assembly hall (Fig. 88).[10] Two of the principal
elements of the *Nightwatch* are already found here: the central position
of captain and lieutenant in front of the other men and the movement
of part of the company toward the viewer. The relationship is even
closer with two of De Keyser's preparatory drawings for his painting
(Fig. 87).[11] These drawings have two more features that return in the
Nightwatch: the man at the very right pointing to the left with his
outstretched arm[12] and an informal scene at the left that breaks the
monotony of standing and that includes a man seated on a bench
placed in a position and in a direction similar to the railing in Rembrandt's *Nightwatch*.

De Keyser's composition had its own antecèdent in a work by Cornelis Ketel that had been painted long before, in 1588, less than a
decade after the reorganization of the militia guilds (Fig. 83).[13] Different is the placement of the ensign, who here occupies the center of
the composition (or rather what was the center before the painting

[10] Thomas de Keyser, *Officers and Men of the Company of Captain Allaert Cloeck
and Lieutenant Lucas Jacobsz Rotgans*, Rijksmuseum, Amsterdam (Cat. no. C381;
canvas 220 × 351 cm., dated 1632). For the painting see OLDENBOURG 1911, pp. 22-
45. According to SCHAEP 1630-50s, in 1653 the painting was hanging in the Kloveniersdoelen: "Voor in 't Voorhuijs, boven de trap gaende na de grootte Sael", therefore
not in the Voetboogsdoelen as DEL COURT-SIX 1903, pp. 83, 84, and the older catalogues
of the Rijksmuseum state.

[11] Of the two drawings, one (RIEGL 1931, pl. 50) was formerly in the Albertina,
Vienna (present location unknown); the other one is in Copenhagen (No. Tu 85.5,
black chalk, pen, and brown ink, 201 × 407 mm.). They both seem to be studies by
De Keyser, the one in Copenhagen preceding the one formerly in Vienna. They may
have been intended as models (*patroonen*) for the sitters before they approved the
commission, such as the one made by Van Ravesteyn in 1618 (MARTIN 1923-24b., pp.
193-198). KRONIG 1909, pp. 109-111, stated that the *Nightwatch* was influenced by
the drawings (both ill. p. 111) and supposed that the differences between drawings and
painting in format and therefore in composition were due to an unexpected change in
space available for the painting (he may have had a very good point; it would imply
that life-size depiction was required). See also MEIJER 1888, p. 229; RIEGL 1931, pp.
172, 173; and BAUCH 1957, p. 15. According to MEIJER 1888, p. 229, the ex-Vienna
drawing is dated: 1630 27 NOVEB; this precise dating suggests that it was a *patroon*.

[12] Rembrandt may have adopted the motif from Leonardo's *Last Supper* (WEISBACH
1926, pp. 345, 350), and may have done so in order to "improve" De Keyser's gesture.

[13] Cornelis Ketel, *Officers and Men of the Company of Captain Dirck Jacobsz Rosecrans and Lieutenant Pauw*, Rijksmuseum, Amsterdam (Cat. no. C378; canvas 208
× 410 cm., dated 1588). As DE JONGH 1963 observed, the painting originally was
larger on either side, the ensign having been in the center of the composition. Probably
at the left at least one, at the right at least three figures were cut off.

was clipped), flanked by captain, lieutenant, and sergeants. The similarities that do exist were introduced by Ketel for the first time: the militiamen are represented standing, life size, and full length; captain and lieutenant are placed near the center; the members of the company in two groups at either side are both dominated by a sergeant; space is also closed in the background by a wall with an archway in the center and protruding sections at the sides. Also a tentative effort is made to place the figures in space and partly behind each other, and the mannered stances of the figures convey elegance and potential movement. Rembrandt probably knew this painting well, even if it was hanging in another *doelen*, that of the Voetboogschutters.[14]

Not only did Rembrandt adopt an existing composition, he also took over details from earlier examples.[15] The movement of a crowd-like group of militiamen, so different from the predominantly static appearances of men in the other paintings in the assembly hall, had also been an essential feature of a militia piece of uncertain date known only from a drawing attributed to Cornelis Ketel (Fig. 84).[16] The

[14] The line Ketel-De Keyser-Rembrandt has been drawn frequently (RIEGL 1902, pp. 194, 196; KRONIG 1909; OLDENBOURG 1911; SCHMIDT-DEGENER 1916a., pp. 80-83; RIEGL 1931; TÜMPEL 1970; and others). Schmidt-Degener probably exaggerated when writing that Rembrandt owed more to the painting by Ketel than to that by De Keyser.

[15] In spite of the similarity between the motifs of men and soldiers in front of an archway turning to one side in the *Nightwatch* and in the print *The Capture of the Duke of Aerschot* by Hogenberg in the war chronicle of Baudartius of 1615 (and in the copy after it by Frisius), it seems more likely that Rembrandt developed his composition from the precedents mentioned, substituting an arch for an archway with doors, from observation of reality, and for the sake of associations with the functions of the militia (see Chapter VI), than that he was *angeregt* by that print (similarity noted by Colin Campbell, as reported by SCHÖNE 1973, pp. 91, 92, with ill., and TÜMPEL 1970, p. 174). Furthermore, whatever similarities exist between the *Nightwatch* and the drawing *Procession of Cosimo I de'Medici* by Johannes Stradanus or the print by Philips Galle after it, these similarities (possibly with the exception of the placement of the drummer) were caused separately by traditions operative in the Netherlands in the context of militia pieces and processions. It is unlikely that this drawing or print served Rembrandt as an example, as was proposed by ANONYMOUS 1935 (acc. to Reznicek written by Schmidt-Degener), REZNICEK 1961, "Stellingen" no. 6, and REZNICEK 1977, pp. 99-103. The similar position of the drummer may be coincidental or may be derived from Stradanus.

[16] Pen and brown ink and wash, heightened with white, 290 × 390 mm. (Rijksprentenkabinet, Amsterdam, inv. no. '05.97). SIX 1906 considered the drawing a study for the lost militia piece of Captain Herman Rodenborg Beths, mentioned by Van Mander as painted by Ketel in 1581. SCHMIDT-DEGENER 1916a., pp. 83, 84, agreed, and discussed the drawing for its features prototypical of the *Nightwatch* (see also MIRANDE-OVERDIEP 1943, p. 459). The drawing is probably connected with another commission and the attribution needs to be reviewed. BOON 1978, no. 329 also doubts the rela-

militiaman trying to protect himself against the shot going off right in front of him (no. 22 in the diagram of Fig. 2) is taken over from the militia company painted ca. 1623 by Jan Tengnagel which has been lost but is known from a drawing (Fig. 86).[17]

The choice of this specific model of the Ketel-De Keyser tradition was appropriate. Whether Banning Cocq or Rembrandt made the decision, Rembrandt's preference for a unified composition with emphasis on one or perhaps a few leading figures is found in all his work and undoubtedly also agreed perfectly with Banning Cocq's (and Van Ruytenburgh's) preference for playing dominant roles.[18]

---

tionship with the painting described by Van Mander, but tentatively accepts the attribution.

[17] For Tengnagel's painting see also Chapter VI, under "Arms and Costumes, The Central Musketeer", and its notes 37, 49, and 53. There is no reason to think that Rembrandt for his drummer may have been influenced by the print by Jacques de Gheyn after Goltzius (BARTSCH, 1791, III, p. 70, no. 3; ill. HOLLSTEIN VII, p. 178) as TÜMPEL 1973, p. 172, suggested.

[18] SCHMIDT-DEGENER 1916a., pp. 66, 67, made this observation.

VI

The Subject: Reality,
Allusion, Symbolism

In this role portrait, Rembrandt portrayed eighteen Amsterdam citizens as members of their militia company, and defined their image by a great variety of means. He portrayed the sitters, yet made them perform specific actions; he added some figures that were members but were not portrayed, and others that were not members at all of Banning Cocq's company; he liberally provided arms, armor, and costumes, and created a meaningful setting. Every detail said something about the sitters and the role they had chosen to play.[1]

To understand the image Rembrandt and the sitters wished to project, it is necessary to establish the painting's degree of reality and that of fantasy, and the similarities and differences between the subject matter depicted here and in other militia pieces of that time and of previous generations. Wherever Rembrandt introduced novel features, their sources must be established. Parallels, whether in reality, in other militia pieces, or in other realms of art, may provide a clue to the meaning of details, and may help to clarify the image of the men and of their role.

PORTRAITS OF OFFICERS AND MEN

Stepping resolutely forward, Captain Banning Cocq is dressed in the formal black of the upper class. His costume is outfitted with elegant

---

[1] The concept of the role portrait is discussed, to my knowledge for the first time, by BAUCH 1967, pp. 140, 141, 150. Correctly, Bauch characterizes *The Anatomical Demonstration of Dr. Tulp* as a "Rollenporträt", but in his effort to contradict Heckscher, he underestimates the allegorical references and other allusions in the painting. The conclusion of VAN DE WAAL 1956a., p. 88, quoting C. S. Roos, that the *Syndics* are just "five gentlemen in black", and nothing more, does not take into consideration the characterization they derive from their role as members of a defined group. See also Introduction and its notes 6 and 7.

tassels under the knees, a finely worked lace collar, and his shirt is decorated with gold brocade. His red sash, probably of silk, is bordered with gold, its lower end swinging energetically.[2] The rapier at his side, the partly gilded steel gorget barely visible under the collar, and his baton indicate his militia role, the latter distinguishing him as captain. As we learned from the caption to the drawing made for his album (Fig. 43), he orders his lieutenant to make his company march. The process of speaking and, by implication, the giving of the order is expressed by the gesture of his left hand and by his slightly parted lips.[3] In his right hand he holds his left glove by one finger. Rembrandt put so much emphasis on this glove, particularly by setting it off against the bright yellow costume of the girl to the left of center, that it must convey a specific idea. Possibly it signifies challenge or victory.[4] Ban-

[2] The significance of colors of sashes within the Amsterdam militia needs to be investigated further. It is unlikely that they are those of the company (MARTIN 1935-36, I, p. 160) because blue sashes are found in militia pieces of many different companies. They therefore may refer to the Krijgsraad, whose colors were blue and gold (see Chapter III and its note 25), but then officers of the militia in Hoorn also wore blue sashes with gold trim (see the color illustrations to VAN DER SLOOT-KIST 1970). HELLINGA 1956, pp. 12, 13, saw, possibly correctly, the color red as emblematic for the city of Amsterdam, and black for "unadorned distinction" ("sobere deftigheid") but connected black also, unconvincingly, with "wisdom".

[3] See Chapter 1 and its note 2. That Banning Cocq is represented as giving an order is accepted on the evidence of this contemporary caption in his album. An unidentified draughtsman (perhaps still of the seventeenth century) copying the head only, closed the mouth, probably because out of context the "speaking" mouth seemed inappropriate (black chalk; Kunsthalle, Bremen, no. 1953/51, as perhaps by Jan Lievens). The "speaking" gesture of the left hand serves Rembrandt also as a means to establish a connection between the viewer and the captain with his entire company (VAN DE WAAL 1956, p. 97).

[4] Although the glove is depicted as belonging to Banning Cocq (it matches his other glove), symbolically it could be the adversary's. It therefore may indicate the captain's acceptance of the challenge to defend the city (adversary's gauntlet picked up; a verbal suggestion made by Stephanie Dickey), the intent to challenge (Banning Cocq's gauntlet ready to be thrown down), or victory achieved (Banning Cocq's or the enemy's gauntlet picked up after victory; the latter interpretation is HELLINGA's 1956, pp. 14, 15; SCHÖNE 1973, p. 91, simply calls the glove a "Fedehandschuh"). A glove held in this manner may convey different concepts in portraits of different sitters. SCHMIDT-DEGENER 1916b., pp. 36, 37, referred to the glove held in a similar way by Don Carlos in his portrait by Velasquez (of ca. 1626/27, Prado, No. 1188); he added: "the captain does not do it sufficiently unobtrusively to be distinguished. Spanish grandezza is endowed with more simplicity and ease". A glove is held in the same way by one of Rubens' two sons in their portrait by their father in the Liechtenstein Collection, Vaduz, by the elegantly dressed boy painted by A. van Gaesbeeck (Rijksmuseum, Amsterdam, no. A113), and in a portrait of 1641 attributed to B. van der Helst (National Gallery, London; MAC LAREN 1960, no. 4691); a glove in the same shape is lying on the floor in Rembrandt's

ning Cocq's civic distinction is emphasized by the black costume, elegant boots, and hat. His role in public life and in the militia are thus fully intertwined. Contemporaries may have interpreted this fusion in different ways, from being simply an expression of the dual function of a distinguished citizen in Amsterdam's life, to conveying the need for military strength and civic independence in defense of the city's welfare against threats from any adversary.[5]

Many of these motifs are traditional formulae. The walking, the gesture, the concealed gorget, the emphasis on stature, and even the act of speaking are also found in De Keyser's painting of 1632 (Fig. 88). The gesture of the hand, also expressing speech but more emphatically than the parted lips, was already used by Ketel in the same context (Fig. 83). Rembrandt himself represented the act of preaching of Cornelis Anslo in the portrait that he painted while working on the *Nightwatch* by means of the same gesture made with an almost identical hand (Fig. 80). New was Rembrandt's emphasis on Banning Cocq's energetically stepping forward and the motion of his body. He achieved this emphasis by counterbalancing the captain's right hand holding the glove and the baton on one side with his left leg and its swinging tassel on the other. He paid equally careful attention to the features of Banning Cocq, and undoubtedly made a good likeness of him (Fig. 10) as we can conclude from a comparison with a second portrait made nine years later by Bartholomeus van der Helst (Fig. 11).[6]

Portrait of a Standing Man in Kassel (Br. 216). Maerten Soolmans of Rembrandt's portrait of 1634, interpreted by SCHMIDT-DEGENER 1914, p. 40, as a "preformulation" of Banning Cocq, also holds one of his gloves by the fingers, but in a different way.

[5] SCHMIDT-DEGENER 1916b., pp. 35-37, was of the opinion that Banning Cocq's stature as regent was stressed more than his role as captain (see also MARTIN 1947, p. 38, and others).

[6] The assumption of SCHMIDT-DEGENER 1916a., p. 67, that Banning Cocq's likeness was unsatisfactory, and was felt by himself as such, is unfounded. For Van der Helst's *The Governors of the Handboogsdoelen* and its copy by Lundens (Fig. 44), see Chapter II and its note 12. Banning Cocq is not so dashing as nine years before and a little fuller in the face, and he has trimmed his moustache and goatee more closely, but the similarity is obvious, particularly in the eyes, one being slightly larger than the other. No other portrait of Banning Cocq is known. The suggestion by SCHMIDT-DEGENER 1914b., p. 40, and SCHMIDT-DEGENER O.-H. 1914 that the standing man of Rembrandt's portrait of 1639 in Kassel (Br. 216) represents Banning Cocq has not been accepted. Hofstede de Groot and MÜLLER HOSTEDE 1970, p. 240, interpreted the painting as a self-portrait of Rembrandt, also without convincing. Although the sitter looks older than twenty-eight years, he may well be Andries de Graeff as DUDOK VAN HEEL 1969 suggested. The portrait drawing (*ubi?*) reproduced by WIJNBEEK 1944, p. 144 and MEIJER 1968, p. 4, is based on the *Nightwatch*.

Van Ruytenburgh shares the place of honor with Banning Cocq. Since no other portrait of him exists, we can only surmise that his likeness is as good as that of his captain. But here the similarity between lieutenant and captain stops. Portrayed in profile rather than frontally, listening instead of speaking, and marching slightly behind his captain in spite of being at his side, he is no match for his superior, not even in height, as in daily life he neither attained the latter's social position nor equalled his personal achievements.[7] But by virtue of his bright yellow costume with bluish-white silken sash he contrasts brilliantly with his superior and outshines him. The riding boots, the steel gorget that is fully visible, the partisan, represented in stunning foreshortening that dazzled contemporaries,[8] and the brightness of the costume evoke the activities of the militia, particularly its festive parading, more readily than Banning Cocq's distinguished black apparel.

The lieutenant's stance and motion, and the position of his partisan with the blade pointing downward and forward had been established by tradition in painting, and undoubtedly were based on actual customs and rules. Rembrandt's detailed rendering of the costume and of the partisan seems by and large accurate. The yellow costume, complete with yellow leather hose, riding boots outfitted with spurs, and a yellow leather jerkin, is of a French style particularly favored by the nobility in the circle of Prince Frederick Henry in The Hague.[9] Since Van Ruytenburgh had strong ties with The Hague, the costume may very well reflect his own sartorial preferences.[10] The partisan is an elegant, beautifully wrought one, its blade ornamented and partly gilded, its short pole decorated with what look like brass nails and a cross pattern, the transition of blade and pole embellished with a tassel. Rembrandt probably depicted an existing partisan of the same type as one made in Amsterdam in 1626 for Gustavus Adolphus II, King of Sweden, preserved in Stockholm (Fig. 60).[11] The tassel and the fringe of the lining of the gorget, as well as the string of beads on his hat, and the borders of his gloves and stockings, alternate blue and gold, and therefore display the colors of the Kloveniersdoelen and the

[7] See Chapter II.

[8] BALDINUCCI 1686, p. 78; HDG 1906, no. 360; SLIVE 1953, pp. 104-115.

[9] According to SCHMIDT-DEGENER 1916b., p. 36.

[10] Van Ruytenburgh lived in The Hague and Vlaardingen from about 1647 until his death in 1652 (see Chapter II and its note 16), and seems to have had a home in The Hague in the 1630s (DUDOK VAN HEEL 1981).

[11] Kungl. Livrustkammaren, Stockholm (inv. no. 3767ᵃ). I am grateful to R.B.F. van der Sloot for having drawn my attention to this partisan.

Amsterdam Krijgsraad.[12] The coat of arms of Amsterdam held by a rampant lion embroidered in the border of Van Ruytenburgh's jerkin refers even more pointedly to Amsterdam and its militia. This coat of arms with its three crosses of St. Andrew received particular emphasis by its *impasto* execution and by the shadow of Banning Cocq's hand that seems to hold or to present it.[13] Rembrandt wished to make clear that captain and lieutenant and their company were in action for the sake of Amsterdam.

A poem by Jan Vos, although made about another portrait of Banning Cocq, conveys the image that the captain presented to those who saw him in the *Nightwatch*: "This is Van Purmerlandt, one of the main pillars on which the Town Hall rests; his unflinching courage does not succumb to savage force on the borders of the river Y, . . . his loyalty provides a shield for the capital of the watercities. There are no stronger city walls than the loyalty of governing authorities".[14]

[12] For blue and gold as colors of the Kloveniersdoelen and Krijgsraad, see Chapter III and its note 25. These heraldic colors have not been evaluated previously for the interpretation of the *Nightwatch* and other militia pieces. Although a number of paintings painted for the Kloveniersdoelen include blue and gold tassels (*The Company of Captain Albert Joncheyn* by an unidentified painter, Hist. Museum, Cat. no. C387, see note 30 of this chapter; *of Captain Jan De Bisschop* by Aert Pietersz, no. C391, BLANKERT 1975-79, no. 335; *of Captain Albert Bas* by Flinck, no. C371; *of Captain Roelof Bicker* by Van der Helst, no. C375), such tassels are also found in paintings made for other guilds or *doelens* (*The Company of Captain Abraham Boom* by C. P. Lastman and A. [?] van Nieulandt painted for the Voetboogsdoelen, no. C406, BLANKERT 1975-79, no. 221; *of Lieutenant Pieter Hasselaer* by Van der Voort for the Handboogsdoelen, no. C408, BLANKERT 1975-79, no. 491). Blue and gold in tassels therefore may have referred to the Amsterdam militia in its entirety, and probably in standards as well, though only one of the other militia pieces in the assembly hall, *The Company of Captain Van Vlooswijck* by Nicolaes Eliasz (Fig. 40) displays a blue and gold banner (of a different design). The reasons for the supposition of HELLINGA 1956, p. 13, that the colors blue and yellow stand for "the use of the pleasure of the world" are not clear.

[13] VAN DIJK 1758 (ed. 1760, pp. 60, 61) was the first to describe this coat of arms; since then it has been mentioned frequently.

[14] Jan Vos made the poem on the portrait of Banning Cocq by Van der Helst, therefore probably on his likeness in the *Governors of the Handboogsdoelen* of 1653 (Fig. 11). The poem (apparently published by J. van Duisburg in 1658, which I have not verified) was already quoted in connection with the *Nightwatch* by VAN DIJK 1758 (ed. 1760, p. 60); also quoted by DE GELDER 1921, p. 154. According to Van Dijk the poem runs as follows:

Dit is van Purmerlandt, een van de Hooft-Pilaren,
Daar 't Raadthuis vast op staat, zyn ongekreukte moedt
Laat zich niet aan het Y, door woest gewelt, vervaaren.
Een die de Vryheid mind ontziet geen Hartebloedt.

Ruytenburgh largely shares Banning Cocq's role, and the poem there-fore can be applied to both.

Of the two other officers, only Rombout Kemp at the right (no. 5, Fig. 17) is known from another portrait. He is one of the six regents of the Nieuwe Zijds Huiszittenhuis painted in or about 1651 by Jacob Backer (Fig. 18).[15] There Kemp is seated in front of a table, fully visible and in a place of honor. Although he is now about eight years older, his features are clearly recognizable and testify to the abilities of both artists. The comparison also indicates that in Rembrandt's portrait the sitter seems to have more life, that his muscles and skin have more tension and his eyes more sparkle. The liveliness cannot be credited only to his greater youth or his speaking role.

Kemp wears an elegant, contemporary black costume, a mill-stone collar, and a broad brimmed hat similar to the one worn by Banning Cocq. The costume accords well with his stature in Amsterdam, and we may assume that he is depicted the way he was known to his contemporaries. His halberd, which he carries over his shoulder with the blade pointing forward, is also of a contemporary type (Fig. 66).[16] Before painting the hat, Rembrandt had made him don a helmet with impressive plumes. The latter are still present in the painting, although not attached to any helmet. A recent find indicates that Kemp indeed owned a helmet with feathers.[17]

It is most uncommon for seventeenth-century militia pieces to por-

---

Zyn trouw verstrekt een Schildt voor 't Hooft der Watersteeden.
Geen sterker Wallen, dan de Trouw der Overheden.

Is the word "Hooft" in "Hooft-Pilaren" meant as a pun on Banning Cocq's relationship with the Hooft family?

[15] Rijksmuseum, Amsterdam (Cat. no. C442); HAAK 1972, p. 51; BLANKERT 1975-79, no. 19. See also illustration in VAN SCHENDEL-MERTENS 1947, Fig. 26. The uni-dentified portrait by Nicolaes Eliasz in the Museum in Kiev (Cat. 1961, no. 138; according to J. Kuznetsov *in litteris* a copy, the original being in Sebastopol) may be another likeness of Rombout Kemp, as S. J. Gudlaugsson suggested (ms. note in Rijks-bureau voor Kunsthistorische Documentatie, The Hague). For Kemp's life, see Chapter II.

[16] Kon. Nederlands Leger- en Wapenmuseum "Generaal Hoefer", Leiden (inv. no. L. 170). I am grateful to R.B.F. van der Sloot for referring me to this halberd.

[17] The helmet is visible in an X-ray radiograph (see Chapter I). Dudok van Heel writes me (letter May 9, 1980) that Kemp's militia accoutrements were preserved with care after his death. In his estate they are listed as "A richly appareled box, in which two white plumes, a black bunch of feathers, a blue silken veil with golden trim" ("een rycke doos daerinne / Twee witte pluymen / Een swarte vederbos / Een syde blauwe sluyer met goude kant"). He may have worn the last item as lieutenant since it recalls the sash Van Ruytenburgh sports.

tray the two sergeants in different costumes and carrying different arms. In contrast to Kemp, Reijer Engelen (no. 4, Fig. 16) wears a cuirass and a gauntlet, and his head is covered with a fancy helmet reminiscent of the Italian Renaissance. His halberd likewise is at least a century old.[18] Whether Engelen himself owned these antiques or whether they were Rembrandt's contribution we do not know, but certainly the two sergeants are meant to convey a contrast between past and present. We shall come back to this difference below when discussing arms and armor and costume. Here, however, we may speculate that the contrast between the dignified clothing of Kemp and the antique dress of Engelen also reflects their personalities. The former was successful, civic-minded, responsible; the latter had a scattered career, misrepresented his age, even came in touch with the law.[19]

The ensign, Jan Cornelisz Visscher, dominates the scene at the upper left. His standard, representing the colors under which the company gathered, cannot have been left to the discretion of the artist, and is represented as it must have looked. It consists of five fields, the central one bearing the coat of arms of Amsterdam; three of the fields are dark blue, and two are yellowish, therefore displaying the heraldic colors of the Kloveniersdoelen and of Amsterdam's War Council.[20] These colors are also found in Visscher's jacket and his sash. These must have been owned by Visscher, and most likely are represented true to their appearance, since, according to another recent find, they appear later in the inventory of his mother who survived him.[21]

Only one of the men of the company is represented in full. The man loading his musket to the left of center (no. 10) must have been a prominent citizen, and a prominent member of the company, and probably paid for the distinction of being portrayed in full.[22] His action

[18] A similar halberd, an Italian work of about 1510, is in the Kretzschmar von Kienbusch Collection, New York (Cat. 1963, no. 496).

[19] For Reijer Engelen's life, see Chapter II. SCHMIDT-DEGENER 1916b., pp. 38, 39, compares the two sergeants in a similar way in spite of not knowing the identity of the sergeant at the left. There is no reason to think with him that the face is that of a sick man.

[20] The blue of the banner in the copy by Lundens is in some areas a more distinct dark blue than in the *Nightwatch* itself. For the colors blue and gold, see above, note 12, and Chapter III and its note 25.

[21] Found by Dudok van Heel (letter, May 9, 1980, and discussion, June 1980). In the painting his costume seems to display various shades of the same colors, as was customary at the time (noted by SCHMIDT-DEGENER 1916b., p. 38; see also MARTIN 1947, p. 43). For Visscher, see Chapter II.

[22] MARTIN 1947, p. 40, remarked on his prominence; for further discussion, see below under "Arms and Armor, the Central Musketeer".

and his costume are of primary significance for the meaning of the entire painting and will be discussed below in the context of other similar elements.

We may assume that the other portraits in the painting, in spite of being limited to head or head and shoulders, are not less trustworthy and lifelike than those of Banning Cocq and Kemp, where the verisimilitude can be checked. This is true in particular of Reijer Engelen (no. 4, Fig. 16), the man at the very right above the drummer (no. 29, Fig. 23), the man deflecting a shot (no. 22, Fig. 21), and the standing man just to the left of the outstretched hand of Sergeant Rombout Kemp (no. 25). If he is identical with the sitter in a painting by Gerrit Bleeker, Rembrandt endowed him with more vigor and alertness.[23] The facial features of three other men in the background under the archway (nos. 18, 20, 23) are not equally detailed, but they also convey liveliness and alertness. All sitters were portrayed in action rather than in motionless pose as is usually the case in the militia pieces of Rembrandt's contemporaries. Rembrandt made action a vital means of portraiture in this painting, and in some figures even subordinated features to action.[24] Since action is a fundamental element of the entire painting, it will be discussed in greater detail below.

The role portrait was not a new genre for Rembrandt. In 1632 he had portrayed eight Amsterdam citizens as if they were participating in an anatomical demonstration. Much closer to the *Nightwatch*, however, because also dressed in old-fashioned costume and surrounded by objects that identify his profession and indicate its historic roots, is the portrait of *Joànnes Uyttenbogaert* that Rembrandt etched in 1639.[25] In this print, commonly called *The Goldweigher* (Fig. 81), Rembrandt had represented the receiver-general of the States General in action, with historical references and allegorizing allusions to sixteenth-century representations of tax collectors and the Calling of St. Matthew by Massys and Marinus van Reymerswaele. The print, as a role portrait, anticipates the *Nightwatch*, which, however, is far more complex.

[23] See Chapter II and its note 22.

[24] Portraits are fused with action (TÜMPEL, 1970, p. 174; "Rembrandt vereinigt Porträt und deutende Handlung in einer Szene"; similarly 1977, p. 81).

[25] SLATKES 1973, p. 256, pointed to similarities between the etching as a history subject and the *Nightwatch*. Rembrandt may have made the etching (BARTSCH, 1791, 281, 250 × 204 mm.) for Uyttenbogaert in recognition of the latter's help in securing the fee that the Prince of Orange owed him for his paintings. For a comparison of Rembrandt's and Jan Lievens' portraits of Uyttenbogaert, see CAMPBELL 1978, pp. 18, 19.

POWDERBOY, DRUMMER, AND EXTRAS

Rembrandt defined the role of the militiamen partly by expanding the group of eighteen portrayed sitters with as many as sixteen figures. Among these, some are placed so prominently that they seem to compete with the sitters, while others are clearly subordinated to them. The former, among them the girl with the fowl and the partly hidden musketeer, are heavily charged with symbolism and allusions; the latter have the simple function of identifying these portrayed militiamen as members of a company that comprises many more than eighteen citizens.

The ten supernumeraries (supers or extras), all men, are almost entirely hidden by figures standing in front of them, their faces being only partly visible.[26] Although one (no. 27) is in the middle distance, the others are in the very background.[27] Two carry a musket (nos. 6, 27), two others are helmeted (nos. 19, 21). A fifth one is probably a fragmentary self-portrait (no. 17, Fig. 15).[28] The other painters who received commissions for the assembly hall portrayed themselves in their militia pieces, and we may therefore assume that the head covered with a beret, of which no more than one eye, part of the nose and part of the forehead are visible, is indeed Rembrandt's humorous equivalent. The other figures, like true extras, are not characterized

[26] All figures in the *Nightwatch* other than portraits have been called *figuranten* in Dutch, *Figuranten* or *Statisten* in German. These terms and the English equivalent (extras, supernumeraries, supers) should be applied only to the eleven secondary background figures (nos. 6, 15, 16, 17, 19, 21, 26, 27, 28, 31, and [34]) since the other additions (nos. 11, 12, 13, 14, 30) play a more significant role than would be appropriate for extras (two of them, nos. 13, 14, are personifications). WEISBACH 1926, pp. 345, 356, differentiated between *Figuranten* and *Statisten*, but underestimated the roles of the extras in the background (*Statisten*) as well as the drummers and powderboy in the foreground (*Figuranten*). NEUMANN 1902, p. 274, already stated that with the extras (*Statisten*) Rembrandt wished to create the illusion of a moving crowd. TÜMPEL 1970, p. 168, included our nos. 11-14 and 30 among the *Statisten* but called them also *Figuranten* (p. 169).

[27] Usually the man in the middle distance is considered one of the paying sitters, which is unlikely (see Chapter I, note 12). TÜMPEL 1970, p. 168, also observed that the added figures were distinguished from portraits by the partial visibility of their faces.

[28] Although this hypothesis made by MARTIN 1923-24a. has been received with skepticism (MARTIN 1947, p. 34), it seems to be confirmed by the head cover (perhaps a beret), the shape of the eye, and by the increasing evidence that each militia piece in the assembly hall of the Kloveniersdoelen included a self-portrait of its painter (see DE BRUYN KOPS 1965). The man whose face is partly hidden behind Kemp's arm (no. 27) cannot be Rembrandt's self-portrait, as tentatively suggested by HIJMANS-KUIPER-VELS HEIJN 1976, p. 61, because there is no likeness and because that man is a musketeer.

at all. The pikes in the right distance suggest the presence of more men there hidden behind those in the foreground.[29]

The *Nightwatch* is not the only militia piece including such extras as a synechdoche for the large section of the company that was not portrayed. As early as about 1603-06, an unidentified artist added some figures visible only by their hats and the pikes they carry behind the portrayed members of *The Company of Captain Albert Joncheyn (?)* (Fig. 85).[30] Similarly, Jacob Backer in his painting for the Kloveniersdoelen included, rather shyly, two pikemen in the background turning the backs of their heads toward the viewer. Van der Helst also placed some partly visible faces in the background of his work for the assembly hall.[31] Rembrandt, however, included more of them, and by placing some of them behind others and a little lower, he suggested that still more are present there.[32] More significantly, he fully integrated them with the portrayed figures.

Rembrandt added the boy with a powder horn at the left, seemingly running out of the painting, and the drummer entering the pictorial space from the right for other reasons than to convey numerical size. They intensify the impression of an actual event and of the activity and movement of the entire group, and emphasize specific characteristics and activities of the company of Banning Cocq. The boy (Fig. 29) is a powder monkey assisting the musketeers by running back and forth to supply them with powder, and by his haste and the purpose of his mission he emphasizes that shooting is their business and adds briskness to their action. Furthermore, with his battered helmet, which is much too big for him, complete with ear flaps and scarf, and a thin smile on his face, he adds a humorous note to the seriousness of these earnest citizens. A similar running boy providing the same service to militiamen, although depicted with less sophistication in spite of greater detail, is found in Sybrant van Beest's representation of militiamen in action to pay homage to Queen Henrietta Maria departing from Sche-

[29] Not all pikes stand against the wall as Martin and others seem to have thought.

[30] Historisch Museum, Amsterdam (BLANKERT 1975-79, no. 600A; RIEGL 1931, pl. 42). The painting may have been made for the Kloveniers, probably in 1603 or 1606. TÜMPEL 1970, pp. 168, 172, overlooked this precedent of extras.

[31] MARTIN 1947, p. 35, treats the steward, the provost, and the artist himself in Van der Helst's painting as *Figuranten*, whereas in fact they should be considered "added portraits".

[32] Whether a limited, local elevation (perhaps a typical Amsterdam bridge) or a horizontal level changing into steps is meant is not clear. VAN REGTEREN ALTENA 1955 explained the differences in height by assuming that Rembrandt represented some people as seated on horseback.

veningen to England. In that painting of 1643, the youthful powder carrier is accompanied by a second boy bringing a gin flask, who therefore caters to other needs of the men (Fig. 70).[33] Furthermore, in Amsterdam, boys with powder kegs, powder charges, and powder horns assisted militiamen at the occasion of the entry of Maria de'Medici in 1638, as we know from prints in Van Baerle's book commemorating the event (Fig. 69).[34] Although such caddies may have been a common sight when the militia fulfilled its public duties, not one other painter had used the motif to enliven a collective portrait of citizens as militiamen and to introduce an allusion to their actually serving in this capacity in the streets of the city.[35] The small child on the strip that was cut off (no. 34) fulfilled the same function (Fig. 26).

The drummer (Fig. 30) also adds activity and movement, and by association, a reference to festive parading or the call to assemble and start to march.[36] Occasionally, drummers, like stewards of the *doelens* (with the function of innkeepers) were portrayed along with the militiamen, but with little or no indication of their profession.[37] Never had one been included with similar emphasis, performing his skill in the very foreground. For centuries, drummers had accompanied sol-

[33] Gemeentemuseum, The Hague (no. 4-1862; Cat. 1935, no. 39). Signed and dated *S. Beest fc. An° 1643.*

[34] BARLAEUS 1638, after p. 12 and after p. 22. SCHMIDT-DEGENER 1916b., pp. 41-43, and SIX 1919 already interpreted the powder boy in the *Nightwatch* in this sense with reference to Van Baerle's prints and Van Beest's painting. MARTIN 1947, p. 29, and 1951, pp. 5, 8, also mentioned both.

[35] Already MEIJER 1886, p. 200, stated that the powder boy was introduced out of "obedience to a sense of nature and truth". A similar function is performed by the running errand boy in a wall decoration with portraits of ca. 1630 attributed to Bartholomeus van Bassen (Rijksmuseum; STARING 1965, fig. 2). TÜMPEL 1970, p. 170, characterized the powder boy in the *Nightwatch* as "indirekte Verkörperung der Cloveniere" (but there is no reason to believe with him, p. 173, that Rembrandt was "stimulated" for this motif by the prints in BARLAEUS 1638). The boy in the portrait of five militiamen of Rotterdam by Ludolf de Jongh (destroyed but known from the watercolor by D. Moens of 1807, Archives, Rotterdam) was not necessarily a powder boy as SCHMIDT-DEGENER 1916b., p. 49, supposed.

[36] For his identity, see Chapter II and its note 25.

[37] Tengnagel's lost painting (below and notes 49 and 53) included the portraits of two drummers, identified as such in the key but portrayed without instruments (DEL COURT-SIX 1903, p. 69); *The Company of Captain Jan Jz Karel* by Gerrit Pietersz, called Sweelinck of 1604 (Rijksmuseum no. C592) includes one, and so does *The Company of Captain Gijsbert van de Poll* by Johann Spilberg of perhaps 1653 (Rijksmuseum, no. C395) where he is accompanied by a piper. For the two paintings see R. Ruurs in BLANKERT 1975-79, nos. 431 and 410 respectively, and for the latter also below note 123.

diers and militiamen on many different occasions, and they had preceded rhetoricians when their groups met for competitive performances. Although in Amsterdam at the time of the *Nightwatch*, such
events belonged to the past, the drummer in the painting probably
was associated by Rembrandt and the viewers with both his lapsed
and his contemporary functions. His costume has sixteenth-century
features, and therefore seems to refer both to the past and to an
abstraction. He seems to belong partly to the same world as the girl
with the fowl and the shooting boy in the center of the painting.[38]

ARMS AND COSTUMES; THE CENTRAL MUSKETEER

In the *Nightwatch*, arms and costumes served Rembrandt in his por-
trayal of individual figures. In this respect they have been discussed
above. They also are a vital part of the painting as a whole, because
they help to define the image of the Kloveniers and of Amsterdam's
militia. Some figures, like the central musketeer, oddly hidden behind
the captain, are part of that definition and will therefore be discussed
here as well.

Rembrandt's sitters are more heavily armed and better protected
than those portrayed in the other militia pieces in the hall. Furthermore, the armament is highly unusual. It was customary to portray
lieutenants with beautiful ceremonial partisans, for sergeants to be
equipped with halberds as signs of their rank, and for a number of
militiamen in each painting to be holding muskets.[39] The profusion
of helmets, however, their elaborate designs, and the prominently
demonstrated active manipulation of muskets in the *Nightwatch* was
most uncommon.

The most prominent weapon in the *Nightwatch* is the musket. Four
of the portrayed men are represented as musketeers (nos. 9, 10, 24,
[32]). A fifth person in the very center of the painting (no. 14), partly
silhouetted against the girl in yellow, is shooting a musket. The smoke
of his musket and of others that have been fired is wafting between
and around the figures. It is clearly visible to the left of his own
helmeted head, behind the head of Van Ruytenburgh, and behind the
head of the girl in yellow.[40] The motif is not unique in militia pieces,

---

[38] See below for a discussion of the girl in gold.

[39] See VAN DER SLOOT-KIST 1970, with illuminating examples of the partisans.

[40] Only the recent restoration and cleaning of 1975-76 revealed the presence of smoke;
formerly, these passages were thought to be due to discoloration of paint or opaqueness
of varnish. There are other patches of smoke: to the left of the head of Banning Cocq
(no. 1), behind the head of Van Ruytenburgh (no. 2), and on either side of the head

but there is a world of difference between the last puffs of smoke hesitantly emerging from a gun just fired in Eliasz' painting in the *groote sael* (Fig. 40) and the smoke enveloping figures in the *Nightwatch*.

Four of the five musketeers are shown in action. One, directly to the left of the standard in the background (no. 9), holds a burning slow match; his action is not further defined.[41] Three in the foreground, however, are prominently placed and carry out three specific steps in the handling of the musket. The musketeer in red (no. 10, Fig. 7) is charging his musket by transferring powder into its muzzle from one of the wooden cartridges attached to his bandolier. The figure behind Banning Cocq (no. 14) is shooting his gun to the right.[42] The third one (no. 24, Fig. 22) is clearing the pan by blowing off the powder that remained there after his last shot. These actions do not imply that the musketeers were really shooting their firearms while they were starting to march. On the contrary, the statutes regulating the actions of the Amsterdam militia allowed shooting only under special circumstances, and the beginning of a march was not among them.[43] Rather than representing an actual event, Rembrandt selected three basic steps of the many required to handle the musket.[44]

The same three steps are illustrated in manuals of arms, particularly Jacques de Gheyn's *Exercise of Armes*, first published in Amsterdam in 1607 and reprinted frequently until 1640 with texts in different languages.[45] Three corresponding prints (Fig. 62) show the accuracy

---

[41] of the man with the furket (no. 9). Rembrandt represented smoke surrounding a head in a similar way in his drawing *The Smoker* of 1643 (Private Collection, Holland; BENESCH 1954-57, IV, no. 686). The 1975-76 cleaning has failed to confirm Schmidt-Degener's supposition that more muskets are lying on a rack in the background at the right.

[41] His furket (SCHMIDT-DEGENER 1916b., p. 40; MARTIN 1947, pp. 40, 43) has been mistaken for a burning glass (BAUCH 1957, p. 23; SCHÖNE 1972, p. 90, and TÜMPEL 1970, p. 163).

[42] The lower part of his furket is visible to the right and above the right foot of the girl in yellow; his helmet is inappropriate for a musketeer, but nos. 9 and 24 wear them also.

[43] See the articles 12-15 of the "Nieuwe Ordonnantie op de Wachten" of 1651 (NOORDKERK 1748, p. 151); SCHMIDT-DEGENER 1916a., p. 61, had noted the restriction. Shooting was permitted on the occasion of triumphal entries, but presumably only once the companies were on location, and on other specific occasions (see Chapter III).

[44] Already NEUMANN 1902, p. 254 (1924, pp. 277, 278), characterized actions in militia pieces and, by implication, shooting as *attributiv*.

[45] That three successive stages were represented was first noted by MARTIN 1947, p. 28, 1949, p. 227, and 1951, p. 6 (with reference to De Gheyn's *Exercise*); mentioned by HELLINGA 1956, p. 10, as the three "most important 'tempi' of the handling of the

of Rembrandt's representation, particularly of the musketeer charging his gun and the one blowing the pan. The former, indeed, holds his musket off the ground as De Gheyn specifically instructs him to do,[46] and his musket and bandolier with charges are accurately rendered (as is demonstrated by preserved examples, Figs. 61, 64). The latter has taken care to remove the end of the slow match from the cock of his musket before blowing off the powder so that he now holds both ends of the slow match between his fingers.[47]

Triple and quadruple illustrations of various aspects of one object as a means of rendering its essence, and the simultaneous illustration of successive steps of instruction were well-known artistic devices.[48] Different stages of handling the musket also had been represented simultaneously before for the same purpose. In the lost militia piece by Jan Tengnagel of ca. 1623 (Fig. 86), five of the musketeers represent, from left to right, successive postures of the musket.[49] The painting

---

musket"; again by GERSON 1966 and 1973, p. 16; SCHÖNE 1972, pp. 88-90; and with more detail by TÜMPEL 1970, p. 170, and succinctly 1977, p. 84. De Gheyn's *Exercise of Armes* has been reprinted with an excellent commentary on its historic context and on the arms represented in KIST 1971. The attribution of the prints to Robert de Baudous (p. 21) rather than to Jacques de Gheyn is convincing. Kist refers also to the supplement to De Gheyn's manual by A. van Breen (1618).

[46] The instruction to plate 24 of De Gheyn's instructions to the *muskettier* reads: "how he shall charge the Musket out of the charges, letting the Musket rest yet trayle, but no waye suffering the Musket to come to the ground, if he be not to wearie".

[47] Instruction to plate 20: "how he shall blow pouder of the pann lidde if any were remained there on, for more assurance". The similarity between the three musketeers and De Gheyn's prints does not imply that Rembrandt used the prints as examples. He must have relied mainly on his own observations. Already Martin (see note 45 above) pointed out differences between Rembrandt's and De Gheyn's corresponding figures. TÜMPEL 1970, p. 170, overemphasized Rembrandt's dependence on De Gheyn.

[48] For instance, the three views of a book in Dürer's portrait of Erasmus (BARTSCH, 1791, no. 107; see FRAENKEL 1963), and the triple view of a ship in a *Marine* attributed to Pieter Savery (in 1970 with P. de Boer, Amsterdam; Cat. March-June 1970, without no.). A painting formerly attributed to Rubens (Berlin no. 797, destroyed) and related works illustrate two and three different postures of the riding school. The custom of drawing a head, skull, animal, etc. from two, three, or more different views for instructional purposes was widespread in model books for draughtsmen (e.g. VAN DE PASSE 1643, pt. 1, pp. 35, 37, pt. 2, pp. 17, 19, 21, etc.).

[49] Drawing by Colin (Jacob Colijns?) in ms. Egerton 983, f°. 33, British Museum, London (171 × 359 mm.; for the volume of drawn copies of militia pieces, see Chapter II and its note 8). Tengnagel included himself in the painting with a partisan in spite of not being a lieutenant (second man from the right). For the lost painting and the drawing after it, see DEL COURT-SIX 1903; SCHNEIDER 1921; and Swoboda in RIEGL 1931, p. 152. BAUCH 1957, p. 16, and TÜMPEL 1970, p. 171, recognized Tengnagel's role, the first in general, the latter stressing the representation of successive stages of

was of an unusual type, being a group portrait of musketeers without captain and lieutenant and therefore lacking the allusion to the entire company and the element of hierarchy found in militia pieces in Amsterdam. Other artists represented different successive stages of the handling of the musket in one painting. Nicolaes Eliasz (Fig. 40) placed a musketeer filling his musket at the left, a second one who has just fired his gun at the right, and Jacob Backer lets a man fill his musket before some guns that go off in the far distance (Fig. 41). Van der Helst gave a militiaman ready to shoot a prominent place (Fig. 42), and refers, also in the distance, to shooting itself. Only Tengnagel and Rembrandt, however, represented three successive stages with the clearly discernable intention to symbolize all the properties of the subject. Tengnagel represented the stages in an additive, posed and emblematic fashion in the limited context of a group of musketeers, whereas Rembrandt depicted them as taking part in the action of a company in motion.

Rembrandt characterized musketry not merely by simply letting three men perform three successive stages of its handling. He expressed the shared symbolic functions of the musketeer charging his musket at the left and the one blowing the pan at the right by putting them in similar costumes which, mainly because of the slits in the trousers and sleeves (clearly visible in the figure at left), belong to the sixteenth century.[50] Furthermore, he allowed the central musketeer to play a special role.

This musketeer in the very center shoots his musket, thereby demonstrating the principal function of the weapon. He is not a member of the company; he is probably still a youth; his face is not visible; the direction of his step and of his firing is contrary to that of the other men. Yet, he shares one characteristic with the two other musketeers: his costume is not contemporary, but dates either from the first half or the middle of the sixteenth century, and therefore removes him from reality into the historical or allegorical realm. The oak leaves on his helmet refer to victory and thus convey the supremacy of his firearm.[51] There can be no doubt about this musketeer: unlike the

---

the handling of the musket in Tengnagel's lost painting as an antecedent to the *Nightwatch*.

[50] SCHMIDT-DEGENER 1916b., p. 42, and MARTIN 1947, p. 30 ("early sixteenth-century costume"). A small shield attached to the left arm of the musketeer blowing the pan possibly carrying the emblem of the Kloveniers or of the Krijgsraad may add to his symbolic charge (already observed by SCHMIDT-DEGENER 1916b., p. 49).

[51] SCHMIDT-DEGENER referred to the traditional symbolism of the oak leaves and the

other two, who were portrayed militiamen endowed with a symbolic function, he is purely allegorical. He personifies musketry.[52] His symbolic role explains the direction of his step and firing, which is not in touch with the reality of the company and negates its action.

His seemingly erratic action may have further symbolic significance. It may suggest the disruptive, deadly forces inherent to the weapon, forces that were tamed and civilized by the art of musketry. The Kloveniers served this art, and by their traditional adherence to rules and regulations they kept these forces under control. The youth of the musketeer therefore may be interpreted as stressing the lack of sophistication of his unbridled action and, in contrast, the gesture of the dignified musketeer making an effort to redirect the line of fire as emphasizing the reasoned and artful manipulation of the weapon by the Kloveniers.[53] The author of the poem of 1659 on the order of St. Michael (Fig. 56), which had its seat in the Kloveniersdoelen, expresses this very concept when he recalls that the art of weaponry had a tradition going back as far as classical antiquity, and that thanks to this art and its traditions "no Klovenier will shoot in the wild".[54]

Rembrandt stressed the role of the musket for two reasons. First, when the guild of the Kloveniers was founded in 1522, it was given this firearm as its privileged weapon. Its seventeenth-century successor institution continued that association in distinction to the two other *doelens*, which in name identified with the crossbow and the longbow.

---

presence of the latter in the chain of the "king" of the Kloveniers. Traditionally, "kings" were crowned with wreaths (JACOBS 1887). The frieze of a gate of the Handboogsdoelen in Amsterdam was decorated with a wreath placed between bows and arrows (destroyed; drawing by H. P. Schouten, Atlas Splitgerber no. 660, Archief, Amsterdam). Schmidt-Degener dated the costume to ca. 1570. For descriptions, see MARTIN 1947, pp. 19, 38, 39, and VAN SCHENDEL-MERTENS 1947, p. 41; for a different iconological interpretation, see HELLINGA 1956, p. 13.

[52] NEUMANN, while recognizing the symbolic nature of the shooting (1902, p. 254; see above note 44), stressed (1902, p. 312; 1924, p. 340) that Rembrandt did not want to represent an episode, but that action and attitude of the youth were merely an answer to the artist's wish for certain silhouetting forms in the area; SCHMIDT-DEGENER 1916b., p. 46, called the figure a *Figurant*; WEISBACH 1926, p. 345, saw clearly that the action of this musketeer and the one shooting in Van der Helst's painting of 1643 is "sinnlos und auch nicht rationalistisch erklärbar. Es ist eine den Schützenberuf symbolisierende Handlung". Probably by oversight or for the sake of brevity, TÜMPEL 1977, pp. 84, 134, n. 79, treats him as one of the militiamen. For the meaning of the Landsknechten-tracht, see GUDLAUGSSON 1938, p. 14.

[53] Tengnagel had represented the same motif in his painting of ca. 1623 (see notes 37 and 49 above), as noted by TÜMPEL 1970, p. 171.

[54] I owe the suggestion for this interpretation of the uncivilized action of the young man to Richard S. Sylvester. For the poem perhaps by Vondel, see above, Chapter IV and its note 13.

Secondly, since the end of the sixteenth century, the musket was the most effective weapon and in current use by all militiamen, whatever the special weapon of their *doelen*. Muskets are also found in militia pieces painted for the Voetboogsdoelen and the Handboogsdoelen. Gradually the musket became a symbol of armed defense and the militia as such. When the government of Amsterdam decided to present a souvenir to those militiamen who had stood guard in the new Town Hall on the day of its opening, July 29, 1655, it gave each one a silver spoon with a handle in the shape of a musket (Fig. 63).[55]

The pikes in the distance at the right and the men handling them (nos. 20, 23, 25, 29) indicate the role of the pike in Amsterdam's militia. In spite of the correctness of the representation of certain positions, in this case no effort has been made to illustrate actual successive stages in the handling of that weapon.[56] The pikes also fulfill a significant function in the composition and spatial arrangement of the painting. Large groups of pikes and lances had served this purpose ever since the Roman mosaic of *The Battle of Alexander and Darius*, and had been used so effectively by Velasquez in his *Surrender of Breda* that in Spain the painting became known as *Las Lanzas*.

Helmets abound in the *Nightwatch*. No fewer than nine men wear helmets,[57] whereas not one of the numerous other men portrayed in the five other militia pieces in the same assembly hall is wearing one. Not only the quantity is without parallel; Rembrandt also placed helmets on a sergeant (no. 4) and two musketeers (nos. 9 and 24), who usually did not wear helmets, at least in group portraits.[58] Furthermore, none of these helmets is of the common type actually worn by the Amsterdam militia and occasionally included in group portraits, like Govert Flinck's militia piece of 1648, or Johann Spilberg's of 1653 (Fig. 89).[59] Particularly unusual and striking is the one worn by Reijer Engelen, a partly gilded parade helmet of a Renaissance type, provided with wings as if designed for Mercury (Fig. 16), already mentioned

[55] FREDERIKS 1948, II, no. 243, pl. 77, describes and illustrates one of these spoons in a private collection and mentions the existence of a second one. The drawing by Gerrit Lamberts (1776-1850), here reproduced, was described by JOCHEMS 1892, no. 507.

[56] The correctness of the postures of pikemen nos. 20 and 25 was pointed out by MARTIN 1947, p. 45; the compositional and spatial function of the pikes was discussed by MARTIN 1947, p. 45, and particularly by SCHMIDT-DEGENER 1942.

[57] Nos. 4, 7, 9, 18, 19, 21, 23, 24 and 29.

[58] Musketeers do not wear helmets in Jacques de Gheyn's *Exercise of Armes*. I do not know of any portrait of a lieutenant with a helmet. See also following note.

[59] In Flinck's militia piece painted on the occasion of the Peace of Westphalia, three musketeers wear helmets (Rijksmuseum, no. C1; BLANKERT 1975-79, no. 154).

above. Almost equally elaborate and fanciful is the one worn by the pikeman (no. 23) right above Van Ruytenburgh.

Rembrandt also included liberally other types of arms and armor. He provided four men with cuirasses (nos. 4, 7, 20, 25) and two each with a shield and a sword (nos. 8, 18).[60] Sergeant Engelen's breastplate and gauntlet are as inappropriate and out of date as his helmet. His halberd is also an antique, as we saw. The heavy sword emerging over the hat of Van Ruytenburgh—it is not clear by whom it is held—is also old-fashioned. It may refer to a ceremonial function because it is also found in other militia pieces.[61]

Of course, these pieces of arms and armor, like the muskets, have a symbolic meaning. First, however, the question should be answered whether these militiamen did wear such varied gear in 1642, including antique costumes and out-of-date arms and pieces of armor. Did Rembrandt perhaps represent these men with their apparel as they looked? Apparently in the first half of the seventeenth century, it gradually happened that no uniforms were prescribed anymore for militiamen, not even for official occasions. Many a militiaman may have owned costumes, like Visscher, or helmets, as Kemp did,[62] and other pieces of arms and armor. Barlaeus gives a vivid description of the appearance of the militia participating in the joyous entry of Maria de'Medici in 1638: "They were partly armed with pikes, partly with muskets, and they were covered with helmets and harnesses. As for their clothing, it varied in accordance with either rank or individual preference; but there was no one who had not made an effort to appear in very beautiful apparel".[63]

---

[60] A volume of prints illustrating the handling of shield and sword was published in 1618 as a supplement to De Gheyn's *Wapenhandeling* (see above note 45). The retrospective nature of shields and swords in the *Nightwatch* was stressed by SCHMIDT-DEGENER 1916b., p. 41.

[61] A similar large sword is included in Van der Helst's *Company of Captain Roelof Bicker* of 1643 (Fig. 42) and in Spilberg's *Company of Captain Gijsbert van de Poll* of 1653 (?) (Fig. 89). Particularly in the latter painting the ceremonial function is obvious. SCHMIDT-DEGENER 1916b., p. 48, noted our lack of knowledge about this ceremonial function; VAN SCHENDEL-MERTENS 1947, p. 44, pointed out that it is not clear who is holding the sword in the *Nightwatch*.

[62] See above, under "Portraits of Officers and Men".

[63] BARLAEUS 1639 (French edition), p. 26: "Ils estoyent armez en partie de picques, en partie de mousquets, & couverts de casques & cuirasses. Quant aux habits ils estoyent divers, ou selon la qualité des charges, ou selon la volonté d'un chacun; mais il n'y avoit personne qui ne se fust efforcé d'y paroistre en tresbel equippage". The Latin edition (1638, p. 10) says: "Arma illis diversa, hastae vel sclopeta majora. Habitus vel pro ordinum ratione, vel ex arbitrio aliis alius. Pectus, tergum, brachia, femoraque ferreo thorace, caput galea tecti". That not many were fully armed appears from the

Some of these costumes and arms certainly dated from the past. Any costumed performance is bound to include them, but particularly the militiamen cultivated objects from the past in their doelens, to commemorate the distinguished traditions of their institutions, their ideals, and achievements. In the last two decades of their existence, the Kloveniers and the other two successors to the medieval militia guilds in Amsterdam were tradition-bound. Their "retrospective" attitude is demonstrated in the portraits of the governors of two of the *doelens* (Figs. 36, 44). Objects from the treasury that emphasized the traditions are ostentatiously displayed in two of the paintings, and in one of them (Fig. 44), three sons of the governors hold arches that were out of use and stand on a range that no longer existed.[64] These archers therefore were not existing in reality at the time they were painted (1653), but evoked the past. The old-fashioned costumes and arms in the *Nightwatch* did the same, and the viewers understood this.

Some of these costumes and arms probably were created by Rembrandt; others, it is likely, were seen at that time used and worn by these or similar militiamen at festive occasions. Van Baerle's description, the accoutrements of Visscher and Kemp owned by them and represented in the painting, and the general retrospective tendency of the militia leads to this conclusion. The *Nightwatch* probably was closer to the truth with regard to clothing and arms and armor than the neat uniformity of contemporary militia pieces would suggest.[65]

Dutch translation of the last sentence (1639, p. 13): "Zommigen staecken van den hoofde tot hun voeten toe in 't harnas". The Latin text was already used for the *Nightwatch* by NEUMANN 1902, p. 288, the Dutch one by MARTIN 1947, p. 29, and 1949, p. 227. That no uniforms were prescribed is also stated by MARTIN 1935, p. 160.

[64] As pointed out by SCHMIDT-DEGENER 1916b., p. 46, and TÜMPEL 1970, p. 169. The latter (pp. 173, 174) writes of the "historisierende Tendenz" of costumes and arms.

[65] GUDLAUGSSON 1938, pp. 45, 105, n. 73, came to this conclusion. He referred to the persistence of pantomimic features in processions of militiamen, and to specific instances of old-fashioned feathered caps worn by a militiaman in a group portrait of 1591 by Cornelis Cornelisz van Haarlem, a young man portrayed as an ensign in a family portrait by Van Mierevelt, and men participating in a shooting-the-bird competition perhaps painted by Jan Miense Molenaer (Antwerp, Museum, no. 679). Gudlaugsson's observation has unduly been neglected; recently, only GERSON 1973, p. 16, gave some credence to Rembrandt's costumes. Earlier, Louis Gillet had overemphasized the degree of reality in the *Nightwatch*, but saw correctly that Rembrandt made a group portrait into a history painting: "devant ce spectacle quotidien de la rue d'Amsterdam, une parade de bourgeois en armes, empanachés et pacifiques, Rembrandt (ce que nul n'avait fait!) songe aux guerres récentes et aux gloires de la patrie. Il y voit quelque chose comme une 'Marche héroïque'. Il lui donne le rhythme d'une sorte de Marseillaise"

Their uniformity of civilian and military dress may have reflected a wishful image rather than reality.

There are other significant differences in this respect between the *Nightwatch* and contemporary militia pieces. The other paintings rarely show helmets or pieces of armor, and if they do, these are seldom shown as worn or handled by the militiamen. In the militia piece by Jacob Backer (Fig. 41), which was the counterpart to Rembrandt's on the same wall, cuirasses and other parts of harnesses and a helmet are placed in a pile in the foreground. This heap fulfills the emblematic function of symbolizing the militia's role as protector of Amsterdam's citizens. In contrast to others, Rembrandt let objects in spite of their symbolism be used fully, thereby integrating action and symbolism. Furthermore, his contemporaries did not include old-fashioned costumes or weapons in their group portraits of militiamen, but only in portraits of the governors of the *doelens*.

If Rembrandt's *Nightwatch* reflects the contemporary practice of using varied and old-fashioned costumes and arms, this, of course, does not imply that his painting is a mirror of reality. By no means. We saw that Rembrandt orchestrated the musketeers to symbolize musketry. Likewise he gave Wormskerck (no. 8) and one of his colleagues (no. 18) shields and swords, and included the pikes, in order to refer to the traditional tripartite structure of the armament of the militia: musketeers, pikemen and *rondassiers* (men armed with swords and shields).[66] Furthermore, he linked past and present. Captain, lieutenant, and Sergeant Kemp with their contemporary costumes and arms embody the militia and what it stands for at that time. Sergeant Engelen, on the other hand, represents the past, and alludes to the antiquity of the Kloveniers and the values of its traditions. Rembrandt introduced the contrast to demonstrate the ties between the present and the past.

Costumes and weapons in the *Nightwatch*, while partly based on actual customs during parades, symbolize basic aspects of the Kloveniers and Amsterdam's militia: types of weapons, with musket having priority, devotion to Amsterdam, distinction between officers and men, the antiquity of the institutions and their glorious past. The old-fashionedness of many costumes and arms serves two purposes: to

(GILLET 1913, pp. 149, 150; Gillet is not read by art historians, but HELLINGA 1956, p. 6, admired the passage).

[66] Jacques de Gheyn's *Exercise of Armes* (see above note 45) has three parts (muskets; pikes; swords and shields).

allegorize concepts like the art of musketry and armed protection, and to allude to the traditions and glorious history of Amsterdam's militia and the Kloveniers. But the emphasis Rembrandt put on these antiques resulted partly also from his own bias. He loved old costumes and arms, and grasped this opportunity to include as many pieces as possible. Some of the pieces of arms and armor he may have owned and depicted from life. We know that by 1656 he owned many cuirasses, helmets, pikes, shields, and even a small canon and "a giant's helmet".[67]

THE GIRLS IN GOLD

Pride in the distinguished past of the Kloveniers and the Amsterdam militia was emphatically conveyed by the girl in gold and her barely visible companion. Although few would agree with Renoir and discard the rest of the painting while keeping her,[68] as a center of light and action both surprising and mysterious, she irresistibly draws the viewer's attention (Figs. 8, 9). She is dressed in an elegant, imaginary costume consisting of a finely brocaded robe and a separate shoulder piece also decorated with brocade. The long garment is bright yellow, the shoulder piece primarily greyish blue with yellow areas. On her head rests a bejeweled golden band with a golden chain attached to it; from her ear hangs a pear-shaped pearl. The head of her companion is covered with a different headband or cap, possibly also of gold, and her equally elegant robe is of a bluish green color.[69]

[67] He then owned, according to the inventory, "33 pieces, antique hand weapons and wind instruments", "60 pieces, Indian hand weapons, arrows, shafts, assegais and bows", "13 pieces, arrows, bows, shields, etc.", "4 crossbows and footbows", "5 antique helmets and shields", "One small metal cannon", "20 pieces, halberds, swords and Indian fans", "One giant's helmet", and "5 cuirasses" (FUCHS 1968, p. 79, FUCHS 1971, pp. 79, 80, and STRAUSS-VAN DER MEULEN 1980, pp. 381-385, nos. 312, 313, 315, 319, 320, 335, 339, 341 and 342). Rembrandt is often supposed to have used his own collection for the *Nightwatch*. It should be added that the helmet in Rembrandt's self-portrait of 1634 in Kassel (Br. 22) has an unusual crest similar to those of nos. 9 and 29 in the *Nightwatch*.

[68] VOLLARD 1938, p. 227.

[69] The most detailed description of the costume and apparel of the girl in yellow was given by SCHMIDT-DEGENER 1916b., pp. 43, 44, with corrections by VAN SCHENDEL-MERTENS 1947, p. 40. The former mistook the fowl for a rooster (the legs have no spurs), but rightly contradicted MEIJER 1886, p. 200, who thought the "rooster" was meant as a pun on the captain's name. The second girl was called "sister" of the first, without grounds, by SCHMIDT-DEGENER 1916b., p. 44, and "sister" or "friend" by MARTIN 1947, p. 39.

The most prominent of various objects attached to her waistband contrasts sharply with this sophisticated elegance: a large white fowl, most likely a chicken, is hanging upside down by its claws, its head hidden behind the musket which is being charged by the militiaman in red. Equally unexpected is the object she is carrying in front of her, probably a large drinking horn of which the mouth with its silver rim is clearly visible. Some other objects attached to her waistband are partly hidden. Since they are meant to attract less attention than the chicken, the horn and the costume, they are probably subordinated to them.[70]

The significance of the fowl and of the drinking horn has long been recognized.[71] The fowl, its head and therefore its identifying features obscured (similar to the invisible head of the symbolic musketeer in the center) is included for the sake of its claws that receive full emphasis. These claws are a late and reduced derivation of the larger claw of a bird of prey that was the emblem of the Kloveniers. A claw could be seen everywhere in the Kloveniersdoelen at the time, in the stained glass windows, on dishes, on a gate, in the decoration of the

[70] A handle-like object to the left of the claws (perhaps the handle of a knife or part of a pistol), a bejeweled pouch hanging from two cords (perhaps a purse or bullet pouch), a flat leather bag (perhaps a flask or gunpowder pouch; according to HELLINGA 1956, p. 14, a bit and symbol of *temperantia*) and a smaller container with two compartments mostly hidden by the same musket (perhaps a powder flask). VAN SCHENDEL-MERTENS 1947, p. 40, characterized the objects hanging from the waistband as "precious miniature armament". Finally a piece of material (perhaps silk) with a golden knob is also attached to the waistband. The parallel lines above the head of the girl in yellow have been interpreted as the feathers of a peacock pie carried by her companion (SCHMIDT-DEGENER 1916b., p. 44; MARTIN 1947, p. 39; TÜMPEL 1970, p. 69, and 1977, p. 85; and others). These lines, however, seem to me to have been part of a different headgear of the girl in yellow (perhaps feathers or branches) planned by Rembrandt but subsequently abandoned and overpainted. The "feathers" apparently were not visible when Lundens painted his copy; later cleanings have revealed the *pentimento*. See also VAN SCHENDEL-MERTENS 1947, p. 41; BULLETIN 1976, pp. 46, 47.

[71] This role of the drinking horn and of the claws of the girl's fowl was tentatively suggested by SCHMIDT-DEGENER 1916b., pp. 45-47 (with references to contemporary representations of the claw on objects mentioned, although not realizing that the claw of the emblem was that of an eagle). Subsequently, the emblematic function of the claws was accepted without further discussion by BENESCH 1935, p. 32, by characterizing the claw as "redendes Symbol des Doelen" (also BENESCH 1957, p. 67), treated as an attractive hypothesis by VAN GELDER 1946, p. 265 and by MARTIN 1947, p. 39, accepted by MARTIN 1951, pp. 2, 8, and, with emphasis and elaboration, by TÜMPEL 1970, p. 170, who also indicated the significance of the invisibility of the head of the fowl. For the eagle's claw as emblem inherited by the Kloveniers from their predecessors the crossbow militia guild, see Chapter III.

silver mount of the drinking horn (Fig. 58) and in the links of the collar which honored the winning "king" at the Shooting-the-Parrot competitions (Fig. 59). In former times, the militiamen of the Kloveniers had themselves portrayed in costumes embroidered with the emblem (Fig. 57).

The girl in gold and, by implication, her companion are therefore emblem carriers. As such, they personify the company and the Kloveniers. It is for that reason that Rembrandt awarded them a central place in the composition.[72]

Where did the idea originate of including this personification in this way, and what other concepts did the two girls embody? The origin has been sought both in reality and in artistic tradition. It has been suggested that Rembrandt derived the idea from the actual presence of children among soldiers and militiamen marching,[73] that he represented in them the daughters of the stewardess performing their mother's task,[74] or that they fulfilled the traditional function of sut-

[72] TÜMPEL 1970, p. 170, was the first to state that the reason for Rembrandt to emphasize the girls by means of light, color, and composition as a second focus of the painting was their role as personification of the Kloveniers. Shortly earlier, Jan Emmens had characterized the girls as "allegorical in-sets", in keeping with the Baroque phenomenon of inserting personifications and allegories into historical subjects (CHICAGO 1969, p. 79).

[73] First VETH 1914, p. 565, and then SCHMIDT-DEGENER 1916b., p. 44, referred to children called *troosjens* running between soldiers; MARTIN 1947, pp. 28, 29, and BAUCH 1957, p. 11, adopted it. However, Veth relied on H. Betz (*Historisch Leesboek*, The Hague, 1906) who misinterpreted his own source (Doedijns in *Haagsche Mercurius* of 1699). Doedijns did not write specifically about boys and girls mingling with militiamen, but in general about children, among them girls (also called *trosjes*) appearing in the presence of marching soldiers. Schmidt-Degener, with reference to TER GOUW 1871, p. 455, rightly indicated that the word *troosjens* was used for young girls in general. Undoubtedly children always have mingled with soldiers or militiamen as soon as orders were loose enough to let them do so, but *troosjens* should be omitted from discussions of the *Nightwatch* and other militia pieces. They are not children from the public or the audience that are represented in these paintings but specific emblem carriers conveying symbolism. The misinterpretation leads to statements like that of HAAK 1969, p. 179, characterizing the girl as "just a market girl . . . all dressed up to accompany the militia on parade". Although NEUMANN 1902 recognized the symbolism of various details of the *Nightwatch*, he was of the opinion that Rembrandt introduced the girl for the sake of color and light.

[74] SCHMIDT-DEGENER 1916b., p. 45, probably based on BONTEMANTEL-KERNKAMP 1897, p. 182, under reference to the wife of the steward included in three paintings by Van der Helst. The comparison does not convince because in all three the militiamen are gathered around a table, the ceremonial meal being the central theme. It is equally unlikely that they are the daughters of one of the officers. Sons were occasionally included in militia pieces (Van der Helst, *The Governors of the Handboogsdoelen*;

lers.[75] It is unlikely that children playfully joining militiamen furnished the prototype for these elegantly appareled girls performing their symbolic task. The hypothesis that they were sutlers has the advantage over the others inasmuch as Rembrandt could have based himself on a long tradition of representations of "The Gunner and the Sutler" or of sutlers among camp followers.[76] The nature of sutlers, however, in life as in art, seems difficult to reconcile with the refined dresses of costly materials and sophisticated jewelry, and with the venerable drinking horn and renowned emblem epitomizing the institution and traditions of the Kloveniers. The idea of representing the claws by hanging a chicken from the belt of one of the girls may have come to Rembrandt from traditional representations of sutlers (Fig. 75), but not her primary role as emblem carrier. The origin of that role has to be sought in traditions closer in nature to the Amsterdam militia with its prestigious membership, duties, and social functions.

Their origin can be established. Parallels in Flemish paintings of the beginning of the seventeenth century point the way. In Denys van Alsloot's representations of the annual procession of militia companies and rhetoricians on May 31, 1615, in Brussels, held that year in honor of Archduchess Isabella and therefore celebrated with more than usual splendor, well-dressed boys and girls accompany the procession (Fig. 73). Some of them carry baskets, apparently with food. Their function must have been primarily ceremonial and symbolic.[77] This is also

Spilberg, *The Company of Captain Gijsbert van de Poll*; possibly in Van der Helst, *The Company of Roelof Bicker*), but girls apparently not. Furthermore, Banning Cocq was childless, and although Van Ruytenburgh had two daughters, he also had a son who would have been represented before the girls had a chance.

[75] GLÜCK 1907, p. 18, supposed that she was "eine Zwergin, die der Schützengilde etwa Marketenderinnendienste zu leisten pflegte"; TÜMPEL 1970, pp. 170, 172, interprets the girls as stewardesses of the *doelens* dressed up like sutlers ("als Marketenderinnen verkleidete Doelenwirtinnen").

[76] In the opinion of TÜMPEL 1970, pp. 168-170 (and also briefly 1977, p. 84), the girl is based on the visual tradition of sutlers with fowl and other objects; he referred to prints by J. Amman, Pieter de Jode, Willem Buytewech, Enea Vico, J. Th. de Bry and others. Although I was of the same opinion (in lectures in the 1960s and early 1970s), I do not accept this dependence of the girl of Rembrandt's *Nightwatch* on these prototypes and her association with the sutlers any more. GERSON 1973, p. 32, also expressed doubts. TÜMPEL's reference to Bylert's painting of a sutler (1970, fig. 114) may prove that the subject was acceptable in that medium, but it does not support his interpretation of the girl in the *Nightwatch*. On the contrary, the plain, not to say vulgar appearance of Bylert's woman is an argument against it.

[77] They are found in the first and the second of a series of six large canvases painted in 1616; versions of the first are in the Prado and in the Musées Royaux des Beaux-Arts in Brussels, of the second in the Victoria and Albert Museum and in Brussels. For

apparent from their presence at the landing of Maria de'Medici in Antwerp on August 4, 1631. In the painting representing the event (Fig. 74), probably by Matheus Vroom, a boy and a girl—he in sixteenth-century costume with a feather in his beret and carrying a jar on a stick, she in Sunday dress with a small earthenware pot and a large wooden spoon hanging from her waistband—are standing near two messengers in the foreground while to the right Maria de'Medici is greeted by a woman probably personifying the city of Antwerp. To the left the militia of the city, complete with ensigns, drummers and pikemen, is firing its muskets and standing guard.[78] Probably ceremonial as well is the role of the finely dressed girl with a pitcher in the painting of militiamen in front of the gate of their doelen in Leiden attributed to Hendrick van der Burch.[79]

These parallels, however, do not imply that Rembrandt borrowed the idea from any of these paintings. Rather, his girls in gold are based on the same tradition. The dressed-up children joining the militia in paintings by Van Alsloot, Vroom, and Van der Burch are closely related to figures in plays and processions staged by the rhetoricians, and must have been derived from them. Like the girls in Van Alsloot's paintings, those of the *Nightwatch* also can be understood only as derived from the traditions of the rhetoricians.[80] When chambers of rhetoric (or societies of rhetoric, Rederijker Kamers) met for their

the second, and for bibliography of the series, see KAUFFMANN 1973, pp. 3-7. First mentioned in comparison with the *Nightwatch* by GUDLAUGSSON 1938, p. 105, notes 72 and 73; also by MARTIN 1949, p. 226, and 1951, p. 7. Since these children carrying mainly foodstuffs and cooking utensils are present at the visit of rulers, they may symbolize the rights and privileges that traditionally rulers reaffirmed by means of joyous entries even if the occasion was not a "joyeuse entrée", properly speaking.

[78] The painting, first mentioned in this context by MARTIN 1951, p. 8, exists in at least three versions. The best one is in Dresden (no. 113, signed *MV* and therefore attributed to Matheus Vroom, dated *1632*; panel, 64.5 × 92 cm.), a second one belongs to the city of Antwerp (Cat. Museum 1948, no. 636), a third one (panel, c. 68 × 100 cm.) recently appeared at two auctions (Pisa, 30.X.1960, no. 80, and Brussels, 16.V.1962, no. 139). Martin referred to the second one.

[79] The painting was first mentioned in connection with the *Nightwatch* by VAN SCHENDEL-MERTENS 1947, p. 40, fig. 31; see also MARTIN 1951, p. 8. The painting is now in the Museum Lakenhal, Leiden.

[80] As was noted by GUDLAUGSSON 1938, pp. 44-45, 104, 105. About the *Nightwatch*, p. 45: "Es ist wohl nicht unwichtig, sich dieser Gepflogenheit [roles played by children in processions of militia companies and influenced by customs of rhetoricians] zu erinnern, da nur daraus eine Begründung für die Existenz des 'rätselhaften' Mädchens auf Rembrandts Nachtwache gegeben werden kann". MARTIN 1951, pp. 7, 8, adopted the idea. For an introduction to the influence of performances by rhetoricians on painting, see the excellent study KERNODLE 1947.

traditional competitive festivities, the so-called *landjuwelen*, one of the first performances was the "entry" (*intrede*). Members of each visiting chamber entered the town in procession enacting a pre-established theme. Each chamber was preceded by two persons carrying its emblem (or blazon, *blazoen*) to present it to the host chamber. A characteristic example is provided by the fourteen chambers participating in the *landjuweel* organized in Haarlem in 1606 to raise money for the *oudemannenhuis*, the nursing home where Frans Hals would later live and work. The elaborate descriptions and detailed prints of this event published the next year in Zwolle by Zacharias Heyns show that eleven of the chambers during their entry were preceded by boys or girls carrying the *blazoen* of their chamber (Figs. 71, 72).[81] The girls and boys were dressed in costumes, and sometimes represented mythological figures such as Mercury or Pallas Athena. Most of them had special headgear like fancy caps or wreaths. At the end of the entry they presented their emblem to the host chamber, "Trou moet blijken" (or "Faithfulness must prove itself").

The girls in the *Nightwatch* as costumed emblem carriers resemble closely those preceding the chambers of rhetoric entering Haarlem in order to compete with other chambers.[82] That Rembrandt may have derived them from this custom is supported by the following considerations. First, the parallels between militia companies marching and processions of chambers of rhetoric were not limited to the emblem carriers: the rhetoricians were preceded not only by these youths, but also by a drummer and an ensign. The visual similarity, therefore, between citizens marching as militiamen preceded by ensign and drummer, and citizens doing the same in the role of rhetoricians, also preceded by ensign and drummer, must have been particularly striking.

[81] CONST-THOONENDE IVWEEL 1607. In this remarkably detailed report and its supplement of 1608, all the events are described, poems and *sinnespelen* printed, and fourteen entries illustrated in large fold-out prints (one as long as ca. 114 cm., all ca. 13 cm. high). Since the book is not rare, quite a number of copies must have been printed. Often the prints have been cut up. Informative for the procedures of an elaborate, late *landjuweel* in the Southern Netherlands is SCHADT-KISTE 1620, with illustrations of some *blazoenen* and their presentation (procession of young women with torches, men in costumes, etc.). Although the painting of the rhetoricians' chamber of De Fonteynisten of Dordrecht in the museum in Dordrecht (panel, 33 × 200 cm., cat. 1928, no. 144) is largely a copy after the corresponding print in this book, it seems contemporary because of the three citizens added at the right. It therefore may relate the actual colors of the procession represented.

[82] This parallel between the *Nightwatch* and emblem carriers of chambers of rhetoric has not been drawn before. Gudlaugsson pointed in the right direction and came close to observing the parallel (see note 80 above).

Furthermore, the ties between the rhetoricians and the militia had always been close.[83] Militia companies and rhetoricians often held their competitions and performances together. Before 1580, competitions between militia companies invited by host towns were organized similarly to those of the rhetoricians. Prizes were similar, and militia guilds even entered towns and presented emblems to host guilds in a similar way.[84]

Rembrandt undoubtedly was familiar with the tradition of the competitive performances of chambers of rhetoric and the main stages of the ceremonies, including those of entering the city in procession and of offering the emblems to the host chamber. The events in Haarlem were not an isolated phenomenon. Although the customs varied, the *landjuwelen* had firm traditions that had been established in the Middle Ages and that lasted until his time. From the large cities the *landjuwelen* and the similar *refereinfeesten* had disappeared by 1642, but in smaller places they continued to flourish as old-fashioned yet lively events.[85] Still in 1641 in Rijnsburg, six chambers of rhetoric from The Hague and elsewhere came together to perform for two weeks. Each chamber entered the small town complete with drummer and ensign, and presented its emblem to the host chamber.[86] He also may have known of the older tradition of the same custom of the militia guilds, although those seem to have been discontinued toward the end of the sixteenth century.

Rembrandt was not the only one to introduce a young person symbolizing a militia company among the men portrayed. The provincial painter Maerten van der Fuyck depicted in 1660 a boy in that role among the militiamen of the town of Den Briel, thereby following the same tradition as Rembrandt.[87]

[83] For the relationship between rhetoricians and militia guilds, and for bibliography on the subject, see Chapter III and its note 22.

[84] Van Autenboer 1962, p. 79; see also Ter Gouw 1871, pp. 502-515.

[85] Schotel mentions the following *refereinfeesten* in which chambers of rhetoric from different towns participated: 1610 in Katwijk, 1611 in Gouda, 1613 in Leiden, Haarlem, and Amsterdam, 1615 in Ketel, 1616 in Gouda and Leiderdorp, 1624 in Amsterdam, 1629 in Haarlem, 1641 in Vlissingen and Rijnsburg, and others until the end of the century (Schotel 1871, II, respectively pp. 13; 10; 6; 12, 17; 21, 230; 34; 37; 40; 23, 230; 28; 63; and 80; see also Worp 1908, II, p. 23).

[86] Reijnsburchs Angier-hoff 1641.

[87] Gudlaugsson 1938, p. 105, n. 72, was the first to mention Van der Fuyck's painting in the context of the *Nightwatch*, without making the connection with the emblem carriers. The boy is certainly not dressed up as Amor (Martin 1951, p. 8). His bow and quiver with arrows symbolize the militia company and its traditions, the hare probably the activity of shooting. The seal of the militia guild of Arendonk in

It is now clear also why the girl in gold has a companion rather than being alone, why the two girls walk rather than stand, and why they move in a direction different from that of the company. During the entries of the chambers of rhetoric, and presumably also when militia guilds presented their coats of arms, not just one but two persons carried the emblems and preceeded the procession. The two emblem carriers in the *Nightwatch* are only partially visible, and their speedy steps are going in the wrong direction. As a matter of fact, they would seriously hamper the movement of Banning Cocq's company. As in the case of the shooting musketeer in the center, Rembrandt introduced this dichotomy to indicate that the girls belong to a different reality.

Their symbolic nature probably also explains their size. Both the girls, like the symbolic musketeer, are on a smaller scale than the militiamen. It is this smaller scale that makes us see them as girls rather than women in spite of the mature features of the one dressed in gold and the haunting incongruity of her face and her size.[88]

The role of the girls as personification of Kloveniers also explains the colors of their costumes since, as discussed above, blue and gold were the heraldic colors of the Amsterdam War Council and of the Kloveniers. Undoubtedly the blue and gold of the costume of the foremost girl, and therefore also the greyish blue color of the second one, refer to these institutions. Rembrandt emphasized the gold of the dress not only as a luminous key element of the composition and the painting as a whole. He wished to stress also this symbolic function of the gold.

Although added to Banning Cocq and his men as personifications of their company and the Amsterdam militia, they fulfill a different and more complex role than the usual personification added to a history scene or a group portrait.[89] Their associations with the waning traditions of competitive performances of chambers of rhetoric and

---

Flanders displays two crossed muskets and a rabbit-like animal (SCHATTEN 1966-67, no. 45).

   [88] It is possible that Rembrandt, consciously or subconsciously, endowed the girl in gold with a certain resemblance to Saskia, which is observed by many who see the painting. Saskia died in June 1642, shortly after Rembrandt finished the painting or while he was still working on it. For the symbolic musketeer, see above in this chapter.

   [89] As mentioned above (note 72), Tümpel and Emmens discussed the girl in gold as an added personification. Rubens frequently added personifications or classical gods to his historical figures in the Medici Series; Lucas de Heere made figures of War, Peace, and Plenty share the space and the action of worldly figures in his portrait of *The Family of Henry VIII* (Dent-Brocklehurst Collection).

militia companies added connotations of tradition-oriented, theatrical competitiveness to their role as personifications. Their derivation expanded their meaning. Rembrandt must have intended this, and we may assume that a good number of his contemporaries understood the meaning of the two emblem carriers.

Yet, there is ambiguity, particularly in the foremost girl's superficial similarity to a sutler. This ambiguity may be intended. Those who did not understand them as personifications of the militia and its glorious past were free to think of sutlers and their unchanging role in the military life of men. Rather than intended as a pun, their double associations allowed for interpretations on different levels.

In the context of the primary background of the girls in gold, the role of the drummer becomes clearer.[90] With his sixteenth-century costume, he belongs to the realm of *landjuwelen* and their entries. Drummers, as we saw, played an important role on those occasions. Rembrandt's drummer probably strengthened the references just summarized. But he was also a common sight in Amsterdam when the militia performed. He therefore may be interpreted as emphasizing and enlivening the past as well as the present activities of the militia. Furthermore, he served to close the composition of the painting toward the right.

THE ARCHWAY

The massive wall and its monumental archway also contribute vitally to both the formal qualities and the meaning of the painting.[91] This gate did not exist in Amsterdam.[92] Its features, more Renaissance than Baroque,[93] were created by Rembrandt. In doing so, he undoubtedly was guided partly by paintings of his predecessors, partly by arches and gateways he knew. He seems to have been influenced by Cornelis Ketel's *Company of Captain Rosecrans* of 1588 (Fig. 83).[94] There the men are standing in front of sturdy architectural structures flanking

[90] See above in this chapter under "Powderboy, Drummer, and Extras".

[91] For the pictorial function of wall and archway, see Chapter V.

[92] MEIJER 1886, p. 201, stated already so; most writers seem to have agreed (from SCHMIDT-DEGENER 1917a., p. 5, to KOOT 1969, p. 58 and MÜLLER HOFSTEDE 1970, p. 240), with the exception of MARTIN 1935, p. 161, who was of the opinion that the archway was "based on reality" (but later he considered it imaginary: 1947, pp. 30, 33). VAN DILLEN 1934, p. 102, thought the gate was the Haarlemmerpoort, apparently without checking.

[93] CLARK 1966, p. 85.

[94] See Chapter V.

a gate that occupied the very center of the painting before the canvas was curtailed on either side. Because of the size of the gate and the two heavy closed doors, probably a city gate is represented. It was the first duty of the militia to guard these gates. Rembrandt adopted Ketel's background device, changed its shape and spatial function, but did he retain its association with city gates? Gates to the *doelens*, at least in Amsterdam, were much smaller.[95] Furthermore, in those paintings in the assembly hall in which the *doelens* are represented in the background, the entrance door of the meeting building rather than a monumental arch is depicted. The massive high walls on either side of the archway are also inappropriate for *doelens*, whereas they accord well with the function of city walls. The same is true of the window with its heavy bars. Its placement to the right, in spite of its height, may imply a reference to the militia's duties as guardians of the city since in Amsterdam in the seventeenth century the militia had guard rooms or separate guardhouses to the right of the gateway.[96] For all these reasons, the archway and adjoining walls probably were meant to be thought of in the first place as an imaginary monumental gate in a solid city wall.[97]

That the gate is imaginary is confirmed by the steps in front of it. The steps are only there to justify the different height of the placement of some of the figures, and were not found in Amsterdam in front of any of its arches.[98]

The archway always has been supposed to be open, and the dark, almost black tone that fills the arch invariably is assumed to suggest space under the arch and beyond it. This reading is based on the assumption that Rembrandt wished to suggest the actual movement of the company through the archway toward the viewer, and that whatever lies beyond the arch is invisible. The sophisticated analysis and ground plan of the architecture and of the placement of the figures

[95] The entrance gate of the St. Jorisdoelen in Leiden, which was depicted by Hendrick van der Burch and Domenicus van Tol (Lakenhal, Leiden, nos. S.1536 and S.433), and which still exists, is about as large as the archway in the *Nightwatch*, but was built only in 1645 and lacked the defensive features of the walls. KOOT 1969, p. 58, considers the archway in the *Nightwatch* an imaginary concept of a *doelen* gateway.

[96] JOCHEMS 1892, p. 82, note 2.

[97] DYSERINCK 1890, p. 272, already spoke of a stadsmuur. The massive windowless structure to the right in Backer's *Company of Captain Cornelis de Graeff* may also suggest a city wall, as DE GELDER 1921, pp. 43, 44, observed.

[98] The steps, which are difficult to see, are not curved (SCHMIDT-DEGENER 1917a., p. 8, 9; WEISBACH 1926, p. 343; and others), but run horizontally (VAN SCHENDEL-MERTENS 1947, p. 46). The 1975-76 cleaning leaves no doubt in this respect.

made in 1916 by Schmidt-Degener showing graphically the militiamen marching forward through the archway have never been challenged and have often been praised for their clarity.[99] But the space beyond the arch that he included in his plan is not indicated in the painting, and none of the figures is placed beyond the arch, although some may be standing under it. Although not representing closed gates or another physical barrier, the impenetrable darkness may very well symbolically emphasize and complete the image of the wall as a city enclosure rather than contradict or interrupt it.[100] In that case, this darkness is the equivalent to the emphatically closed doors of Ketel's painting of half a century before (Fig. 83).[101] Furthermore, if the darkness stresses enclosure rather than passage, it is one more element in this painting that refers to the militia's duties as protector of the city.[102]

The archway does not seem to allude to city gates only. The temporary triumphal arches erected in Amsterdam and in other cities at appropriate occasions left traces in the formulation of this archway and of the space in front of it, as well as in its meaning. Particularly the combination of the archway with a bridge in front of it bordered by a banister seems to reflect acquaintance with one of the triumphal arches constructed in honor of Maria de'Medici in 1638 (Fig. 68).[103] Even if these similarities were accidental, the arch seems to fulfill the image of a triumphal arch, and to signify glory to the militiamen placed in front of it, particularly to Banning Cocq and Van Ruytenburgh.[104]

[99] SCHMIDT-DEGENER 1916b., p. 33, and 1917a., p. 7 (drawn by Huib Luns); the former taken over by BAUCH 1957, p. 13.

[100] It is true, as NEUMANN 1902, p. 268 (1924, pp. 292-3) observed, that in etchings, Rembrandt frequently placed figures in action in front of arches enclosing dark space, but this darkness suggests either a wall (B. 74, 77) or an interior (B. 43, 49, 76).

[101] Thomas de Keyser placed the men in front of a wall flanked by recessed spaces on both sides (*The Company of Captain Allaert Cloeck*, 1632; Fig. 88). Nature and structure of the building are not clear.

[102] The interpretation of the darkness in the archway as space beyond the arch probably has contributed to the origin and subsequently to the acceptance of the title of the painting, and the title the *Nightwatch* in its turn may have prevented questioning the meaning of this darkness.

[103] See Chapter III. Influence of Maria de'Medici's arches on the *Nightwatch* was seen by SIX 1919, ALTENA 1955 and SNOEP 1975, pp. 44, 168, notes 58, 59. Although one high bridge with steps existed near the Beurs (MEIJER 1886, p. 201; SIX 1919) it was not placed parallel to an archway. SCHMIDT-DEGENER 1916a., p. 73, reproduced the print from Van Baerle's *Medicea Hospes*.

[104] SCHMIDT-DEGENER 1916a., pp. 70, 71, quoted a description from 1560 likening the marching militiamen to a "solemn triumph"; TÜMPEL 1970, p. 174, qualified the arch in the painting as a *Hoheitsmotiv*. See also HAVERKAMP-BEGEMANN 1973, p. 7, and GERSON 1973, p. 32 ("semble un arc triomphal").

In one sense, these citizens take the place of the dignitaries whom they themselves honored from time to time.

Rembrandt himself provides parallels to both these meanings in other works of his. What other than a city gate could be the archway behind Athena in her representation as Bellona in the painting of 1633 in New York (Fig. 78)?[105] Similarly, the corner of a wall that, in its bold stones and masonry, resembles the archway of the *Nightwatch*, placed close to the standard-bearer Floris Soop in his portrait of 1654 (Fig. 77), was probably also intended as a reference to a city gate.[106] The arches in his portraits of a poet (Jan Hermansz Krul) and a physician (Jan Antonides van der Linden), on the other hand, can only stand for glory.[107] Outside of Rembrandt's work, the stone structure behind Giovanni da Castaldo, General of Charles V, in his portrait in full armor by Titian, conjures up the general's military might, and the arch with its dark space behind a lieutenant portrayed by Aert de Gelder (Fig. 79) symbolizes this man's responsibilities toward his city, probably Amsterdam.[108]

In one other instance Rembrandt made an archway fulfill the same triple function. In *The Triumph of Mordecai* (Fig. 76), a large archway linking left and right of the composition stresses the center, represents also a city gate, and serves to convey the idea of triumph. Formally and in individual motifs, the etching has so much in common with the painting that it probably was made at the same time, or ca. 1641-42. These similarities may have been more than purely formal analogies, and they may have been enhanced by a parallelism in subject

[105] BREDIUS-GERSON 1969, no. 467. The spatially awkward juxtaposition of architectural elements in the background and the discrepancy between the architecture and the chair in front of it may be due to an influence from backdrops used in *tableaux vivants* (for that practice, see KERNODLE 1947, p. 105).

[106] BREDIUS-GERSON 1969, no. 275. With his right shoulder and right leg (left from our point of view) placed closer to the viewer, he is represented in the attitude of stepping. Soop was a neighbor of Jan Six. His identification is due, once more, to Miss VAN EEGHEN (1971, pp. 173-181).

[107] Rembrandt painted the *Portrait of Jan Krul* in Kassel (BREDIUS-GERSON 1969, no. 171) in 1633, etched the posthumous *Portrait of Jan Antonides van der Linden* (B. 264) about 1665 after the painting by Abraham van den Tempel in Leiden (loan from Mauritshuis; the arch was not or is not anymore depicted in the painting).

[108] Titian's *Portrait of Giovanni da Castaldo* is in the Residenzgalerie, Salzburg. Aert de Gelder's undated portrait (LILIENFELD 1914, no. 175, "after 1690") is in the Gemäldegalerie Alte Meister, Dresden (Cat. 1966, no. 1792, *Der Mann mit der Partisane*). The darkness of the space under the arch is clearer in the print after the painting made by A. Riedel in 1754 than in photographs. The foreshortening of the partisan and the arch in the background may have been influenced by the *Nightwatch*.

matter between the two works, between the historic role of the militia in Amsterdam and that of Mordecai rescuing the Jews. Holland associated the past, particularly the history of the Jews, with its own recent history and struggles, and the militia thought of itself as the victorious protector of the freedom of the citizens. The parallel between Mordecai, who had delivered the Jews from the destruction plotted against them by Haman, and the Amsterdam militia, who had protected the city in the past and most recently against the Spaniards, presented itself readily. As a matter of fact, in the 1620s, in a conflict between the militia and the city government, some likened the role of the militia to that of Mordecai. Whether Rembrandt introduced the similarity between painting and etching because of the links in subject matter or not, as a group portrait of militiamen in front of a triumphal arch, the *Nightwatch* undoubtedly was felt to allude to the history of the Netherlands and to the recently gained independence and freedom.[109] It was an idea to which Rembrandt would come back in a purely historical rather than in an essentially contemporary parallel, namely, in *The Conspiracy of the Batavians*.

ACTION

Rembrandt subordinated figures and objects with their complex allusions to one feature unifying the entire painting: action.[110] Banning Cocq and Wilhem van Ruytenburgh march forward, the captain "ordering his lieutenant . . . to let his company of citizens march", and the militiamen are in the process of forming company, while some citizens (powderboy, drummer) lend them support. From this unified action, Rembrandt purposefully excepted those figures that are exclusively symbolic; the girls in yellow and the musket-shooting boy in the center move in a different direction.

Rembrandt intensified the action by emphasizing the participation of everybody, whether walking or standing and whether fully visible

[109] Similarity between the etching and the *Nightwatch* has been discussed frequently since NEUMANN 1902, pp. 268 ff., most recently by HAVERKAMP-BEGEMANN 1973, with emphasis on the parallels and possible links in meaning of the two works. At the time of my writing the latter, I did not know of the perceptive analysis of formal similarities between the two works made by Madlyn M. Kahr in her dissertation *The Book of Esther in Seventeenth Century Dutch Art*, 1966, pp. 131-138 (with, p. 137, reference to Flavius Josephus as source for crownless Mordecai).

[110] RIEGEL 1882, p. 133, already stressed the significance of the specific action in the *Nightwatch*, and sees it as something that Frans Hals could not achieve. See also NEUMANN 1902, pp. 258-260.

or only partially. He stressed action in gestures, attitudes of heads, direction of glances, and in the movement of clothing and objects. Banning Cocq's elegant sash and the tassel attached to his left leg are swaying, the cartridges of the loading musketeer swing out, and so does the cape of the ensign.[111] A dog is participating in the action and barking fiercely.[112] The action is so intense that a nineteenth-century observer thought that the Spartans entering the Battle of Thermopylae could not have been more agitated.[113]

Action is as much the subject of the *Nightwatch* as the portraits. This stress on action distinguishes the painting in a fundamental way from its predecessors and contemporary militia pieces: whereas other artists tried to reconcile posed portraits with an allusion to the sitters' role as militiamen, Rembrandt integrated the portraits with the action required of them as members of the company. The ambiguous references to movement in Ketel's painting, and the hesitant stepping in De Keyser's militia piece of 1632 are the closest parallels yet worlds removed from the emphasized action of the *Nightwatch*.[114]

The dominating role of action and its life-like quality have created the impression that Rembrandt represented or commemorated a specific event.[115] When historians started to raise the question as to the

[111] Earlier, Rembrandt had used the same device to express Belshazzar's startled rising from his seat to see God's handwriting on the wall (*Belshazzar's Feast*, dated 163-, from middle 1630s, London, National Gallery). Belshazzar's sudden rise upsets a wine goblet and makes his chain swing away from his chest. Related is the "frozen movement" of falling objects Rembrandt loved in the 1630s: shepherd's crooks hanging in mid-air in the *Annunication to the Shepherds* (BARTSCH, 1791, no. 44, 1634), falling knife in *Abraham Sacrificing Isaac* (BREDIUS, 1935, no. 498, 1635, Leningrad), and falling sword in *The Resurrection of Christ* (BREDIUS, 1935, no. 561, 1639, Munich; I owe the list to Barbara D. Boehm, paper, 1980).

[112] The dog is a traditional element of militia pieces. Ketel's group of 1588 has an enormous muzzled black dog, probably symbolizing vigilance and faithfulness (DE JONGH 1963). Despite Rembrandt's probable awareness of its symbolic function, this mongrel, loudly barking at the militiamen, is a humoristic and light-hearted interpretation of the tradition.

[113] KOLLOFF 1854, p. 453: "die Spartaner des Leonidas, die zu den Waffen rannten, um den Engpass der Thermopylen zu vertheidigen, zogen gewiss nicht heftiger und stürmischer dahin, als diese honneten amsterdamer Bürger zum Scheibenschiessen aufbrechen".

[114] See Chapter V.

[115] The actuality of the scene depicted by Rembrandt in the *Nightwatch* was overemphasized by MARTIN, particularly in 1949 and 1951; his reconstruction of the order of the "festive procession" does not convince. SCHMIDT-DEGENER 1914-1917, while contributing more to a correct understanding of the painting than anyone else for

purpose of this movement, they thought the company was marching toward the place where the competition of Shooting the Parrot was going to take place.[116] Later, the periodic marching to enliven kermisses was considered the principal reference.[117] This interpretation was given up in favor of the supposition that the joyous entry of Maria de'Medici in 1638 or that of Henrietta Maria in 1642 was thought to have been the occasion that brought the company into action.[118]

Rembrandt represented neither an actual event, nor did he or his sitters want to commemorate a special occasion. Rembrandt borrowed features from actual customs, like marching out armed and in costume,

---

decades after him, occasionally overestimated the effect of actual events (Maria de'Medici's entry) on the painting. His reconstruction of the site was based on the assumption that it represented an existing site, and therefore failed.

[116] Around the middle of the nineteenth century, Banning Cocq's company was thought to be preparing itself for "Shooting the Parrot" (POTGIETER 1844, p. 148; KOLLOFF 1854, p. 453; VOSMAER 1877, p. 221).

[117] NEUMANN 1902, pp. 161-162 (1924, pp. 285-286) was of the opinion that Rembrandt might have thought of a departure for a parade on the occasion of a kermis. As Neumann remarked, the fancy costumes and weapons excluded marching out for more mundane tasks like guarding gates or extinguishing fires (probably in reference to RIEGEL 1882, pp. 134-6, who was of the opinion that the *Nightwatch* in essence represented action during a watch to face disturbance or danger). The supposition of SCHÖNE 1972, p. 91, that an appeal to the citizens of Amsterdam to rally against Spain is alluded to is unfounded.

[118] The hypothesis that the *Nightwatch* represents or commemorates the participation of Banning Cocq's company in the ceremonies welcoming Maria de'Medici in 1638, proposed first by SIX in 1909, and elaborated by him in 1919, was generally accepted (particularly by MARTIN 1935-36, I, pp. 160, 218, and MARTIN 1947, with reservations by KOOT 1947, p. 14), in spite of the serious scepticism of NEUMANN 1924, p. 286, n. 2, that was based mainly on the same considerations that made KOK 1967 finally refute the hypothesis convincingly. (SCHMIDT-DEGENER 1916b., p. 30, and 1917a., pp. 2, 3, had accepted only the general influence of this triumphal entry; LUNS 1936, p. [12], and VAN GELDER 1946, pp. 260, 261, doubted the relationship; BAUCH 1957, pp. 17, 18, accepted only the possibility of some influence). The painting cannot commemorate either the triumphal entry of Henrietta Maria, Queen of Great Britain, and Frederick Henry, Prince of Orange and their married young daughter and son on May 20, 1642, because (even if one accepts that the visit was planned long enough in advance to allow Rembrandt to finish the painting before June of that same year) to welcome the party, the captains rode out with burgomasters and aldermen rather than with their companies (BONTEMANTEL-KERNKAMP 1897, pp. 195-197). The connection between the *Nightwatch* and this triumphal entry was first made by NIEUWENHUYS 1834, pp. 8, 9, tentatively accepted by HOFDIJK 1874-75, pp. 155, 156, and with more reservation by MEIJER 1906, p. 428, but had already been rejected on various grounds by SCHELTEMA 1853, p. 102, and by MEIJER himself (1886, p. 208). For the interpretation by CARROLL 1976, see the Preface.

and depicted the action similar to what the public saw at such occasions.[119] His contemporaries undoubtedly associated the action in the painting and the painting as a whole with occasions like triumphal entries and parades on Sundays and at kermis time, but we may assume that neither Rembrandt nor his public thought that the painting recorded one specific event, or even referred to it. The traditions that helped to shape the painting, the symbolism and allusions that Rembrandt conveyed, and the different nature of reportage, at that time almost exclusively limited to prints and drawings, preclude it.

In Flanders existed a tradition of representing group portraits of militiamen engaged in actual activities, with a high degree of verisimilitude in the depiction of event and setting. The *Ommegangen* painted by Van Alsloot belong to that tradition, and so does David Teniers' group portrait representing members of the Antwerp magistracy and of the St. George militia guilds of the city at the moment that the former leaving the town hall are greeted by the latter.[120] This Flemish tradition did reach the Northern Netherlands, but was modified. In the few paintings that portray men in commemoration of an event, traditional motifs and compositions prevail rather than representation of the event itself, which is only referred to. The group portrait of Captain Abraham Boom, his lieutenant, and seven members of the Amsterdam detachment sent off in 1622 to defend Zwolle painted by Claes Pietersz Lastman and Adriaen van Nieulandt, follows the tradition of men standing on a line parallel to the picture plane, with a skirmish in the distance as a reference to the occasion.[121] Similarly,

[119] Since the late nineteenth century, authors have stressed the point that a specific event is not represented, for instance: RIEGEL 1882, p. 136 ("zwar beruht das Werk in allen seinen einzelnen Theilen völlig auf der Wirklichkeit, . . . als Ganzes besteht es nur in der Phantasie"); MEIJER 1886, p. 201 (noted that militia pieces do not represent facts, but are group portraits occasionally painted in commemoration of an event in which the sitters took part, and enlivened by action according to the artist's fantasy); SCHMIDT-DEGENER 1916b., p. 30 (with reference to paintings by Sybrand van Beest and Paulus Lesire that do represent events but are not group portraits); WEISBACH 1926, p. 342 ("[The painting does not represent] ein einmaliges Erlebnis bei einer bestimmten historischen Gelegenheit, an einem bestimmten Ort und zu einer bestimmten Stunde", but Rembrandt, using elements from reality, transferred "das Ganze in eine Sphäre des Phantastischen"); SCHÖNE 1972, pp. 90, 91.

[120] For Van Alsloot's paintings, see above in this chapter under "The Girls in Gold". Teniers' painting is almost contemporaneous with the *Nightwatch*: it dates from 1643 (Hermitage, Leningrad; ROSENBERG 1895, p. 38, fig. 34). Teniers also included portraits of Archduke Ferdinand and others in his representation of *The Shooting-the-Bird Ceremony in Brussels* of 1652 (Museum, Vienna; ROSENBERG 1895, p. 48, fig. 44).

[121] Rijksmuseum, Amsterdam, cat. no. C406; see also note 12 of this chapter.

Flinck's and Van der Helst's group portraits of *The Company of Captain Jan Huydecoper* and *The Company of Captain Cornelis Witsen*, both commemorating the Peace of Westphalia (Vrede van Munster), do not differ significantly from traditional, nonevent-connected militia pieces, and both refer on *cartellini* to the event commemorated.[122] *The Company of Captain Gijsbert van de Poll* (Fig. 89), formerly thought to have been painted on the occasion of the appointment of the captain to colonel and his statutory retirement from the company, belongs to the tradition of banquet portraits of militiamen, and represents neither the appointment nor the leave taking of the captain.[123]

Interpretation of the action in the *Nightwatch* as representing an actual marching-out for a specific event denies its Dutch rather than Flemish origins; it depends unjustifiably on nineteenth-century artistic concepts. If the paintings by Lastman, Flinck, and Van der Helst are seen as analogy, and the action construed as alluding to the joyous entry of Maria de'Medici in 1638, it should be pointed out that the *Nightwatch* does not contain one detail that specifically refers to this event. Banning Cocq was not involved in that occasion, at least not as captain. His vanity would have made him refer with great emphasis to even a tenuous association of himself or of the painting with that significant event, either in the painting itself or in the album recording his noteworthy deeds.

Rembrandt turned action that had been only a symbolic attribute in the work of De Keyser (Fig. 88) into a primary characteristic and a vehicle for further allusions. He demonstrated the viability of arms and armor as symbols of virtuous defense of freedom and order by letting them be used. By making those figures that are purely sym-

---

[122] Rijksmuseum, Amsterdam, cat. nos. C1 (BLANKERT 1975-79, no. 154) and C2 respectively.

[123] Formerly *The Company of Captain Gijsbert van de Poll* by Johann Spilberg (Fig. 89) was thought to have been painted on the occasion of the appointment of Jan van de Poll to colonel and to commemorate his retirement from the company because of that appointment, which took place on August 25, 1650. His brother Gijsbert was appointed captain on October 29 of the same year. The two brothers are seated in the foreground, Jan as colonel at the far right, Gijsbert as captain at his left. The painting glorifies the two brothers but does not refer to the specific events of appointments. It partakes in the tradition of banquet portraits of militiamen. It probably was painted in 1653 rather than 1650. (For the reinterpretation of the painting, see R. Ruurs in BLANKERT 1975-79, no. 410). The titles given to the three paintings mentioned in this paragraph and to Spilberg's militia piece in ALL THE PAINTINGS 1976 and to no. 154 in BLANKERT 1975-79 overemphasize the narrative and are misleading. They stem from a tradition which endeavors to see the paintings as recording events.

bolic—the musket-shooting boy and the girls in yellow—perform their own act among the citizens, he made them their equals, thereby intensifying the validity of the concepts they symbolize. By the same token, he emphasized their symbolic nature by giving their action a direction contrary to that of the citizens.

Conclusion

The *Nightwatch* shares basic characteristics with the numerous other group portraits of Dutch citizens represented in their roles as members of militia companies, yet differs fundamentally.

Since the beginning of the sixteenth century, distinguished men in Holland had wished to be portrayed as members of the militia. When the *Nightwatch* was painted, they were well aware of the historic role played by the militia in Holland's liberation from the Spanish tyranny. As citizens of Amsterdam they proudly realized that their militia now had to protect the independence of Holland's wealthiest and most successful city, a world power by itself.[1] They were flattered to be associated with the militia's traditions and functions, its social events, its elegant quarters and spacious shooting ranges, and to be portrayed with their peers who all belonged to Amsterdam's elite.

The *Nightwatch* fulfilled the same function as six other group portraits painted about the same time for the same newly built assembly hall of the Kloveniersdoelen. Rembrandt had to accept the same conditions of size and location. Like the other painters, Rembrandt adopted an existing formula for his composition. The main features of that formula were the central position of captain and lieutenant and the unifying action of forming company. Rembrandt also borrowed many details of the arrangement of figures and of their individual roles from his predecessors.

Yet, Rembrandt completely transformed a subject steeped in tradition and bound by conventions. He reformulated fundamental characteristics, not merely superficial features. He fused past and present, portraiture and action, reality and symbol. The action dominating the entire scene was a radical innovation. It referred to contemporary customs and events, like joyous entries and Sunday marches, and simultaneously symbolized the company's vitality. Rembrandt dressed

---

[1] Already NEUMANN 1902, p. 255 (1924, pp. 278, 279) wrote about the "Nationalstolz" and "Lokalpatriotismus" evident in the *Nightwatch* and other militia pieces. Although the history of the appreciation of the *Nightwatch* is not a subject for this book, I should like to mention that in my opinion, this seventeenth-century patriotism has influenced present-day Dutch admiration for the painting.

a number of his sitters in old-fashioned costumes, others in contemporary dress, and gave them historical as well as contemporary arms; he thereby symbolized the values the musket had in his time, and illustrated the heroic past of this company and Amsterdam's militia in general. The arch also alludes to past and present duty of citizens to protect the city by guarding its gates, and simultaneously symbolizes triumph (and formally helps to unify the composition). Some of the other painters only alluded to armed action in their militia pieces, and included weapons as attributes rather than as part of the men's apparel. All avoided overt action.

In contrast to others, only Rembrandt represented the past and its impact on his time in a group portrait of a militia company. He emphasized historic ties by personifying the company in a motif that was virtually obsolete in 1642, but which for centuries had been in use. Formerly emblem carriers playing the role of the girl in the golden dress and her companion had personified groups of rhetoricians and militiamen. By means of reintroducing these young women in a prominent place, Rembrandt did not merely allude to the past, he made it the center of his painting.

The contemporary viewer understood the symbolism and the references to concepts and events that Rembrandt wished to convey. But the viewer also had feelings and thoughts that were not explicitly expressed in the painting. He experienced these as associations based on his own knowledge and on circumstances surrounding the painting. He knew that captain and lieutenant were distinguished regents, and that the other sitters were mostly successful, wealthy wholesale dealers, mainly drapers, who all lived close together in a small quarter of the city, and thus shared more than their membership of the same company. He also knew that almost all were Protestant, that some of them had leading positions in civic institutions, and that the ensign was a well-read bachelor, and he knew other aspects of the sitters' lives. His knowledge of these and similar facts was an essential part of his interpretation of the painting. Furthermore, his interpretation of the painting as a whole was affected by its setting. The distinction and grandeur of the hall emphasized the social distinction and worldly success of the sitters; the purpose of the building and the presence of six more similar paintings expressed the role of the militia and stimulated the viewer's pride in civic virtues of the past and the present.

Rembrandt's intentions and the viewer's associations endowed the painting with a clear message. The *Nightwatch* expressed forcefully the preparedness of the individual men represented and thereby of

Amsterdam's citizens to defend the independence of the city against any adversary, including the Dutch republic itself. The willingness to fight for Amsterdam's rights may have been inherent in other group portraits of militiamen, but was not stated overtly. Only Rembrandt did so, in a most emphatic manner. Furthermore, while representing customs alive at the time, he emphasized the historic foundations of the city's ambitions, and left no doubt about the successful outcome of any action that might have to be undertaken. For their contemporaries, this group portrait of eighteen men undoubtedly signified a glorification of Amsterdam, the most successful and powerful city-state of its time.

The sitters had expected a group portrait, and had paid for it. Were they disappointed? Some contemporaries did criticize Rembrandt for "making more work of the overall subject he preferred to depict than of the individual portraits which he was commissioned to do".[2] However, no discontent on the part of the sitters has been recorded. Rembrandt kept his reputation as portrait artist and later received two equally significant commissions for group portraits from other distinguished Amsterdam citizens, the *Anatomical Demonstration of Dr. Deyman* (1656) and *The Syndics* (1662). The sitters of *The Syndics* lived in the same "block" as the men portrayed in the *Nightwatch*, were also drapers and shared the high office of overseer of the cloth trade and manufacture with some of the men in the *Nightwatch*. They would not have resorted to Rembrandt if their neighbors and peers had not been satisfied with his work.[3] If anyone's vanity was hurt in the *Nightwatch*, he may have realized that in a different way he re-

[2] For Van Hoogstraeten's text, see Chapter V and its note 6. NEUMANN 1902, p. 224 (1924, p. 248) considered the commission an "artistic misunderstanding" since Rembrandt was not interested in a series of portraits; according to him, Rembrandt wanted to tell a story rather than paint a group portrait (1902, p. 273; 1924, p. 297).

[3] VAN EEGHEN 1957, p. 65, established the names of the sitters. My supposition that sharing precinct and profession by the "Syndics" and the sitters of the *Nightwatch* indicated absence of serious criticism, was made but not published in HAVERKAMP-BEGEMANN 1949, p. 16; for "waardijnen van de lakenen" portrayed in the *Nightwatch*, see Chapter II and its note 28. MARTIN 1908, pp. 734, 753, wondered whether the "Syndics" gave Rembrandt the commission out of compassion with the forgotten artist or perhaps because he charged less than others, but was quick to reject these hypotheses himself. It seems fair to say that although Rembrandt did not fall out of favor as a painter of individual portraits during the course of the 1640s and afterwards, his patronage changed. In the 1630s he was the portraitist for many fashionable people, in the 1650s for those who recognized his talent independently of fashion. As a group portraitist he remained esteemed in those circles whose members had personal knowledge of his talents in this respect.

ceived more than he had bargained for, and that a lack of finesse in facial features was compensated by the expression of ideas and associations he cherished. No one before had defined his image as militiaman, and the role and significance of the militia in Amsterdam, as well as Rembrandt. No wonder that according to a contemporary artist, the *Nightwatch* was the basis for Rembrandt's fame.[4]

[4] BALDINUCCI 1686, p. 78: "[Rembrandt] avendo dipinta una gran tela . . . [the *Nightwatch*] . . . si procacciò sì gran nome, che poco migliore l'acquistò giammai altro artefice di quelle parti" ("Having painted a large canvas [the *Nightwatch*] he acquired such a great name that never any artist of that region did little better"). For Baldinucci's reference, see also Introduction.

Bibliography

Listed are those titles of articles and books that have been referred to in the notes. Further bibliography on the *Nightwatch* is found in BENESCH 1935, pp. 89, 90; H. van Hall, *Repertorium voor de geschiedenis der Nederlandsche schilder- en graveerkunst sedert het begin der 12de eeuw tot het eind van 1932.* The Hague, 1936, pp. 563-565; vol. 2 (. . . *tot het eind van 1946*), The Hague 1949, p. 322; and in the *Bibliography of the Netherlands Institute for Art History* (covering the years 1943-1972 and being continued).

ADÈR 1976-77

R. Adèr. *Van Intocht tot Uitvaart* . . . Exhibition Catalogue. Rotterdam, 1976-77.

VAN AGT 1953

J.J.F.W. van Agt. *De Nederlandsche monumenten van geschiedenis en kunst.* Vol. 8, *De provincie Noord Holland,* pt. 1, *Waterland en omgeving.* The Hague, 1953.

D'AILLY 1934

A. E. d'Ailly. *Catalogus van Amsterdamsche plattegronden.* Amsterdam, 1934.

D'AILLY 1947

A. E. d'Ailly. "De Toren Svych Wtrecht, het een en ander over zijn naam en zijn gevelsteen". *Jaarboek* . . . *Amstelodamum,* 41 (1947), pp. 42-50.

ALINGS 1962

H. W. Alings. " 'D'Oyevaer' en 'Het Groninger Wapen', twee verschillende huizen". *Maandblad* . . . *Amstelodamum,* 49 (1962), pp. 85-87.

ALL THE PAINTINGS

Department of Paintings of the Rijksmuseum. *All the Paintings of the Rijksmuseum in Amsterdam, A Completely Illustrated Catalogue.* Amsterdam, 1976.

ALTENA 1955

J. Q. van Regteren Altena. "Quelques remarques sur Rembrandt et la Ronde de Nuit". *Actes du XVIIᵐᵉ Congrès International d'Histoire de l'Art, 1952.* The Hague, 1955, pp. 405-420.

AMSTERDAM 1952

Amsterdam, Rijksmuseum. *Catalogus van goud en zilverwerken* . . . Amsterdam, 1952.

ANONYMOUS 1935
Anonymous. "Rijksmuseum". *Maandblad Amstelodamum*, 22 (1935), pp. 106-108.

ARCHITECTURA MODERNA 1631
Hendrick de Keyser and Salomon de Bray. *Architectura moderna, ofte, Bouwinge van onsen tyd*. Amsterdam 1631. New ed. with introduction by E. Taverne. Soest, 1971.

VAN AUTENBOER 1962
E. van Autenboer. *Volksfeesten en rederijkers 1400-1600*. Ghent, 1962.

BALDINUCCI 1686
F. Baldinucci. *Cominciamento, e progresso dell'arte dell'intagliare in rame* . . . Florence, 1686.

BARBOUR 1950
Violet Barbour. *Capitalism in Amsterdam in the 17th Century*. Baltimore, 1950.

BARLAEUS 1638, 1639
Caspar Barlaeus (Kaspar van Baerle). *Medicea Hospes, sive Descriptio Publicae Gratulationis, qua Serenissimam Augustissimamque Reginam, Mariam de Medicis, excepit Senatus Populusque Amstelodamensis*. Amsterdam, 1638. French trans., *Marie de Medicis entrant dans Amsterdam* . . . , 1638. Dutch trans. *Blyde Inkomst der allerdoorluchtighste Koninginne, Maria de Medicis, t'Amsterdam* . . . , 1639.

BARTSCH 1791
A. Bartsch. *Catalogue raisonné de toutes les estampes qui forment l'œuvre de Rembrandt, et ceux de ces principaux imitateurs. Composé par Gersaint, Helle, Glomy et Yver. Nouvelle édition entièrement refondue, corrigée et considérablement augmentée*. Vienna, 1791.

BAUCH 1957, 1962
K. Bauch. *Rembrandt van Rijn, Die Nachtwache*. Stuttgart, 1957. Dutch translation by R. Limburg, Rotterdam, 1962.

BAUCH 1960
K. Bauch. *Der frühe Rembrandt und seine Zeit* . . . Berlin, 1960.

BAUCH 1967
K. Bauch. "Ikonographischer Stil". In his *Studien zur Kunstgeschichte*. Berlin, 1967, pp. 123-151.

BAUDOUIN 1973-75
F. Baudouin. "De ontwerper van het Kolveniershof te Antwerpen en de datering van dit gebouw". *Gentse Bijdragen tot de Kunstgeschiedenis*, 23 (1973-75), pp. 183-198.

HAVERKAMP-BEGEMANN 1947
E. Haverkamp Begemann. "Nogmaals: de Nachtwacht". *De Groene Amsterdammer*, 71, no. 35 (30 August 1947), p. 7.

HAVERKAMP-BEGEMANN 1949
E. Haverkamp Begemann. *De waardering van Rembrandt door zijn tijdgenoten*. Typescript. Amsterdam, 1949.

HAVERKAMP-BEGEMANN 1970
E. Haverkamp Begemann. "Eine unbekannte Vorzeichnung zum 'Claudius Civilis' ". In *Neue Beiträge zur Rembrandt-Forschung*, ed. O. von Simson and J. Kelch, Berlin, 1973, pp. 31-43. From lecture Berlin, September 1970.

HAVERKAMP-BEGEMANN 1973
E. Haverkamp Begemann. "Rembrandt's *Night Watch* and *The Triumph of Mordecai*". In *Album Amicorum J. G. van Gelder*, ed. J. Bruyn, J. A. Emmens, E. de Jongh, D. P. Snoep, The Hague, 1973, pp. 5-8.

HAVERKAMP-BEGEMANN 1980
E. Haverkamp-Begemann. "Dutch and Flemish Masters of the Seventeenth Century [in San Francisco]". *Apollo*, 111 (1980), pp. 202-211.

BENESCH 1935
O. Benesch. *Rembrandt, Werk und Forschung*. Vienna, 1935.

BENESCH 1954-57
O. Benesch. *The Drawings of Rembrandt* . . . 6 vols. London, 1954-57. New ed., 1973.

BENESCH 1957
O. Benesch. *Rembrandt*. German ed. Geneva, 1957.

BERLIN 1978
Berlin, Staatliche Museen Preussischer Kulturbesitz . . . *Catalogue of Paintings* . . . 2nd revised ed. Berlin, 1978.

BESCHRIJVING BOYMANS 1862
Beschrijving der schilderijen enz. in het Museum te Rotterdam . . . Boymans. Rotterdam, 1862.

BEUDEKER
C. Beudeker. "Oudheden van Amstelredamme". Ms. Archiefdienst, Amsterdam.

BIJTELAAR 1959
B. Bijtelaar. "Het Sint Joriskoor van de Oude Kerk". *Jaarboek van het Genootschap Amstelodamum*, 51 (1959), pp. 15-36.

BILLE 1961
C. Bille. *De Tempel der Kunst* . . . 2 vols. Amsterdam, 1961.

BLAEU 1651
Joan Blaeu. *Toonneel der Steden van de Vereenighde Nederlanden* . . . [Amsterdam, 1651].

BLANKERT 1975-79
A. Blankert, with R. Ruurs. *Amsterdams Historisch Museum, schilderijen daterend van voor 1800, voorlopige catalogus*. Amsterdam, 1975-79.

BOKHOVEN 1976
J. Bokhoven, *Blijde inkomsten in Amsterdam* . . . Exhibition catalogue. Schiedam, 1976.

BONTEMANTEL-KERNKAMP 1897
H. Bontemantel. *De regeeringe van Amsterdam soo in 't civiel als crimineel en militaire (1653-1672)*. Edited by G. W. Kernkamp. Vol. 1. *Werken*

uitgegeven door het Historisch Genootschap gevestigd te Utrecht, third series, vol. 7. The Hague, 1897.

BOON 1969

K. G. Boon. "De Toren 'Swijgh Utrecht' door Rembrandt getekend". *Bulletin van het Rijksmuseum,* 17 (1969), pp. 119-125.

BOON 1978

K. G. Boon. *Netherlandish Drawings of the Fifteenth and Sixteenth Centuries in the Rijksmuseum.* The Hague, 1978.

BREDIUS 1912

A. Bredius. "Iets over de copie van Gerrit Lundens naar Rembrandt's 'Nachtwacht' ". *Oud-Holland,* 30 (1912), pp. 197-200.

BREDIUS 1935

A. Bredius. *Rembrandt. Schilderijen. 630 afbeeldingen. Inleiding en bewerking van Dr. A. Bredius.* Utrecht, 1935. German ed. Vienna, 1937; English ed. London, 1937.

BREDIUS-GERSON 1969

A. Bredius. *Rembrandt, The Complete Edition of the Paintings.* Revised by H. Gerson. London, 1969.

BREDIUS-DE ROEVER 1885

A. Bredius and N. de Roever. Rembrandt, nieuwe bijdragen tot zijn levensgeschiedenis". *Oud-Holland,* 3 (1885), pp. 85-107.

BROM 1936

G. Brom. "Rembrandt in de literatuur". *Neophilologus,* 21 (1936), pp. 161-191.

DE BRUYN KOPS 1965

C. J. de Bruyn Kops. "Vergeten zelfportretten van Govert Flinck en Bartholomeus van der Helst". *Bulletin van het Rijksmuseum,* 13 (1965), pp. 20-29.

DE BRUYN KOPS 1976

C. J. de Bruyn Kops. "The Framing of Rembrandt's Night Watch in the Past and the New Frame". *Bulletin van het Rijksmuseum,* 24 (1976), pp. 99-119.

BUCHELIUS 1928

A. Buchelius. *"Res Pictoriae"* . . . *(1583-1639).* Edited by G. J. Hoogewerff and J. Q. van Regteren Altena. The Hague, 1928.

BULLETIN 1976

Bulletin van het Rijksmuseum, 24, no. 1 and 2 (1976), pp. 1-119. Various articles on the restoration of *The Nightwatch* translated by P. Wardle and G. Schwartz.

CAMPBELL 1978

C. Campbell. "Portretten en kaerteblaeren, Portraits and Playing-cards". *De Kroniek van het Rembrandthuis,* 30, no. 2 (1978), pp. 3-35.

CARROLL 1976

M. D. Carroll. "Rembrandt's 'Nightwatch' and the Iconological Traditions of Militia Company Portraiture in Amsterdam". Harvard University Dissertation, 1976.

CHICAGO 1973

The Art Institute of Chicago. *Rembrandt After Three Hundred Years: A Symposium—Rembrandt and His Followers . . . 1969.* Chicago, 1973. This work appeared in 1975.

CLARK 1966

K. Clark. *Rembrandt and the Italian Renaissance.* New York, 1966.

COMMELIN 1693

C. Commelin. *Vervolg van de Beschrijving der Stadt Amsterdam.* Amsterdam, 1693.

CONST-THOONENDE IVWEEL 1607

Const-Thoonende Ivweel, bij de loflijcke stadt Haerlem, ten versoecke van Trou moet blijcken, in't licht gebracht . . . Zwolle, 1607. With supplement *Haerlems Juweel . . .* Zwolle, 1608.

COPPIER 1922

A. C. Coppier. "La Mutilation d'un chef-d'œuvre, Ce qu'était 'La Ronde de Nuit' au dix-septième siècle". *L'Illustration*, no. 4135 (1922), p. 541.

COSTER 1642

S. Coster. *Beschrivinge vande Blyde Inkoomste . . . van Haare Majesteyt van Groot-britanien . . . Den 20 May, 1642.* Amsterdam, 1642.

DAPPER 1663

O. Dapper. *Historische Beschryving der Stadt Amsterdam . . .* Amsterdam, 1663.

DELAUNAY 1879

L. A. Delaunay. *Étude sur les anciennes compagnies d'archers, d'arbalétriers et d'archebusiers.* Paris, 1879.

DEL COURT-SIX 1903

W. del Court and J. Six. "De Amsterdamsche Schutterstukken." *Oud-Holland*, 21 (1903), pp. 65-84.

VAN DIJK 1758

Jan van Dijk. *Kunst- en historie-kundige beschrijving en aanmerkingen over alle de schilderijen op het stadhuis te Amsterdam . . .* Amsterdam, 1758.

VAN DILLEN 1934

J. G. van Dillen. "De sergeants en schutters van Rembrandt's schuttersoptocht". *Jaarboek Amstelodamum*, 31 (1934), pp. 97-110.

VAN DILLEN 1974

J. G. van Dillen. *Bronnen tot de geschiedenis van het bedrijfsleven en het gildewezen van Amsterdam.* Vol. 3, *1633-1672.* The Hague, 1974.

DUDOK VAN HEEL 1969

S.A.C. Dudok van Heel. "Het maecenaat De Graeff en Rembrandt". *Maandblad Amstelodamum*, 56 (1969), pp. 150-155; 249-253.

DUDOK VAN HEEL 1980

S.A.C. Dudok van Heel. "Doopsgezinden en schilderkunst in de 17e eeuw;

Leerlingen, opdrachtgevers en verzamelaars van Rembrandt". *Doopsgezinde Bijdragen*, N.R. 6 (1980), pp. 105-123.

DUDOK VAN HEEL 1981
S.A.C. Dudok van Heel. "De schutters van Wijk II op Rembrandt's 'Nachtwacht' ". To be published 1981.

DUTCH CITYSCAPE 1977
Opkomst en bloei van het Noordnederlandse stadsgezicht in de 17de eeuw / The Dutch Cityscape in the Seventeenth Century and its Sources. Exhibition catalogue by R. J. Wattenmaker, D. Carasso, B. Bakker, and others. Amsterdam and Toronto, 1977.

DVOŘÁK 1921
M. Dvořák. *De Nachtwacht*. Vienna, 1921.

DYSERINCK 1890
J. Dyserinck. "De Nachtwacht van Rembrandt". *De Gids*, 54 [4th ser. 8] (1890), pp. 235-276.

DYSERINCK 1893
J. Dyserinck. "De vier overlieden van den St. Sebastiaan doelen door Bartholomeus van der Helst". *Oud-Holland*, 11 (1893), pp. 193-210.

EDELMANN 1890
A. Edelmann. *Schützenwesen und Schützenfeste der deutschen Städte vom 13-18 Jahrhundert*. Munich, 1890.

VAN EEGHEN 1957
I. H. van Eeghen. "De Staalmeesters". *Jaarboek . . . Amstelodamum*, 49, (1957), pp. 65-80. Excerpt in *Oud-Holland*, 73 (1958), pp. 80-84.

VAN EEGHEN 1965
I. H. van Eeghen. "De aantekeningen van Jan Vogelesangh". *Maandblad . . . Amstelodamum*, 52 (1965), pp. 4-7.

VAN EEGHEN 1967
I. H. van Eeghen. "De restauratie van Singel 140-142" and "Singel 140-142 en 't Schap". *Maandblad . . . Amstelodamum*, 54 (1967), pp. 88-93 and 133-140.

VAN EEGHEN 1969
I. H. van Eeghen. "De restauratie van het voormalige Anslohofje". *Maandblad . . . Amstelodamum*, 56 (1969), pp. 199-205.

VAN EEGHEN 1971
I. H. van Eeghen. "De Vaandeldrager van Rembrandt". *Maandblad . . . Amstelodamum*, 58 (1971), pp. 173-181.

VAN EEGHEN 1977a
I. H. van Eeghen. "Rubens en Rembrandt kopen van de familie Thijs". *Maandblad . . . Amstelodamum*, 64 (1977), pp. 59-62.

VAN EEGHEN 1977b
I. H. van Eeghen. "Drie portretten van Rembrandt (Bruyningh, Cater, Moutmaker), Vondel en Blaeu". *Jaarboek . . . Amstelodamum*, 69 (1977), pp. 55-72.

ELIAS 1903-1905
J. E. Elias. *De vroedschap van Amsterdam 1578-1795*, 2 vols. Amsterdam, 1903 and 1905.

ELIAS 1937
J. E. Elias. *Het geslacht Elias, de geschiedenis van een Amsterdamsche regentenfamilie*. The Hague, 1937.

ELIAS 1944
J. E. Elias. "Het Fonds Wormskerck". *Jaarboek . . . Amstelodamum*, 40 (1944), pp. 138-161.

VAN ENST KONING 1836
G. van Enst Koning. *Het Huis te Ilpendam en deszelfs voornaamste bezitters*. Amsterdam, 1836.

FOKKE 1748
S. Fokke. *Korte schets . . . van het tegenwoordig gedrag der burgeren . . .* [Amsterdam], 1748.

FRAENKEL 1965
J. J. Fraenkel. "Dürers ets en Erasmus' Eulogium". *Hermeneus*, 37 (1965), pp. 85-89.

FREDERIKS 1892
J. G. Frederiks. "De Luitenant Ruytenburch van Rembrandt's 'Nachtwacht' ". *Maandblad van het Genealogisch-Heraldiek Genootschap De Nederlandsche Leeuw*, 10 (1892), pp. 27, 28.

FREDERIKS 1948
J. W. Frederiks. *Dutch Silver . . .* Vol. 2. The Hague, 1948.

FREMANTLE 1977
K. Fremantle and W. Halsema-Kubes. *Beelden kijken; De kunst van Quellien in het Paleis op de Dam*. Exhibition catalogue. Amsterdam, 1977.

FRIMMEL 1894
T. von Frimmel. *Verzeichnis der Gemälde in Gräflich Schönborn-Wiesentheid'schem Besitze*. Pommersfelden, 1894.

FROMENTIN 1876
E. Fromentin. *Les Maîtres d'autrefois*. Paris, 1876.

FUCHS 1968, 1971
R. H. Fuchs. *Rembrandt en Amsterdam*. Rotterdam, 1968. English trans. *Rembrandt in Amsterdam*, translated by P. Wardle and A. Griffiths, New York, 1971.

DE GELDER 1921
J. J. de Gelder. *Bartholomeus van der Helst*. Rotterdam, 1921.

VAN GELDER 1946
H. E. van Gelder. *Rembrandt*. Amsterdam [1946].

VAN GELDER 1961
J. G. van Gelder. [Review of *Rembrandt*, by Benesch]. *The Burlington Magazine*, 103 (1961), pp. 149-151.

GERSON 1950
   H. Gerson. "Enkele weinig bekende schilderijen in het Museum Amstel-kring." *Oud-Holland*, 65 (1950), pp. 79, 80.
GERSON 1961
   H. Gerson. *Seven Letters by Rembrandt.* The Hague, 1961.
GERSON 1966
   H. Gerson. "De Nachtwacht". *Openbaar Kunstbezit*, 10, no. 1 (1966).
GERSON 1968
   H. Gerson. *Rembrandt Paintings.* Translated by H. Norden. Edited by G. Schwartz. Amsterdam, 1968.
GERSON 1973
   H. Gerson. *Rembrandt, La Ronde de Nuit.* Freiburg, 1973.
GILLET 1913
   L. Gillet. *La Peinture, XVII^c et XVIII^c siècles.* Paris, 1913.
GILTAY 1977
   J. Giltay. "Een onbekende schets van Rembrandt". *Kroniek van het Rembrandthuis*, 29 (1977), pp. 1-9.
GIMPEL 1918
   C. J. G[impel]. "De Doelens te Amsterdam", pt. 2. *Buiten*, 12 (1918), pp. 404-406.
GLÜCK 1907
   G. Glück. *Niederländische Gemälde aus der Sammlung des Herrn Alexander Tritsch in Wien . . .* Vienna, 1907.
TER GOUW 1871
   J. ter Gouw. *De Volksvermaken.* Haarlem, 1871.
TER GOUW 1880
   J. ter Gouw. *Geschiedenis van Amsterdam.* Vol. 2. Amsterdam, 1880.
GUDLAUGSSON 1938
   S. [J.] Gudlaugsson. *Ikonografische Studien über die holländische Malerei und das Theater des 17. Jahrhunderts.* Würzburg, 1938.
HAAK 1969
   B. Haak. *Rembrandt, His Life, His Work, His Time.* New York, 1969.
HAAK 1972
   B. Haak. *Regenten en regentessen, overlieden en chirurgijns; Amsterdamsche groepsportretten van 1600 tot 1835.* Exhibition catalogue. Amsterdam, 1972.
DE HAAS 1927
   K. H. de Haas. *Een meetkundige reconstructie van het oorspronkelijke formaat van Rembrandt's Nachtwacht.* Rotterdam, 1927.
VAN HAMEL 1946
   J. A. van Hamel. *De Eendracht van het Land 1641, Een schilderij van Rembrandt en een tijdvak.* Amsterdam, 1946.
HAVERKAMP-BEGEMANN
   See HAVERKAMP-BEGEMANN under B.

HdG 1906
C. Hofstede de Groot. *Die Urkunden über Rembrandt* . . . The Hague, 1906.

HELD 1950
J. S. Held. "Debunking Rembrandt's Legend". *Art News*, 48 (1950), pp. 21 ff.

HELD 1965
J. S. Held. *Museo de Arte de Ponce, Fundación Luis A. Ferré, Catalogue.* Vol. 1. Ponce, 1965.

HELLINGA 1956
W. G. Hellinga. *Rembrandt fecit 1642* . . . Amsterdam, 1956.

HIJMANS-KUIPER-VELS HEIJN 1976
W. Hijmans, L. Kuiper, A. Vels Heijn. *Rembrandts Nachtwacht, Het vendel van Frans Banning Cocq, de geschiednis van een schilderij.* Leiden, 1976. English trans., *Rembrandt's Nightwatch, The History of a Painting*, translated by P. Wardle, Alphen, 1978.

VAN HOBOKEN 1971
W. J. van Hoboken. "Wat waren kloveniers?". *Maandblad Amstelodamum*, 58 (1971), p. 7.

HOBUSCH 1927
C. Hobusch. *Deutsche Schützenkleinodien, Eine Beschreibung von Schützenkönigsketten und ähnlichen Ehrenstücken* . . . Zerbst 1927.

HOFDIJK 1874-75
W. J. Hofdijk. *De oude schutterij in Nederland* . . . Amsterdam, [1874-75].

HOLLSTEIN 1949
F.W.H. Hollstein, *Dutch and Flemish Etchings, Engravings and Woodcuts.* Vol. 1. Amsterdam, 1949.

VAN HOOGSTRAETEN 1678
S. van Hoogstraeten. *Inleyding tot de Hooge Schoole der Schilderkonst* . . . Rotterdam, 1678.

JACOBS 1887
E. Jacobs. *Die Schützenkleinodien und das Papageienschiessen, ein Beitrag zur Kulturgeschichte des Mittelalters.* Wernigerode, 1887.

JANSE 1969
H. Janse. *Stads- en dorpskerken in Noord-Holland.* Zaltbommel, 1969.

JANSE 1970
H. Janse. "Kloveniers". *Maandblad* . . . *Amstelodamum*, 57 (1970), p. 176.

JOCHEMS 1888
J. A. Jochems. *Amsterdams oude burgervendels (schutterij) 1580-1795* . . . Amsterdam, 1888.

JOCHEMS, CATALOGUS 1888
[J. A. Jochems]. *Catalogus van de boekwerken, pamfletten, enz. behoorende aan de Historische Verzameling der Schutterij te Amsterdam.* Amsterdam,

1888. 2nd enlarged edition, 1890; 1st supplement, 1894; 2nd supplement, 1903.

JOCHEMS 1892

J. A. Jochems. *Beschrijving der prenten [en teekeningen] van de Historische Verzameling der Schutterij te Amsterdam.* Amsterdam, 1892. 1st supplement, 1896; 2nd supplement by A.J.J. Ph. de Haas, 1907.

DE JONGH 1963

E. de Jongh. "Cornelis Ketel . . . Corporaalschap van kapitein . . . Roosecrans . . .". *Openbaar Kunstbezit*, 7, no. 1 (1963).

JUYNBOLL 1954

W. R. Juynboll. "De reis van Sir Joshua Reynolds in de Nederlanden". In *Varia Historica, Aangeboden aan W. W. Byvanck . . . door de Historische Kring te Leiden.* Assen, 1954, pp. 177-185.

KAUFFMAN 1973

C. M. Kauffmann. *Victoria and Albert Museum, Catalogue of Foreign Paintings.* Vol. 1, *Before 1800.* London, 1973.

KERNKAMP 1897

G. W. Kernkamp. *Amsterdam in de zeventiende eeuw.* Vol. 1, pt. 1. Amsterdam 1897, pp. 126-139.

KERNODLE 1947

G. R. Kernodle. *From Art to Theatre, Form and Convention in the Renaissance.* Chicago, 1947.

KIST 1971

Jacob de Gheyn. *The Exercise of Armes.* Commentary by J. B. Kist. Lochem and New York, 1971.

KNUTTEL 1955

G. Knuttel Wzn. "De Nachtwacht en de Gysbrecht". *Nederlands Kunsthistorisch Jaarboek*, 6 (1955), pp. 151-155.

KOK 1967

M. Kok. "Rembrandts Nachtwacht: van feeststoet tot schutterstuk". *Bulletin van het Rijksmuseum*, 15 (1967), pp. 116-121.

KOLLOFF 1854

E. Kolloff, "Rembrandt's Leben und Werke, nach neuen Actenstücken und Gesichtspunkten geschildert". In F. von Raumer, *Historisches Taschenbuch*, 3rd ser., vol. 5, Leipzig, 1854, pp. 401-582. Annotated reprint by C. Tümpel, Hamburg, 1971.

KOOT 1947

T. Koot. *Rembrandt's Nachtwacht in nieuwen luister.* Amsterdam, 1947.

KOOT 1969

T. Koot. *Rembrandt's Night Watch, a Fascinating Story.* Amsterdam, 1969.

KRONIG 1909

J. O. Kronig. "Thomas Hendricksz de Keyser". *Onze Kunst*, 16 (1909), pp. 77-85, 109-126.

KUIPER-HESTERMAN 1976

L. Kuiper and W. Hesterman. "Report on the Restoration of Rembrandt's

Night Watch". *Bulletin van het Rijksmuseum*, 24, no. 1 and 2 (1976), pp. 14-51.

LEEUWENBERG 1973

J. Leeuwenberg and W. Halsema-Kubes. *Beeldhouwkunst in het Rijksmuseum*. Amsterdam, 1973.

LILIENFELD 1914

K. Lilienfeld. *Arent de Gelder, sein Leben und seine Kunst*. The Hague, 1914.

TE LINTUM 1896

C. te Lintum. *Das Haarlemer Schützenwesen, in seiner militärischen und politischen Stellung* . . . Enschedé, 1896.

TE LINTUM 1910

C. te Lintum. *Onze schutter-vendels en schutterijen van vroeger en later tijd, 1550-1908* . . . The Hague, 1910.

LUGT 1933

F. Lugt. *Inventaire général des dessins des écoles du Nord [au Musée du Louvre]* . . . *Ecole hollandaise*. Vol. 3, *Rembrandt* . . . Paris, 1933.

LUNS 1936

H. Luns. *Rembrandt en 'De Nachtwacht'*. Amsterdam, 1936.

VAN LUTTERVELT 1951

R. van Luttervelt. "Het grafbord van Frans Banning Cock". *Maandblad* . . . *Amstelodamum*, 38 (1951), pp. 24-26.

MACLAREN 1960

N. MacLaren. *National Gallery Catalogues, The Dutch School*. London, 1960, pp. 343-349.

MAK 1944

J. J. Mak. *De rederijkers*. Amsterdam, 1944.

MARTIN 1908

W. Martin. "Über den Geschmack des Holländischen Publikums im XVII. Jahrhundert mit Bezug auf die damalige Malerei". *Monatshefte für Kunstwissenschaft*, 1, pt. 1 (1908), pp. 727-753.

MARTIN 1923-24a

W. Martin. "Rembrandt zelf op de Nachtwacht", *Oud-Holland*, 41 (1923-24), pp. 1-4.

MARTIN 1923-24b

W. Martin. "Jan van Ravesteyn's 'Magistraat en Schutters', 1618, en het ontwerp daarvoor". *Oud-Holland*, 41 (1923-24), pp. 193-198.

MARTIN 1933

W. Martin. "Backer's Korporaalschap uit den Kloveniersdoelen te Amsterdam". *Oud-Holland*, 50 (1933), pp. 220-224.

MARTIN 1935-1936

W. Martin. *De Hollandsche schilderkunst in de zeventiende eeuw*. Vol. 1, *Frans Hals en zijn tijd*. Vol. 2, *Rembrandt en zijn tijd*. Amsterdam, 1935-1936.

MARTIN 1947

W. Martin. *Van Nachtwacht tot Feeststoet* . . . Amsterdam and Antwerp, 1947.

MARTIN 1949

W. Martin. "Een sleutel voor Rembrandt's *Nachtwacht*". In *Miscellanea Leo van Puyvelde*, edited by G. Theunis. Brussels, 1949, pp. 225-228.

MARTIN 1951

W. Martin. "Nachtwacht overdenkingen". *Oud-Holland*, 66 (1951), pp. 1-9.

MEIJER 1886

D. C. Meijer Jr. "De Amsterdamsche schutters-stukken in en buiten het nieuwe Rijksmuseum", pts. 2 and 3. *Oud-Holland*, 4 (1886), pp. 198-211, 225-240.

MEIJER 1888

D. C. Meijer Jr. "De Amsterdamsche schutters-stukken in en buiten het nieuwe Rijksmuseum", pt. 4. *Oud-Holland*, 6 (1888), pp. 225-240.

MEIJER 1896

D. C. Meijer. "Wist Rembrandt op welk licht hij zijn schutterstuk schilderde?". *De Nederlandsche Spectator* (1896), pp. 241-242.

MEIJER 1900

D. C. Meijer. "Het verleden van het Sophiaplein". *Amsterdamsch Jaarboekje* (1900), pp. 80-103.

MEIJER 1906

D. C. Meijer Jr. "Frans Banning Cocq en zijn familiealbum". *Eigen Haard* (1906), pp. 426-430, 444-447.

MEISCHKE 1978

R. Meischke. "Buitenverblijven van Amsterdammers voor 1625". *Liber Amicorum I. H. van Eeghen*. In *Jaarboek Amstelodamum*, 70 (1978), pp. 82-106.

MICHEL 1890

E. Michel. "Francesco [sic] Baldinucci et les biographes de Rembrandt". *Oud-Holland*, 8 (1890), pp. 160-172.

MIRANDE-OVERDIEP 1943

Het Schilder-Boek van Carel van Mander. Translated and annotated by A. F. Mirande, G. S. Overdiep, and others. Amsterdam, 1943.

MOES-VETH 1960

A. J. Moes-Veth. "Rembrandt's Claudius Civilis en de Nachtwacht van terzijde beschouwd". *Oud-Holland*, 75 (1960), pp. 143-156.

MOLTKE 1965

J. W. von Moltke. *Govaert Flinck 1615-1660*. Amsterdam, 1965.

MÜLLER HOFSTEDE 1970

C. Müller Hofstede. "Rembrandt und Amsterdam". *Pantheon*, 28 (1970), pp. 240-243.

NEUMANN 1902, 1924

C. Neumann. *Rembrandt*. Heidelberg, 1902. 4th ed., Munich, 1924.

NIEUWENHUYS 1834

C. J. Nieuwenhuys, *A Review of the Lives and Works of some of The most Eminent Painters* . . . Amsterdam, 1834.

NOORDKERK 1744

[H. Noordkerk]. "Verhandeling over de drie schutterijen en de wakende burgerije der stad Amsteldam". Ms. 1744. Amsterdam, Gemeentelijke Archiefdienst. As by J. Wagenaar in *Oud en nieuw, uit de vaderlandsche geschiedenis en letterkunde*, edited by P. Scheltema, vol. 1, Amsterdam, 1844, pp. 41-118.

NOORDKERK 1748

[H. Noordkerk]. *Handvesten ofte Privilegien ende Octroyen* . . . *der stad Amstelredam* . . . Vol. 1. Amsterdam, 1748.

OLDENBOURG 1911

R. Oldenbourg. *Thomas de Keysers Tätigkeit als Maler*. Leipzig, 1911.

OLDEWELT 1942

W.F.H. Oldewelt. *Amsterdamsche Archiefvondsten*. Amsterdam, 1942.

OSINGA 1961

W.P.J. Osinga. [Articles on Ilpendam and Ilpenstein]. *Nieuwe Noord-Hollandse Courant*, 6 Oct.-29 Dec. 1961.

VAN DE PASSE 1643

C. van de Passe. *'t Light der teken en schilder konst* . . . 1st ed. Amsterdam, 1643. Rpt., introduced by J. Bolten and translated by G. Schwartz. Soest, 1973.

PELINCK 1949

[E. Pelinck]. *Stedelijk Museum 'De Lakenhal' Leiden* . . . *catalogus* . . . *Schilderijen* . . . Leiden, 1949.

PLIETZSCH 1939

E. Plietzsch. "Helldunkel um Rembrandt". *Deutsche Rundschau*, 66, pt. 3 (1939), pp. 94-100.

POTGIETER 1844

E. J. Potgieter. *Het Rijksmuseum te Amsterdam*. 1st ed. Amsterdam, 1844. 3rd ed., edited by L. Simons, Amsterdam, 1915.

PRINZ 1971

W. Prinz. *Die Sammlung der Selbstbildnisse in den Uffizien*. Vol. 1, *Geschichte der Sammlung*. Berlin, 1971.

RAM 1964

B. Ram. "Van Schuttersdoelen tot Doelenhotel", *Ons Amsterdam*, 16 (1964), pp. 265-269.

RAVE 1959

P. O. Rave. "Paolo Giovio und die Bildnisvitenbücher der Renaissance". *Jahrbuch der Berliner Museen*. 1 (1959), pp. 119-154.

Reijnsburchs Angier-hoff 1641
Reijnsburchs Angier-hoff beplant met alle de wercken, ende liedekens, die op't selve Rethorices Beroep verhandelt zijn . . . Leyden, 1641.

Reintges 1963
T. Reintges, *Ursprung und Wesen der spätmittelalterlichen Schützengilden.* . . . Rheinisches Archiv . . . 58. Bonn, 1963.

Renier 1944
G. J. Renier. *The Dutch Nation*. London, 1944.

Reznicek 1961
E.K.J. Reznicek. *Hendrick Goltzius als Zeichner*. Utrecht, 1961.

Reznicek 1977
E.K.J. Reznicek. "Opmerkingen bij Rembrandt". *Oud-Holland*, 91 (1977), pp. 75-107.

Riegel 1882
H. Riegel. "Zur Geschichte der Schütter- und Regentenstücke". In H. Riegel, *Beiträge zur niederländischen Kunstgeschichte*. Vol. 1, *Abhandlungen und Erforschungen zur niederländischen Kunstgeschichte*, Berlin, 1882, pp. 105-162.

Riegl 1902
See Riegl 1931.

Riegl 1931
A. Riegl. *Das holländische Gruppenporträt*. Vienna, 1931. Text and most illustrations first published in *Jahrbuch der kunsthist. Sammlungen des Allerhöchsten Kaiserhauses*, 23 (1902), pp. 71-278.

De Roever 1887
[N. de Roever]. "Twee trommelslagers . . .". *Jaarboekje voor de Schutterij te Amsterdam* (1887), p. 38.

Rosenberg 1895
A. Rosenberg. *Teniers der Jüngere*. Bielefeld and Leipzig, 1895.

Schaap 1936
H. P. Schaap. "De Brielsche schilder Maerten van der Fuijck en diens Doelenstukken". *Oud-Holland*, 103 (1936), pp. 263-267.

Schadt-kiste 1620
De Schadt-kiste der Philosophen ende Poeten waer inne te vinden syn veel schoone leerlycke blosoenen, refereynen ende liedekens . . . Mechelen . . . 1620. Mechelen, 1621.

Schaep 1630-50s
Gerard Schaep Pietersz. "Begin, vervolg, ende verandering van Schutterien, vaendelen, vande Burgerien inde Wijcken." Ms. 1630-50s. Amsterdam, Gemeentlijke Archiefdienst. Also partly published in "De schilderijen in de drie doelens te Amsterdam, beschreven door G. Schaep, 1653", by P. Scheltema, *Aemstel's Oudheid*, 7 (1885), pp. 121-141.

Schatten 1966-67
Schatten van de Vlaamse schuttersgilden. Exhibition catalogue by W. van Nespen and others. Antwerp-Brussels, 1966-67.

SCHELTEMA 1844
P. Scheltema. *Oud en nieuw, uit de vaderlandsche geschiedenis en letter-kunde.* Vol. 1. Amsterdam, 1844.

SCHELTEMA 1853
P. Scheltema, *Rembrand, redevoering over het leven en de verdiensten van Rembrand van Rijn* . . . Amsterdam, 1853.

SCHELTEMA 1885
P. Scheltema. "De schilderijen in de drie doelens te Amsterdam, beschreven door G. Schaep, 1653". *Aemstel's Oudheid* . . . , 7 (1885), pp. 121-141.

VAN SCHENDEL-MERTENS 1947
A. van Schendel and H. H. Mertens. "De restauraties van Rembrandt's Nachtwacht". *Oud-Holland*, 62 (1947), pp. 1-52.

SCHMIDT-DEGENER 1912
F. Schmidt-Degener. "Een voorstudie voor de *Nachtwacht*: de *Eendracht van het land*". *Onze Kunst*, 21 (1912), pp. 1-20.

SCHMIDT-DEGENER O-H 1914
F. Schmidt-Degener. "Portretten door Rembrandt". *Oud-Holland*, 32 (1914), pp. 217-224.

SCHMIDT-DEGENER 1914a
F. Schmidt-Degener. "Het genetische probleem van de Nachtwacht. [Part I] Inleiding". *Onze Kunst*, 26 (1914), pp. 1-17.

SCHMIDT-DEGENER 1914b
F. Schmidt-Degener. "Het genetische probleem van de Nachtwacht. II. Welken vorm gaf Rembrandt aan de Nachtwacht?". *Onze Kunst*, 26 (1914), pp. 37-54.

SCHMIDT-DEGENER 1916a
F. Schmidt-Degener. "Het genetische probleem van de Nachtwacht. III. De uitvloeisels van het onderwerp", section 1. *Onze Kunst*, 29 (1916), pp. 61-84.

SCHMIDT-DEGENER 1916b
F. Schmidt-Degener. "Het genetische probleem van de Nachtwacht. III. De uitvloeisels van het onderwerp", section 2. *Onze Kunst*, 30 (1916), pp. 29-56.

SCHMIDT-DEGENER 1917a
F. Schmidt-Degener. "Het genetische probleem van de Nachtwacht. III. De uitvloeisels van het onderwerp", section 3. *Onze Kunst*, 31 (1917), pp. 1-32.

SCHMIDT-DEGENER 1917b
F. Schmidt-Degener. "Het genetische probleem van de Nachtwacht. IV. De compositie, Inleiding". *Onze Kunst*, 31 (1917), pp. 97-102.

SCHMIDT-DEGENER 1942
F. Schmidt-Degener. *Compositie-problemen in verband met Rembrandt's schuttersoptocht.* Proceedings of the Dutch Academy of Sciences, n.s., vol. 47, pt. 1. Amsterdam, 1942.

SCHNEIDER 1921

H. Schneider. "Der Maler Jan Tengnagel". *Oud-Holland*, 39 (1929), pp. 11-27.

SCHÖNE 1973

W. Schöne. "Rembrandts Mann mit dem Goldhelm". *Jahrbuch der Akademie der Wissenschaften in Göttingen 1972*, Göttingen, 1973, pp. 33-99. With mimeographed supplement, 1973, pp. 1-11.

SCHOTEL 1871

G.D.J. Schotel. *Geschiedenis der rederijkers in Nederland*. 2 vols. 2nd ed. Rotterdam, 1871.

SERLIN 1671

W. Serlin. *Ein Ehrliches Frey-Kunst- und Ritterliches Haupt-Schissen in der Mussquet . . .* Frankfort, 1671.

SICKESZ 1864

C. J. Sickesz. *De Schutterijen in Nederland . . .* Utrecht, 1864.

SIX 1893

J. Six. "Opmerkingen omtrent eenige Meesterwerken in 's Rijks Museum". *Oud-Holland*, 11 (1893), pp. 96-104.

SIX 1906

J. Six. "Een schutterstuk van Cornelis Ketel". *Oud-Holland*, 24 (1906), pp. 105-106.

SIX 1909

J. Six. "Een teekening van Bartholomeus van der Helst". *Oud-Holland*, 27 (1909), pp. 142-148.

SIX 1919

J. Six. "Plaats en tijd van Rembrandt's Nachtwacht". *Onze Kunst*, 35 (1919), pp. 1-20.

SLATKES 1973

L. J. Slatkes. [Book Review of] C. White and K. G. Boon, *Rembrandt's Etchings . . .* , and C. White, "*Rembrandt as an Etcher . . .*". *Art Quarterly*, 36 (1973), pp. 250-263.

SLIVE 1953

S. Slive. *Rembrandt and His Critics 1630-1730*. The Hague, 1953.

SLIVE 1970

S. Slive. *Frans Hals*. Vol. 1. London, 1970.

VAN DER SLOOT-KIST 1970

R.B.F. van der Sloot and J. B. Kist. "Iets over de degengevesten in Hoorn rond het jaar 1650 . . .". *Armamentaria*, 5 (1970), pp. 9-30.

SNOEP 1975

D. P. Snoep. *Praal en propaganda; Triumfalia in de Noordelijke Nederlanden in de 16de en 17de eeuw*. Alphen aan de Rijn, 1975.

SONNENBURG 1978

H. von Sonnenburg, "Rembrandts 'Segen Jakobs' ". *Maltechnik Restauro*, 84 (1978), pp. 217-241.

STARING 1965

A. Staring. "Een raadselachtige kamerbeschildering". *Bulletin Rijksmuseum*, 13 (1965), pp. 1-13.

STECHOW 1966

W. Stechow. *Dutch Landscape Painting*. London, 1966.

STERCK 1900

J.F.M. Sterck. "De inventaris van 'de brieven, 't Silverwerck ende Juwelen doude schutterie toebehoorende', A° 1569". *Amsterdamsch Jaarboekje* (1900), pp. 106-123.

STERCK 1927

J.F.M. Sterck. "Een pastoorsportret op Rembrandt's *Nachtwacht*". In *Rondom Vondel* . . . , Amsterdam, 1927, pp. 41-56.

DE STOPPELAAR 1886

G. N. de Stoppelaar. *Het Schuttengilde van den edelen Handboog confrèrie van St. Sebastiaan te Middelburg*. [Middelburg 1886.]

STRAUSS-VAN DER MEULEN 1980

W. J. Strauss and M. van der Meulen. *The Rembrandt Documents*. New York, 1980.

VAN THIEL 1965

P.J.J. van Thiel. "De Grebbers regels van de kunst". *Oud-Holland*, 80 (1965), pp. 126, 131.

TÓTH-UBBENS 1975

M. M. Tóth-Ubbens. "De Barbier van Amsterdam". *Antiek*, 10 (1975), pp. 381-411.

TÜMPEL 1970

C. Tümpel. "Beobachtungen zur 'Nachtwache' ". *Neue Beiträge zur Rembrandt-Forschung*, edited by O. von Simson and J. Kelch, Berlin, 1973, pp. 162-175. Lecture in Berlin, September 1970.

TÜMPEL 1977

C. Tümpel. *Rembrandt in Selbstzeugnissen und Bilddokumenten*. Rowohlts Monographien, no. 251. Reinbek bei Hamburg, 1977. 2nd ed., 1979.

VAN VALKENBURG 1958-62

C. C. van Valkenburg. "De Haarlemse schuttersstukken . . .". *Haerlem*, *Jaarboek* (1958), pp. 59-68; (1959), pp. 119-128; (1960), pp. 117-125; (1961), pp. 47-76; (1962), 89-98.

VEDER 1914

W. R. Veder. *Het Archief der familie de Graeff*. 1914.

VERREYT 1897

C.C.V. Verreyt. "Rembrandt beoordeeld in het begin dezer eeuw". *De Navorscher*, 30 (1897), pp. 541-544.

VETH 1914

J. Veth. "Ouds en nieuws over Rembrandts Nachtwacht". *De Gids*, 78, pt. 3 (1914), pp. 550-567.

LA VIE EN HOLLANDE 1967
   La Vie en Hollande au XVIIe siècle . . . Exhibition catalogue. Paris, Musée
   des Arts Décoratifs, 1967.
VOLLARD 1938
   A. Vollard. *En écoutant Cézanne, Degas, Renoir.* Paris, 1938.
VOSMAER 1877
   C. Vosmaer. *Rembrandt, sa vie et ses œuvres.* 2nd ed. The Hague, 1877.
VAN DE WAAL 1956a
   H. van de Waal. "De Staalmeesters en hun legende". *Oud-Holland,* 71
   (1956), pp. 61-107. English translation in *Steps towards Rembrandt,* by
   P. Wardle and A. Griffiths, edited by R. H. Fuchs, Amsterdam and London,
   1974, pp. 247-292.
VAN DE WAAL 1956b
   H. van de Waal. "Rembrandt 1956". *Museum, Tijdschrift voor filologie
   en geschiedenis* . . . , 61 (1956), pp. 193-209.
WAETZOLDT 1908
   W. Waetzoldt. *Die Kunst des Porträts.* Leipzig, 1908.
WAGENAAR 1765, 1767
   Jan Wagenaar. *Amsterdam in zyne opkomst, aanwas* . . . Vols., 2 and 3.
   Amsterdam, 1765, 1767.
WEGENER SLEESWIJK 1970
   C. Wegener Sleeswijk. *Vijftien jaar restauratie in de Oude Kerk te Am-
   sterdam.* Amsterdam, 1970.
WEISBACH 1926
   W. Weisbach. *Rembrandt.* Berlin and Leipzig, 1926.
WHITE 1964
   Christopher White. *Biografieën in woord en beeld, Rembrandt.* With a
   preface by K. G. Boon and notes by H. F. Wijnman. Translated by J. M.
   Komter. The Hague, 1964.
WIJNBEEK 1944
   D. Wijnbeek. *De Nachtwacht, de historie van een meesterwerk.* Amsterdam,
   1944.
WISHNEVSKY 1967
   R. Wishnevsky. "Studien zum 'portrait historié' in den Niederlanden". Mu-
   nich University Dissertation, 1967.
WORP 1904, 1908
   J. A. Worp. *Geschiedenis van het drama en van het tooneel in Nederland.*
   2 vols. Groningen, 1904, 1908.

Index

Illustrations

1. Rembrandt, *The Nightwatch*, 1642. Amsterdam, Rijksmuseum.

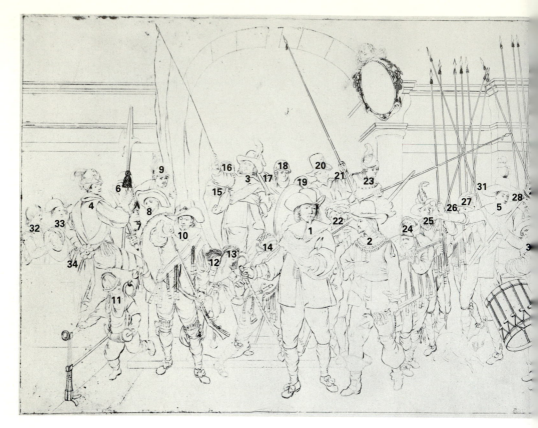

2. Key to the *Nightwatch* on a reproduction of the first state of the print by Lambertus Claessens, 1797, Amsterdam, Rijksmuseum.

*1. Frans Banning Cocq as Captain
*2. Wilhem van Ruytenburgh as Lieutenant
*3. Jan Visscher as Ensign
*4. Reijer Engelen as Sergeant
*5. Rombout Kemp as Sergeant
 6. Musketeer
*7. Helmeted Man with Sword
*8. Man with Shield and Sword (Herman Wormskerck?)
*9. Musketeer with Furket and Slow-match
*10. Musketeer Loading his Musket
 11. Powder Boy
 12. Girl in Gold and Blue
 13. Girl in Gold and Blue
 14. Shooting Youth
 15. Head of a Man
 16. Head of a Man
 17. Self-Portrait
*18. Helmeted Man with Shield and Sword

 19. Head of a Man
*20. Pikeman
 21. Head of a Man
*22. Man Trying to Divert Musket
*23. Pikeman
*24. Musketeer Blowing the Pan
*25. Pikeman (Jacob de Roy?)
 26. Head of a Pikeman
 27. Musketeer
 28. Head of a Man
*29. Pikeman
 30. Drummer (Jacob Jorisz?)
 31. Head of a Man
*32. Bareheaded Musketeer
   (in section removed ca. 1715)
*33. Man with a Hat
   (in section removed ca. 1715)
 34. Child (in section removed ca. 1715)

* Portraits of eighteen officers and members of the militia company of Captain Frans Banning Cocq.

3. Gerrit Lundens, *Copy after the Nightwatch*, ca. 1649. Amsterdam, Rijksmuseum, on loan from the National Gallery, London.

4. Rembrandt, *Studies of an Officer and Other Figures*. Drawing. Paris, Musée du Louvre, Walter Gay Bequest.

5. Rembrandt, *Study of an Officer*. Drawing. Budapest, Szépmüvészeti Múzeum.

6. *The Nightwatch* (detail: Frans Banning Cocq as captain and Wilhem van Ruytenburgh as lieutenant).

7. *The Nightwatch* (detail: militia-man charging his musket).

8. *The Nightwatch* (detail: girls dressed in gold and blue).

9. *The Nightwatch* (detail: girls dressed in gold and blue).

10. *The Nightwatch*
(detail: Frans Banning Cocq).

11. Bartholomeus van der Helst, *The Governors of the Handboogsdoelen* (detail: Frans Banning Cocq), 1653. Amsterdam, Rijksmuseum.

12. *The Nightwatch* (detail: Wilhem van Ruytenburgh).

13. *The Nightwatch* (detail: Van Ruytenburgh's partisan).

14. *The Nightwatch* (detail: Van Ruytenburgh's partisan). X-ray photograph.

15. *The Nightwatch* (detail: Jan Visscher as ensign, and a militiaman; between them, Rembrandt).

16. *The Nightwatch* (detail: Reijer Engelen as sergeant).

17. *The Nightwatch* (detail: Rombout Kemp as sergeant).

18. Jacob Backer, *The Regents of the Nieuwe Zijds Huiszittenhuis* (detail: Rombout Kemp). Amsterdam, Rijksmuseum.

19. *The Nightwatch* (detail: A citizen and Herman Wormskerck [?] as militiamen).

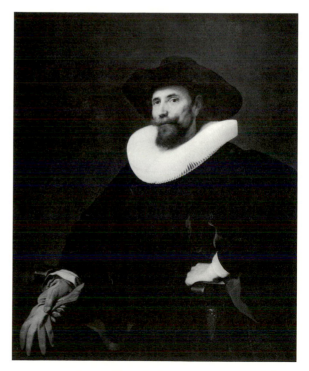

20. Bartholomeus van der Helst,
Herman Wormskerck (?), 1653.
Ponce, Museo de Arte.

21. *The Nightwatch*
(detail: militiaman
deflecting a shot).

22. *The Nightwatch* (detail: militiaman
blowing off the pan of his musket).

23. *The Nightwatch* (detail: militiaman).

24. *The Nightwatch* (detail: militiaman holding furket and slow match).

25. *The Nightwatch* (detail: militiaman, partly hidden behind arm).

26. Gerrit Lundens, *Copy after the Night-watch* (detail: two militiamen and a child).

27. *The Nightwatch* (detail: signature).

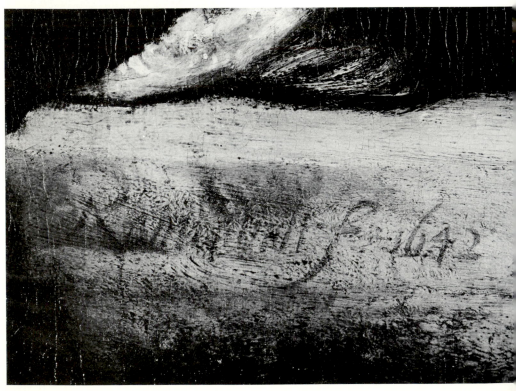

28. *The Nightwatch* (detail: shield with names).

29. *The Nightwatch* (detail: pow-derboy).

30. *The Nightwatch* (detail: drum-mer).

31. Isaac de Moucheron, *Firework Island on Amstel River on the Occasion of the Visit of the Muscovite Ambassadors*, 1697. Etching. Rotterdam, Atlas van Stolk.

32. *The Kloveniersdoelen*. Photograph, ca. 1870. Amsterdam, Gemeentelijke Archiefdienst.

33. Rembrandt, *The Tower Svych Wtrecht*, 1650s. Drawing. Amsterdam, Rijksmuseum.

34. Unidentified artist, *The Groote Sael of the Kloveniersdoelen*. Amsterdam, Rijksmuseum.

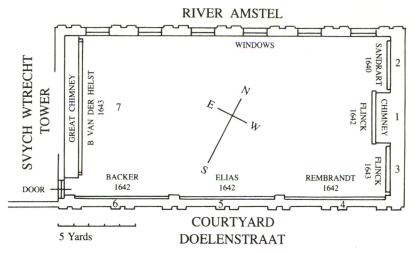

RIVER AMSTEL

WINDOWS

SANDRART 1640 — 2

CHIMNEY / FLINCK 1642 — 1

FLINCK 1643 — 3

SVYCH WTRECHT TOWER

GREAT CHIMNEY

B VAN DER HELST 1643 — 7

N
E — W
S

BACKER 1642

ELIAS 1642

REMBRANDT 1642

DOOR

6 5 4

5 Yards

COURTYARD
DOELENSTRAAT

35. Groundplan of the Groote Sael of the Kloveniersdoelen Indicating Location of the Paintings.
1. Govert Flinck, *The Four Governors of the Kloveniersdoelen*; 2. Joachim von Sandrart, *The Company of Captain Cornelis Bicker*. 3. Govert Flinck, *The Company of Captain Albert Bas*.
4. Rembrandt, *The Nightwatch*. 5. Nicolaes Eliasz, called Pickenoy, *The Company of Captain Jan van Vlooswijck*. 6. Jacob Adriaensz Backer, *The Company of Captain Cornelis de Graeff*.
7. Bartholomeus van der Helst, *The Company of Captain Roelof Bicker*.

36. Govert Flinck, *The Governors of the Kloveniersdoelen*, 1642. Amsterdam, Rijksmuseum.

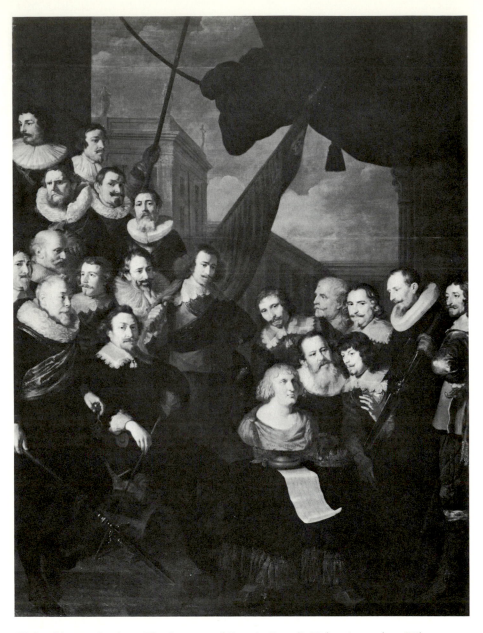

37. Joachim von Sandrart, *The Company of Captain Cornelis Bicker*. Amsterdam, Rijksmuseum.

38. Govert Flinck, *The Company of Captain Albert Bas*, 1645. Amsterdam, Rijksmuseum.

39. *The Nightwatch*, as seen from the center of the assembly hall of the Kloveniersdoelen.

40. Nicolaes Eliasz, called Pickenoy, *The Company of Captain Jan van Vlooswijck*, 1642. Amsterdam, Rijksmuseum.

41. Jacob Backer, *The Company of Captain Cornelis de Graeff*, 1642, Amsterdam, Rijksmuseum

42. Bartholomeus van der Helst, *The Company of Captain Roelof Bicker*, 1639. Amsterdam, Rijksmuseum.

43. Jacob Colijns(?), *Copy after the Nightwatch*, ca. 1649-1655. Drawing after Lundens' copy, in album of Frans Banning Cocq. Amsterdam, Rijksmuseum, on loan from private collection.

44. Gerrit Lundens, *The Governors of the Handboogsdoelen.* Copy after painting by Van der Helst. Paris, Musée du Louvre.

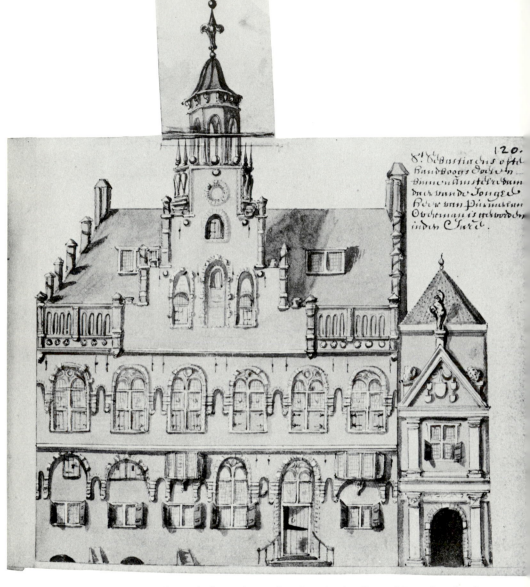

45. Unidentified Artist, *The Handboogsdoelen in Amsterdam*. Drawing in album of Frans Banning Cocq. Amsterdam, Rijksmuseum, on loan from private collection.

46. *Banning Cocq's House, De Dolphijn, at Singel 140-142, Amsterdam (after restoration).*

47. Unidentified artist, *Banning Cocq's Country Estate, Ilpenstein*. Drawing in album of Frans Banning Cocq. Amsterdam, Rijksmuseum, on loan from private collection.

48. Unidentified artist, *Stained Glass Window Presented by Frans Banning Cocq to Church in Purmerland in 1642*. Drawing in album of Frans Banning Cocq. Amsterdam, Rijksmuseum, on loan from private collection.

49. Artus Quellien or his studio, *Coats of Arms of Frans Banning Cocq and his Ancestors*, ca. 1654-58. Terracotta and wood. Amsterdam, Rijksmuseum.

ORDONNANTIEN

Geſtatueert by de E. Heer. van de Krijgſ-
Rade voo2 de twintigh Vaendelen Schuttery binnen deſer Stede
Amſterdam/ waer na ſy luyden hun hebben te reguleren.

I.

Erſtelijck ſullen alle daghen twee Compagnien waken/het eene op den Dam/ ende het ander op Sint Antonis Marckt.

II.

Die op den Dam de Nacht-wacht hebben/ ſullen aldaer met een half Vaendel blijven houden de Hooft-wacht/ ende een Co2poraelſchap aen het Weſt-Indiſche Huys ende Stads Herbergh/ ende een Co2poraelſchap aen de Heylige Weghs Poo2t/ ende des daegs Dag-wacht een half Co2poraelſchap aen de Poo2t/ ende een half Co2poraelſchap aen de Stads Herbergh voo2 de middagh/ ende het ander Co2poraelſchap na de middagh in voegen als voren. **III.**

Van gelijcken oock het Vaendel dat de wacht heeft op Sint Antonis Marckt/ ſal aldaer het halve Vaendel blijven/ houden de Hooft-wacht/ ende een Co2poraelſchap trecken aen de Sint Antonis Poo2t/ ende het ander aen de Reguliers Poo2t/ ende des daeghs een half Co2poraelſchap Dagh-wacht aen de Sint Antonis Poo2t/ ende aen de Regulie rs Poo2t/ het eene Co2poraelſchap voo2 de middagh/ ende het ander Co2poraelſchap na de middagh ut ſupra. **IV.**

Sullen oock alle avonden de verloſſinghe geſchieden p2ecijs ten ſeven uren/ op pene van vijfentwintigh guldens boeten/ te betalen aen 't Vaendel die verloſt wert/ by 't Vaendel dat te laet komt. **V.**

De Boeten die over 't verſupm van de Wacht vallen/ ſullen van nu voo2taen weſen des nacht dertigh ſtupers/ ende des daeghs twintigh ſtupers voo2 yeder perſoon. **VI.**

De p2ovooſten ſullen alle daghen tuſſchen vier en vijf uuren na de middagh/ op het Stadthuys het woo2t halen in een beſloten biljet/ ende aen hunne reſpective Capiteynen b2engen/ ende alle dagen 's mo2gens ten acht uren hunne Capiteynen de Wachten aenſeggen. **VII.**

Alle Paſſagiers in de Stadt komende/ Officieren of Soldaten zijnde/ doo2 de Sch2ijvers van de Compagnie te doen aenteyckenen haer namen ende Herbergen/ende doo2 de Poo2tiers ende Boom-ſtuyters Burgermeeſteren des avondts doen b2engen. **VIII.**

Ende ſullen deſe Wachten haer aenvanck nemen op Maendag den achtſten Auguſti 1650, by de Manhafte Capiteynen Cornelis van Dronckelaer ende Franck van der Meer, ende ſoo voo2ts ſucceſſivelijck na het regiſter van de Krijghs-Rade alle nachten twee Vaendelen. **IX.**

De Capiteyn Majoo2 ende andere Capiteynen van de Soldaten/ ſullen alle Poo2ten/ Boomen en Co2ps du gardens/ die by de Burgers niet beſet zijn/ hebben waer te nemen. **X.**

De Hooft-Officieren ende Adelbo2ſten incluys/ by p2oviſie met het zijdt-ghweer te gaen/ op pene daer toe ſtaende. **XI.**

De Co2poraelſchappen die des nachts de Hooft-wachten hebben/ ſullen des mo2gens ten huyſe van de Heer Burgermeeſter de ſleutelen halen/ ende de ſelfde voo2ts de Dagh-wacht hebben waer te nemen/ ende op hunne Rendebous-plaets gekomen zijnde/ ſullen d'andere alſdan eerſt mogen aftrecken.

Ende dit alles onbermindert de groote ende kleyne O2donnantien op 't ſtuck van de Wachten gemaeckt/ ofte die namaels noch gemaeckt ſouden mogen werden.

Aldus goet gevonden gearreſteert by mijn E. Heeren van den Krijgs-Rade binnen deſer Stede Amſterdam den 7 Auguſti 1650. Onder ſtont

F. Banninck Cocq.

AMSTERDAM, Voo2 Jooſt Hartgers, Boek-verkoper op den Dam/bezijden 't Stadhuys. 1650.

50. *Ordinance to Militia of Amsterdam Issued over Signature of Frans Banning Cocq,* 1650. Amsterdam, Koninklijk Oudheidkundig Genootschap.

51. *House Soli Deo Gloria, at Herengracht 166, Amsterdam, Bought in 1642
by Herman Wormskerck, Portrayed in the Nightwatch.*

52a. Balthasar Florisz, *Map of Amsterdam* (detail: second precinct, residence of men portrayed in *The Night-watch*). Engraving. Amsterdam, Gemeentelijke Archiefdienst.

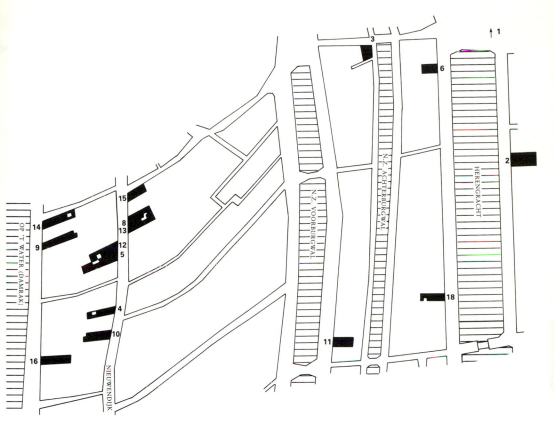

52b. Key to Map, Indicating 1642 residences of fourteen of the eighteen men portrayed in *The Nightwatch*, in order of their listing on the shield of the painting (Established by S.A.C. Dudok van Heel).

1. Frans Banning Cocq—Singel, In 'De Dolphijn' [nos. 140-142] (outside map area); 2. Wilhem van Ruytenburgh—Herengracht, In ' 't blaeuwe huys' [nos. 196-198] (owned by his mother-in-law, outside map area); 3. Jan Cornelisz Visscher—N. Z. Achterburgwal (East), Corner Molsteeg (North) (owned by his grandmother [Spuistraat 125ª]); 4. Rombout Kemp—Nieuwendijk, In 'de Brabantsche Wagen' [no. 199]; 5. Reijer Jansz Engelen—Nieuwendijk, In 'de vergulde Voetboogh' [no. 189]; 6. Barent Hermansz Bolhamer—Singel, near Jan Rodenpoortstoren; 7. Jan Adriaensen Keyser (location of house unknown); 8. Elbert Willem Louwerisz (Elbert Willemsz Swedenrijck)—Nieuwendijk, In 'de drie vergulde Stockvissen' [no. 196]; 9. Jan Claesz Leijdeckers—'Op 't Water', opposite the Papenbrug, In 'de vergulde cam' [Damrak, no. 81] (rented); 10. Jan Ockers—Nieuwendijk, In 'het groene Claverblat' [no. 181]; 11. Jan Pietersz Bronckhorst—N. Z. Voorburgwal, In 'de Blaeuwe Pot' [no. 94]; 12. Harmen Jacobsz Wormskerck—In 'het Groninger Wapen', later called 'de Oyevaer' [no. 201]; 13. Jacob Dircksz de Roy—Nieuwendijk, In ' 't vergulde Spoor' [no. 196]; 14. Jan Aertsz van der Heede—'Op 't Water', North Corner of Zoutsteeg [Damrak, no. 84] (rented); 15. Walich Schellingwou—Nieuwendijk, North Corner of Gravenstraat [no. 198] (property of his step-mother); 16. Jan Brugman—'Op 't Water', In ' 't gulden Hooft' ('de vergulde Hardebol') [Damrak, no. 64]; 17. Claes van Cruysbergen—exact location of house rented by him 'Op 't Water' [Damrak] not known; 18. Paulus Harmensz van Schoonhoven—Singel [no. 97].

53. *Name Stone of the Tower Svych Wtrecht.* Early sixteenth century. Amsterdam, Historisch Museum.

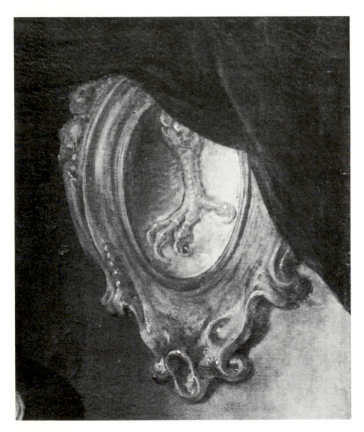

54. Govert Flinck, *The Governors of the 'Kloveniersdoelen,'* 1642 (detail: emblem of the Kloveniers). Amsterdam, Rijksmuseum.

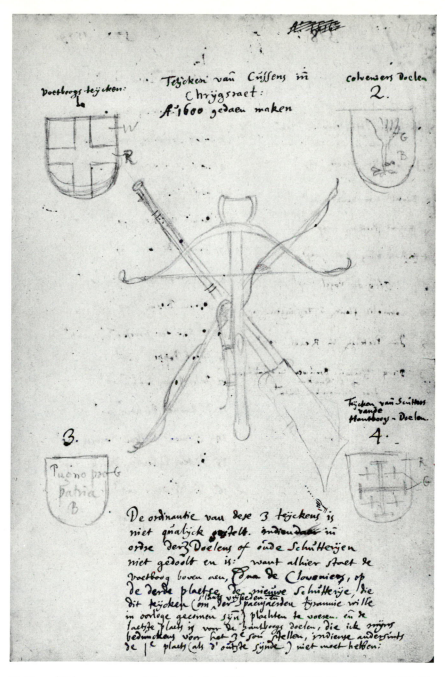

55. Gerard Schaep, *Pillow of the Amsterdam Krijgsraad*, ca. 1600. Drawing, ca. 1630-50. Amsterdam, Gemeente-Archief.

Aen de edele Gebroederſchap der ſchutters-
orde van Sint Michiel, in de Kolveniers doelen.

 E groote Aertsengel Sint Michiel
Bewaeck' zijn trouwe ſchutteryen,
Daer 't edel ſchutters lot op viel:
Een orde van aeloude tijen
Gewettight om den Aemſtelheer,
Zijn burgery, en recht, en wallen
Door 't handelen van haer geweer,
De Kolſbus, tegens 't overvallen
Van laege, of uiterlijck gewelt,
Te veiligen, en af te keeren,
Als 't goet, en bloet, en vryheit gelt.
De Griecken en Romainen leeren
Van outs de wapenhandeling
En 't ridderſpel hun brave zoonen,
Daer elck den palm en prijs ontfing,
Gewaden, penningen, of kroonen.
Zoo ſchiet geen Kolvenier in 't wilt.
Zoo eert de Klaeu den ſchuttersſchilt.

S. D.

't Amſterdam, Ter Druckerye van THOMAS FONTEIN, by de Deventer Houtmarckt. 1659.

56. Unidentified artist, *Eulogy of th*
Order of St. Michael, 1659. Poem by
S. D. Amsterdam, Doelenhotel.

57. Dirck Jacobsz, *Militiamen of th*
Kloveniers Guild (detail: claw and
musket, embroidered emblem of the
Kloveniers).

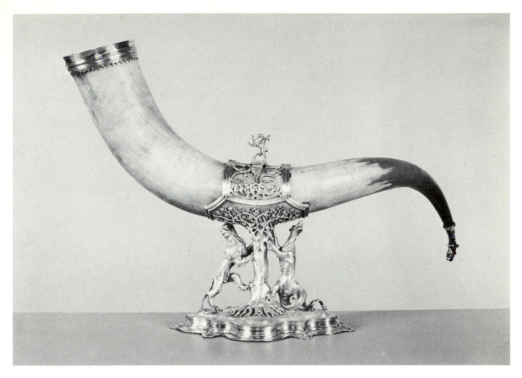

58. *Ceremonial Drinking Horn of the Kloveniers.* Amsterdam, Rijksmuseum.

59. *Ceremonial Collar of the "King" of the Kloveniers, with detail.* Amsterdam, Rijksmuseum.

60. *Ceremonial Partisan*, 1626. Made in Amsterdam for King Gustavus II Adolphus. Stockholm, Kun. Livrustkammaren.

61. *Musket.* Seventeenth century, made in Amsterdam. Stockholm, Kun. Livrustkammaren.

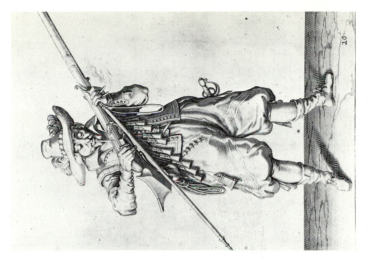

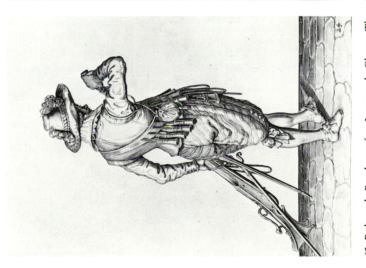

62. Robert de Baudous after Jacques de Gheyn, *Three Postures from "The Exercise of Armes"*, 1607. New Haven, Yale University, Beinecke Library.

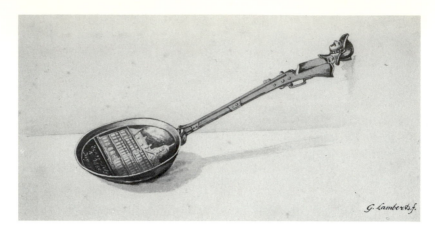

63. Gerrit Lamberts, *Silver Spoon Offered to Militiamen in 1655 at the Occasion of the Opening of the Town Hall.* Drawing. Amsterdam, Historische Verzameling van de Schutterij, K.O.G.

64. *Bandolier with Cartridges for Musket Charges.* Seventeenth century. Amsterdam, Rijksmuseum.

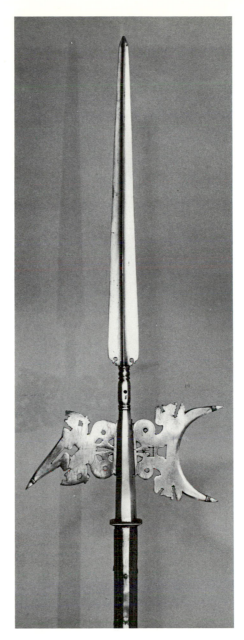

66. *Halberd, Used by the Amsterdam Militia.* Northern Netherlands, Seventeenth century. Leiden, Kon. Nederlands Leger- en Wapenmuseum "Generaal Hoefer".

65. *Furket.* Northern Netherlands, Seventeenth century. Leiden, Kon. Nederlands Leger- en Wapenmuseum "Generaal Hoefer".

67. Unidentified artist, *Procession of Amsterdam Militia on the Dam Square*, ca. 1620-30. Pommersfelden, Graf von Schönborn'sche Gemäldegalerie.

68. Unidentified artist, *Joyous Entry of Maria de'Medici in Amsterdam*. Etching. Amsterdam, Rijksmuseum.

69. *Joyous Entry of Maria de'Medici into Amsterdam* (detail).

70. Sybrant van Beest, *Departure of Queen Henrietta Maria from Scheveningen*, 1643 (detail). The Hague, Haags Gemeentemuseum.

Oude Camer tot
Haerlem.

71. Unidentified artist, *Entry of the Chamber of Rhetoric De Pellicanisten in Haarlem in 1606.* West Berlin, Staatliche Museen, Kunstbibliothek.

72. *Entry of the Chamber of Rhetoric De Aeckerboom in Haarlem in 1606* (detail). West Berlin, Staatliche Museen, Kunstbibliothek.

73. Denys van Alsloot, *Captain, with Attendants and Musketeers of the Guild of the Archers* (detail from *The Ommeganck in Brussels on 31 May 1615: The Senior Guilds*). London, Victoria and Albert Museum.

74. Matheus Vroom(?), *The Landing of Maria de'Medici in Antwerp on August 4, 1631* (detail). 1632. Formerly Dresden, Gemäldegalerie.

75. Willem Buytewech, *The Gunner and the Sutler*. Etching. Amsterdam, Rijksmuseum.

76. Rembrandt, *The Triumph of Mordecai*, ca. 1642. Etching (**Bartsch** 1791, no. 40). Washington, National Gallery of Art, Lessing J. Rosenwald Collection.

77. Rembrandt, *Floris Soop as Ensign*, 1654. New York, The Metropolitan Museum of Art, The Jules S. Bache Collection.

78. Rembrandt, *Bellona*, 1633. New York, The Metropolitan Museum of Art, The Michael Friedsam Collection, 1931.

79. Aert de Gelder, *Portrait of a Lieutenant*. Dresden, Gemäldegalerie Alte Meister.

80. Rembrandt, *The Mennonite Preacher Anslo and His Wife*, 1641. West Berlin, Staatliche Museen, Gemäldegalerie.

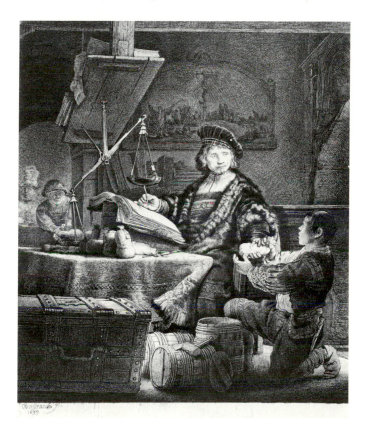

81. Rembrandt, *Jan Uyttenbogaert ("The Goldweigher")*, 1639. Etching (Bartsch, no. 281). New York, The Pierpont Morgan Library.

82. Dirck Jacobsz, *Militiamen of the Kloveniers Guild*, 1529. Amsterdam, Rijksmuseum.

83. Cornelis Ketel, *The Company of Captain Dirck Rosecrans*, 1588. Amsterdam, Rijksmuseum.

84. Attributed to Cornelis Ketel, *A Militia Company*. Drawing. Amsterdam, Rijksmuseum.

85. Unidentified Artist, *The Company of Captain Joncheyn (?)*, ca. 1606. Amsterdam, Rijksmuseum.

86. Jacob Colijns (?), *Ensign and Other Militiamen Affiliated with the Handboogsdoelen*. Drawing, copy after lost painting of 1623 by Jan Tengnagel. London, British Museum.

87. Thomas de Keyser, *The Company of Captain Allaert Cloeck*, 1630 (?). Drawing. Copenhagen, Statens Museum for Kunst, Kongelige Kobberstiksamling.

88. Thomas de Keyser, *The Company of Captain Allaert Cloeck*, 1632. Amsterdam, Rijksmuseum.

89. Johann Spilberg, *The Company of Captain Gijsbert van de Poll*, 1653 (?). Amsterdam, Rijksmuseum.

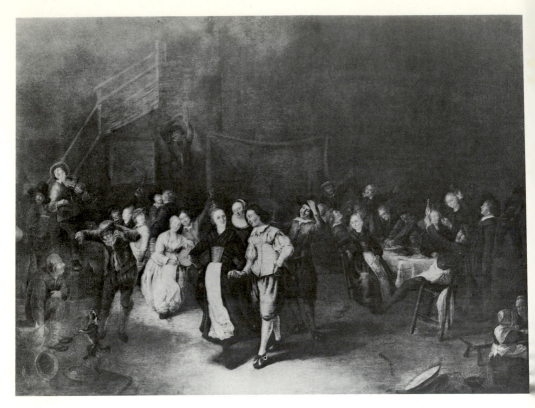

90. Gerrit Lundens, *Country Wedding*, 1649. Formerly Vienna, Coll. Alexander Tritsch.